Cronenberg on Cronenberg

Cronenberg on Cronenberg

REVISED EDITION
EDITED BY

Chris Rodley

faber and faber
LONDON · BOSTON

First published in 1992
by Faber and Faber Limited
3 Queen Square London WC1N 3AU
Revised paperback edition published in 1993
This revised edition published in 1997

Photoset by Parker Typesetting Service, Leicester
Printed in England by Clays Ltd, St Ives plc

A CIP record for this book
is available from the British Library

ISBN 0-571-19137-1

2 4 6 8 10 9 7 5 3 1

Contents

List of Illustrations

Acknowledgements

The major part of this book comprises interviews recorded with David Cronenberg over the last seven years. The first was in Toronto in May 1984, at which time Cronenberg was in lengthy script and design preparation for what was to be his next movie: *Total Recall*. The second occasion was in February 1986, during the filming of *The Fly* at Kleinburg Studios, north of Toronto. The third, also in 1986, took place in London during the final sound mix of *The Fly* at Twickenham. The fourth, and most extensive, was recorded in January 1990 over five days at David Cronenberg Productions in Toronto, just after the completion of the first draft script of *Naked Lunch*. Interviews five and six took place on the set of *Naked Lunch* in Toronto, in February and March 1991. The seventh and final interview took place in Toronto in May 1993 at a time when *M. Butterfly* was in the very last stages of picture editing (small changes were subsequently made to the movie) and prior to its eventual full sound/music mix. Principle thanks, therefore, go to David Cronenberg for his willingness and ability to respond incisively and honestly to continued questioning over a number of years, sometimes in the thick of shooting a movie.

Major thanks also to Sandra Tucker of David Cronenberg Productions, for her support, enthusiasm and unending assistance with all manner of detail concerned with the final preparation of the manuscript and illustrations.

For invaluable editorial guidance and patience, special thanks to Iwona Blazwick and Walter Donohue.

For their permission to reprint quotes from other David Cronenberg interviews, thanks to: Piers Handling and William Beard; Tim Lucas, Paul M. Sammon and *Cinefantastique* magazine; Gill McGreal and the British Film Institute; Karen Jaehne and *Film Comment*; Susan Ayscough and *Cinema Canada*; Mitch Tuchman; *Time Out* magazine.

Stills and illustrations appear by courtesy of David Cronenberg and the British Film Institute, as well as Cinepix Inc., The Mantle Clinic II, M. Butterfly Productions Inc./Geffen Pictures, Quadrant Films, Twentieth Century–Fox, Universal Pictures, Chris Walas Inc., UIP (UK), Columbia Pictures, CBS/Fox Video, Warner Brothers, Miracle Films, Target International and The Recorded Picture Company.

Jenny Holzer's *Truism* © Jenny Holzer. Reprinted by kind permission of the artist.

Foreword
by Dr Martyn Steenbeck

In 1976 I contracted an audiovisual virus. It happened in a cinema. At that time, I believed that few people had been exposed to this particular cinematic phenomenon. However, I was later to discover that large audiences in more than forty countries had also been ravaged by what I had seen. There was no known antidote, and worse, the contagion seemed to spread at an alarming rate among those very unsuspecting souls who had exposed themselves to it for the price of a movie ticket.

It is now clear that in the warm, dark recesses of movie auditoriums everywhere, the virus found little resistance among audiences whose immune systems had grown soporific and complacent on a diet of polite imagination, subtle subtext and decorative gore. We had exposed ourselves to a movie called *Shivers*. Eighty-seven minutes later, life was a different prospect altogether.

The perpetrator, mad scientist, creative genius – depending on your point of view – was Canadian film-maker David Cronenberg, a man (I have since discovered) whose social camouflage resembles a recently graduated dental student with straight As for etiquette, articulation and an uncanny ability to locate painful nerves.

The Cronenberg Condition (I can describe it in no other way) has proved contagious and addictive. Although the director's own viral approach to horror is less a part of the healthy flow of the genre than a parasite or tumour on it, Cronenberg's visions have been appropriated by the main body of the horror/sci-fi genres. It's unlikely that the million-dollar mainstream shock of *Alien* could have been realised without the extreme and uncompromising purity of imagination of the low-budget *Shivers*, made four years earlier.'Body horror' – as convenient a phrase as any with which to satisfy the impulse to imprison and control such phenomena – is now everywhere. But it starts and ends with Cronenberg. The (un)intention is clear: to transpose a sensibility into language: 'Felliniesque', 'Kafkaesque', and now 'Cronenbergesque'.

His practice has no other cinematic parallel that I am aware of. Its true equivalent is to be found in the nature of pure scientific endeavour. Very obviously in the early films, the director is the absentee scientist of the narratives: the man who sets in motion an experiment aimed at short-circuiting the evolutionary process, but is no longer present to witness or fully comprehend its inevitable and unpredictable course. However, this self-reflexive alignment with fictional scientific masterminds is only the beginning. Cronenberg's practice itself is truly scientific. The films are experiments, conducted in a 'pure' sense, with little or no regard for the consequences. The point is to follow the experiment or hypothesis through to the end, unrestrained by social or political considerations.

Furthermore, each film can now be seen as an important and necessary stage in a continuing meta-experiment, which has taken years. In true scientific spirit, the director has been encouraged by each movie to progress and refine that experiment – film to film – as part of a lifetime's commitment towards an end: finding the cure to a disease common to us all. It is called mortality.

Knowing this disease to be incurable, and finding religious belief an unacceptable anaesthetic, each film explores an alternative way of exploring and defusing anxiety about death. Mutation and transformation are offered up as possible cures for a mind/body schism which results from the very incomprehensibility of bodily demise. The fact that these alternatives also lead to death and destruction is perhaps less to do with a deep-rooted pessimism or negativity than the need to seek a hard and realistic optimism. Needless to say, the experiment must continue. The cure is elusive.

Cronenberg sets his experiments in motion but, like his fictional counterparts, has no control over their eventual fate when released into the world. This may account for the observation – or criticism – that what the director says about his films sometimes fails to correspond to how they actually work on certain audiences and critics. However, scientific endeavour often causes unease, due to an unwillingness or inability – endemic to the process – to discuss or perceive effect or implication. It is Cronenberg's enthusiasm for the pure experiment that has distressed some critics: his determination to be unsparing and unflinching; his refusal to dilute what he creates with any considerations outside the demands of a particular narrative.

I have attempted to comprehend the nature of my addiction to the Cronenberg Condition. Like certain other viruses that are pleasurable in the getting, it continually retreats to the safety of the nervous system where it loiters – only to break surface again in another story, on another screen, in another town. It seems incurable, to my mind. The pain is in its emergent melancholia; the pleasure is in its absolute integrity – a rare commodity in commercial movie-making; the joy is in its necessary and perverse sense of humour and play. And the consolation is in its cathartic effect: hopefully personal chaos isn't any more frightening, or more close, than what David Cronenberg projects on that screen.

Note: Psychologist and cinéaste Dr Martyn Steenbeck established a revolutionary media studies course in 1978 at the Schreber Institute in northern Ontario. He dedicated much of his academic life to analysing the impact of violent sexual imagery on the central nervous system. The above is taken from his unpublished journals, lodged with the Schreber Institute by his wife Flavia, shortly after his mysterious death by self-immolation in 1988.

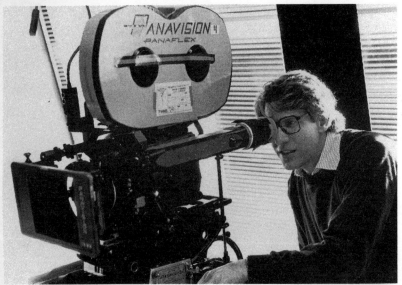

1 Cronenberg lines up a shot for *Shivers* (c. 1974).
2 Cronenberg lines up a shot for *Dead Ringers* (c. 1988).

Introduction

It's an extraordinary feeling when
parts of your body are touched for
the first time. I'm thinking of the
sensations from sex and surgery.

Jenny Holzer

Since David Cronenberg burst on to commercial cinema screens in 1975 with his diabolical début feature *Shivers*, he has been variously dubbed 'the king of venereal horror', 'the Baron of blood', Dave 'Deprave' Cronenberg, and any number of variations on that theme. The cliché of that theme is his responsibility for creating some of the most shocking, perverse, disgusting and truly inventive scenes of horror and bodily mayhem ever conceived for the cinema. This has been coupled with another apparent shock: the perpetrator of these monstrous entertainments is not – as director Martin Scorsese expected – 'a combination of Arthur Bremmer and Dwight Frye as Renfield in *Dracula*, slobbering for juicy flies'. Cronenberg is an articulate, well-educated and quietly spoken man. Shock.

As Cronenberg's career has progressed, his various titles and initial claims to infamy have, to an extent, masked the actual development of a maturing talent. This has been frustrated further by his desire to continue working within, or increasingly to the side of, a genre still regarded by some critics and audiences as unworthy of serious consideration; one which represents the 'low' part of a redundant high/low cultural equation: namely horror.

From the earliest years, certain virtues of what has since been referred to as the 'Cronenberg Project' have been obvious. On the release of Cronenberg's embryonic avant-garde featurette *Stereo* in Britain in 1971, one critic remarked: 'David Cronenberg's first feature is a true "original", defying categorization.' As one film followed another, it also became clear that Cronenberg is an *auteur*, perhaps more in a European than a North American sense: he writes as well as directs most of his material and continues to work outside systems which threaten to wrest control in any important sense from production. Cronenberg was able to enforce a powerful, shocking and alarmingly consistent vision of the world on a series of movies which began as low-budget 'exploiters' and became major motion pictures.

Once past the 'shock value' and content of the movies – and the critical smoke this has produced – two other, very important facets of the Cronenberg Project emerge: integrity and endurance. After *The Fly*, a film which gave the director commercial success at an almost mainstream level, and his widest critical acclaim and audience, he did not sell out, buy in or, in any obvious way, capitalize on that success with his next movie. Instead, he chose to pursue a deeply personal project, already some six years in gestation, a project which by virtue of its subject-matter alone was incapable either of consolidating his newly found position in the movie marketplace or of finding favour with major backers. The difficulties involved in realizing that film – *Dead Ringers* – also forced him, for the first time since his featurette days, to become his own co-producer.

No doubt certain audiences and critics were refreshingly surprised by *The Dead Zone*'s lack of difficult images and provocative, confrontational material. Or, to a lesser extent, *The Fly*'s triumph of love story over special effects. The director's full-throttle return to his desire to 'show the unshowable, speak the unspeakable' with *Dead Ringers* is symptomatic of his integrity – just when they thought it was almost safe to go back into the cinema to see a David Cronenberg movie.

Cronenberg's endurance has often been confused with directorial development. Loyal critics and journalists from schlock-horror days seemed oddly surprised by the fact that Cronenberg – with ever-growing budgets – could improve his craft technically, and could mature from the experience which that brought. It is obvious that, since his early days with Cinepix, his command of all aspects of cinema has grown. The subtext, then, of his followers' surprise was surely that Cronenberg continued to work on the *same* project, which was becoming increasingly complex, refined and highly achieved with each film he made. *Shivers* and *Rabid* were not pragmatic, low-budget strategies, the ideas informing them to be abandoned or diluted when Hollywood recognition was finally bestowed on yet another North American maverick talent: they were not just a phase to be gone through, like adolescence. They were as serious as they were original, elements which were perhaps on the mind of contemporary American director John Carpenter when he observed, 'Cronenberg is better than the rest of us combined.'

What is so unusual about Cronenberg's commercial features is that they should constitute such an absolute progression in one important respect or another. Not one represents a backwards or sideways step, as is so often apparent or necessary in the course of a long career in an entertainment industry uneasy with *auteurs* or 'artists'. Certainly, those directors who have also emerged from an era of contemporary low-budget horror (George Romero, Wes Craven, John Carpenter, Larry Cohen, etc.) have, to a greater or lesser degree, all marked time or diversified with less interesting projects. *Shivers* (1975), Cronenberg's first commercial feature for Cinepix, is perhaps the only real exception to this systematic development, primarily because it is hard to imagine exceeding its raw visceral appeal, repulsiveness and inventiveness. However, after what might be described as the 'shock of the new', the movies have not strayed from a developing film-making practice and philosophical inquiry. The second Cinepix movie, *Rabid* (1976), continued and extended Cronenberg's concern for the breakdown of social order through the eruption of sexuality and disease. Taking its cue from the end of *Shivers*, the film broadened its narrative context from a high-rise community to the entire city of Montreal. *Rabid* not only fits neatly into the genre's concern at that time for the apocalyptic vision, it also forced the director on to the streets and highways and into the shopping malls to stage more ambitious set pieces.

Both *Shivers'* and *Rabid*'s significant financial success (the movies returned $5 million and $7 million respectively for their tiny budgets) was in part due to their hard-sell marketing as exploitation movies. If an exploitation movie is – as defined by its most successful exponent, Roger Corman – a movie in which the subject-matter alone guarantees an audience, whatever the quality of the film, one assumes that it was Cronenberg's resiting of horror from the realm of the gothic to the body that thrilled and shocked audiences. Specifically, given *Shivers'* reputation as the first 'venereal horror' movie, it was the films' interest in sex and violent, playful anarchy rather than their disease-obsessed, philosophical tendencies, that made them function so well as exploitation movies.

The pejorative connotations of exploitation (cheap, poorly executed, not serious) were to plague Cronenberg for some time after the highly productive Cinepix years, despite the next stage of his trajectory. This was made possible by the Canadian tax-shelter years, during which Cronenberg was able to make another four features on ever-increasing budgets: *Fast Company, The Brood, Scanners* and *Videodrome*. Most significantly, Cronenberg was now freed of the negative constraints of low-budget film production – if not its die-hard marketing techniques.

Fast Company (1979) has always been regarded as the aberration in the Cronenberg Project, being non-horror, thematically 'apart', less personal. However, it is important, for four reasons: as a crucial bridge between low- and medium-budget movie-making; for Cronenberg's technical development; as his first experience of working with non-original material; and for the chance meetings with certain crew members, many of whom have stayed with him to work on every movie he has made since. As if to assist the pure *auteurist* Cronenberg case, *Fast Company* is the only movie made by the director not to have been distributed at all at the time of its making.

The Brood (1979) saw Cronenberg refining and personalizing the obsessions of the Cinepix movies, aided by the ability to afford 'name' actors. This was the beginning of Cronenberg's three-picture association with executive producers Victor Solnicki and Pierre David, and with producer Claude Héroux. It was also the beginning of an altogether darker phase of his work. The obsessions remained: medical science's misunderstood endeavours to assist the evolutionary process; the body's capacity to respond independently with transformation, mutation and its own creative diseases; descent into familial, societal or bodily chaos. However, *The Brood*'s evident seriousness of purpose was all but thwarted on its release by Cronenberg's exploitation past. Distributors were unwilling or unable to perceive the maturity of the film's construction, execution and intent, in comparison to the rude, guerrilla schlock surface of *Shivers* and *Rabid*.

Scanners (1980) was to be Cronenberg's first major visible hit, again a development for the director as his first real 'action' picture, though still firmly situated within a world where minds and bodies literally do battle. It was an important development in bringing the director to the attention of the Hollywood community (where action speaks louder than words). This was to assist in the realization of future Cronenberg projects, at this point still some years down the line. *Scanners* again boasted a name cast, some spectacular special effects and, on this occasion, an extremely effective add campaign. But for the limpness of Stephen Lack in the central Scanner role of Cameron Vale (cast primarily for his eyes), the film might have achieved even greater success. Significantly, *Scanners* remains Cronenberg's most easily classifiable movie (almost pure sci-fi) and, apart from the infamous shock of an exploding head, his least disturbing.

Videodrome (1982), the last of Cronenberg's tax-shelter movies, proved pivotal in the director's trajectory. For many, the film remains his most conceptually ambitious, challenging and provocative entertainment. Certainly, the movie was a creative chrysalis from which emerged a director still to achieve his most affecting work. *Videodrome* was important to the developing Cronenberg Project on many fronts. It was the first of his films to be backed by the distribution muscle of a major Hollywood company – MCA/Universal. It was also the first Cronenberg film resolutely to deny generic categorization in its search for a truly contemporary horror – a factor which contributed to its wholly unsuccessful 'sell' in the international marketplace. In addition, it represented the outer limits of Cronenberg's thematic concerns with wacky, well-meaning scientists and renegade, conspiratorial institutions: Professor Brian O'Blivion is the last of the director's absentee innovators, and Spectacular Optical the last menacing, covert operation.

Most significantly, in the character of Max Renn, we see a watershed Cronenberg development, a man in the throes of a more personal mental chaos. We also see, for the first time, a man more intrinsically interesting than the social/political/physical revolution into which he unwittingly stumbles. As Renn part-functions as *Videodrome*'s particular incarnation of the director's *alter ego*, it is intriguing that, at last, this representation is considerably less bland than its equivalents in previous films, most notably Frank Carveth in *The Brood*.

Cronenberg had gone as far as he could at that time with *Videodrome*. Like Renn, the director had to progress to the next stage: shed the old flesh and embrace the new. In part, this was made necessary by virtue of the removal of Canadian tax-shelter advantages. Cronenberg would no longer be able to direct a film a year, should he wish, merely because he was a Canadian director with a track record. For the first time, he was without assured indigenous financial support at a stage in his career and development that demanded high-profile projects and reasonable budgets. Mentally somewhat exhausted from his *Videodrome* experience, Cronenberg stepped into the uncertain light of an entertainment arena dominated by the safe bet and American finance.

The Dead Zone (1983) was an all-too-obvious change in terms of its source material (adapted by another screenwriter from a story by best-selling novelist Stephen King) and its look (non-visceral). However, in Cronenberg's terms, it was the beginning of a new phase of work, primarily characterized by the grafting of an emotional intensity absent from previous work on to the same philosophical concerns. Cronenberg has suggested that the absentee scientist in *The Dead Zone* is God. Leaving aside the need to read consistency into one's own work, this is certainly the last film for which such a case can be made. *The Dead Zone* is also the last Cronenberg film to deal in the real world with the significant societal implications of the main characters' actions and experiences. After *The Dead Zone*, the absentee scientist or experimenter takes centre stage and becomes the main character. The resulting chaos is chiefly sited in the personal, with little or no impact in reality beyond the context of close personal relationships. *The Dead Zone* marks the beginning of a much more personalized, claustrophobic, interiorized and affecting cinema for Cronenberg.

In the performance and face of actor Christopher Walken (as Johnny Smith) can be seen the fusion of a more classic horror (Frankenstein's confused monster) with an increasing sense of melancholia and resignation in the work: the edges of James Woods's portrayal of Max Renn, in fact. And, most surprisingly, *Love Story* in wolf's clothing can be seen in the film's delicate and unfulfilled central love affair. And criticisms of Cronenberg's 'inability' to work with actors or his heartless, unfeeling direction were roundly answered in what Stephen King evaluated as a movie in which, for Cronenberg, 'the warm mixes with the cold to make something entirely new'. Despite being accused by some of an attempted mainstream cinema *coup d'état*, Cronenberg's version of *The Dead Zone* was not intended to divert him from his purpose, nor did it do so. It was not a conspicuous box-office hit, perhaps in part due to its admirably faithful, depressed tone. Johnny Smith's success in apparently saving the world from a doomsday-driven president seems little recompense for the palpable weight of his personal tragedy.

The Fly (1986) was to be the perfect fusion of his work both before and after *The Dead Zone*. Returning to more familiar themes (disease, physical transformation, science), the movie weds gruesome special effects to another central love story, this time between Jeff Goldblum and Geena Davis. Two emergent aspects of the director's work were integrated in one movie for the first time. *The Fly* was also critically and financially a success. It deftly located the centre of Cronenberg's obsession with flesh, disease and transformation, as Seth Brundle (Goldblum) experiences a physical revolution which emerges as a metaphor for the ageing process: the tragedy of mortality, accelerated and made more difficult to accommodate aesthetically by his genetic fusion with an insect. The movie was interestingly once characterized by the director as basically 'three people in a room, talking', confirming the work's drift towards more interior, claustrophobic experiences.

The 'thing that would not die' – Cronenberg's fascination for what goes on secretly inside the human body – inevitably broke surface in the story of Beverly and Elliot Mantle, the identical-twin gynaecologists of *Dead Ringers*. By avoiding the obvious potential to indulge in some distinctly queasy special effects, Cronenberg achieved his most intensely unsettling, melancholic and mature work to date. The mind/body schism is here established literally at the point of physical conception, in a story which investigates one soul split into two bodies – forever one entity and forever two physical beings.

Although the movie showcases some extraordinary motion-control-camera sequences, allowing actor Jeremy Irons (as both Elliot and Beverly Mantle) to appear to interact with himself, the real special effect of the film is Irons's performance itself. Continuing the work with his male leads – beginning most noticeably with James Woods in *Videodrome*, and maintained with Christopher Walken's *tour de force* in *The Dead Zone* and Jeff Goldblum's strangely affecting performance achieved by acting through the layers of five hours' worth of prosthetic make-up – Cronenberg coaxed an amazing effort from Irons for *Dead Ringers*. When the actor finally received an Oscar for his role as Claus von Bülow in Barbet Schroeder's *Reversal of Fortune*, he was to thank – among others – David Cronenberg.

The film was an interior experience, literally. After its opening sequence, the entire movie features only two or three short and unimportant exterior scenes (perhaps in part due to the difficulties for motion-control camerawork). However, *Dead Ringers* was always conceived as an interior story, in that it deals with the mental disintegration of one man made two by an accident of conception.

With *Naked Lunch* (1991) Cronenberg returned home. It may not be a home most of us would be comfortable to live in, but for Cronenberg it was a return to one of his most formative influences – the literary works of William Burroughs. One wonders what Cronenberg would have come up with had he had the chance to make his version of Burroughs's *Naked Lunch* hot on the heels of his low-budget shockers *Shivers* and *Rabid*. Now a more integrated film-maker, and no doubt less intimidated by the importance and influence of the text, Cronenberg approached the impossible task of addressing a cinematic equivalent of *Naked Lunch* by fusing his own fully developed cinematic sensibility (always informed by the imagery of Burroughs) with aspects of Burroughs's life – as well as pieces of Burroughs's text, not all of them from *Naked Lunch*.

As in *Videodrome* and *Dead Ringers*, the film concentrates on mental states, this time of would-be writer Bill Lee – played with an intense and uncharacteristic quietness by Peter 'Robocop' Weller. Originally planned as Cronenberg's first foreign-location movie (most exteriors were originally to be shot in Tangiers), the production became yet another of the director's interior journeys when the Gulf War prevented filming in North Africa. Tangiers was brought to the studio in Toronto, further emphasizing and clarifying a basic dynamic of the script: a disturbing confusion (as in *Videodrome*, but here more successfully integrated) of reality with hallucination, and with personal disintegration.

Given the 'difficult' subject-matter of the film's literary pedigree and its formal strategy (a random technique which pre-figured the 'cut-up' and 'fold-in' approach of Burroughs's later novels), a low-budget route might seem the most sensible approach to filming *Naked Lunch*; drug addiction, homosexual sex and violence, and the process of writing have hardly been mainstays of commercial cinema over the last ten reactionary years.

By the time *Naked Lunch* had opened in North America, Cronenberg's next film was – uncharacteristically since the tax shelter days – already in place. Adapted from the highly successful Tony Award winning play *M. Butterfly*, and to be released internationally through Warner Bros, Cronenberg joked at the time that it was to be his 'sell-out' movie. Perverse, wishful thinking.

The film *M. Butterfly* is, at the very least, extraordinary proof of how auteurism, in the most interesting sense of the word, operates in cinema. A true story inspires a huge Broadway hit. The author is hired by the producer to write the movie script version of his own international success. Then the project is put in the hands of the most specific of auteurs in North America. Retire to a safe distance and watch the fireworks. This is no sell-out.

As great American movie auteurs have proved in the past, when working with either intransigent material or within the very specific requirements and formulas of genre film-making (such as the configuration Sam Peckinpah/the western), it is the tension between director and material that produces the shocks and surprises, and puts a different spin on either familiar or popular subjects. With *M. Butterfly*, Cronenberg has unlocked aspects of David Henry Hwang's story of a French diplomat's love of a diva from the Beijing opera – only to discover years later that she's a man – which would forever have remained subordinated to the play's main political thrust. The director brings not *the* meaning, but *a* meaning to the material and in so doing, has transformed M. *Butterfly* into an experience that is at once genuinely Cronenbergesque and different.

Above all, one is struck by the perverse nature of its epic sweep. Despite spectacular locations, elaborate exterior set pieces and all the usual trappings of an exotic foreign shoot (Cronenberg's first), M. *Butterfly* evinces the director's absolute control of a story he sees as essentially interior. At times, the backstreets of Beijing feel no more real than the backstreets of Tangiers in *Naked Lunch*. Even the Great Wall of China might have been constructed by production designer Carol Spier. It seems to serve the film, the characters and the story. It does not provide Cronenberg with easy spectacle. His gaze will not be distracted. Lovers of the David Lean school of location movie-making – or latterday Bertolucci – may legitimately wonder why Cronenberg bothered going there in the first place, so tantalizingly glimpsed are the wonders almost on view. But Cronenberg has always been more interested in the actual butterfly than in its natural habitat.

The third in a row of Cronenberg adaptations, *Crash* looks like a ruthless riposte to M. *Butterfly*'s lukewarm reception. If critics and audiences alike were unwilling or unable to delight in that film's ambitions and achievements, *Crash* comes on like unrepentant, quintessential Cronenberg. What is initially so startling about the movie is that, in a film culture drenched in so-called high concept conflations of sex and violence, *Crash* arrives as the first real truth-or-dare movie of an over-excited 90s. If nothing else, it highlights the tame, middle-aged or childish nature of most 'shockers' out there in a noisy, cynical marketplace.

Toronto is once again the site of physical and mental transformation, as car-crash victim James Ballard stumbles into a subterranean culture intent on redefining our relationship to the automobile in radical, psychosexual ways. Based on J. G. Ballard's excoriating techno-sex novel, Cronenberg's cool, spare treatment of a truly disturbing and dystopic premise manages to be as confrontational as the original was when it first appeared over twenty years ago. In every important respect, the movie represents its director's wholehearted return to his uncompromising, dangerous roots. It is a movie like no other, from a voice which continues to 'show the unshowable. Speak the unspeakable.'

Cronenberg has always been violently opposed to any notion that he might consider censoring his own thoughts and images. As a result, since *Shivers* the movies have prompted volumes of critical and theoretical reaction and analysis – proof enough of the director's continuing ability to touch sensitive and difficult nerves with unique surgical skill. Much of this analysis has been ideologically at odds with what the films – as opposed to the director – seem to be saying, using an array of equally effective theoretical tools with which to dissect the films and expose their heart.

Mainly focusing on textual analysis and issues of representation, such ripostes continue to be parried by the director's primary concern for the making of art. In the Cronenberg Project, the creation of art must ultimately free itself of specific – and potentially paralyzing – political, social and cultural concerns. Only then can it first reach the viscera, before being filtered to the mind – something Cronenberg believes horror must achieve in order to be called horror. And to qualify as art.

The schism between Cronenberg's stated intentions and certain readings of the films is impossible to heal. It has become a matter of art versus dogmatic theory; social responsibility versus unhindered imagination; censorship versus freedom to create; perhaps even mind versus body. Ironically, this situation is exacerbated by the director's very ability to articulate the concerns which so explicitly function as organizing factors in his own clearly formed project. Whether the films evince a high degree of phallic panic or not, Cronenberg is one of the most original, confrontational and necessary cinematic voices we have. His undiminished desire to provoke and disturb, both with the movies and with what he says about them, must mean that this schism will remain.

Martin Scorsese was not alone when he said that Cronenberg doesn't understand what his own films are about (to which Cronenberg was to reply later, 'I hope I don't'). However, unlike those unsympathetic critics of Cronenberg who hold the same view, Scorsese also observed that this doesn't matter: 'If what he says doesn't gel with the work, it's what he needs to get himself to that final product. What he says doesn't matter. It's the work that really counts. It's the work that says it.' Perhaps Scorsese is also the best person to conclude: 'Sometimes I don't even want to see his pictures when they come out. But I finally get there, and it's a cathartic experience for me to go through. Cronenberg is twentieth century. *Late* twentieth century. Cronenberg is something that unfortunately we have no control over, in the sense that we have no control over the imminent destruction of ourselves. That's what is so clear about his work. So frightening. So upsetting.'

Chris Rodley, September 1996

3 Polymorphous perversity in *Stereo*.
4 Three bodies, two souls in *Dead Ringers*.

CHAPTER I

Embryo: The Earliest Years

David Cronenberg was born on 15 March 1943 in Toronto. Unlike certain other Canadian movie directors who have achieved a degree of international success and recognition, he continues to avoid the obvious temptation: the country's all too porous border with America. Cronenberg still lives in the city of his birth, and to date has not made a movie outside Canada. Becoming yet another invisible Canadian in that cinema city on the West Coast of the United States is only one of the many expectations he has confounded.

As Cronenberg has observed: 'To a general public, a person who makes horror films must be a culpable freak. When people meet me, they're surprised that I'm not a slathering maniac and that I'm not particularly brutal.' On the evidence of his particular strain of venereal or biological horror, one might reasonably expect of the perpetrator stories of a traumatic, deprived or repressive childhood and upbringing. On the contrary, Cronenberg was not subjected to the many clichéd formative family experiences often found lurking in the adolescence of a 'driven' film-maker, religious or otherwise. There was no Roman Catholic guilt or oppressive Calvinism on offer to fuel a rebellion or fire a self-help cinematic voyage. There was no poverty; no lack of being understood. And no sneaky trips to the cinema to steal production stills of Citizen Kane.

In what sounds a relatively idyllic childhood, one does find two familiar trouble-spots – a sense of isolation, or 'outsiderness', and the inevitable: death. Cronenberg has always referred to the deaths of his father and later of his mother as influencing him personally while denying their specific impact on his work and its content.

His early education was at Dewson Street Public School, Kent Senior School, Harbord Collegiate and North Toronto Collegiate. In 1963 he entered the University of Toronto as an Honours Science student, only to abandon the course a year later in favour of Honours English Language and Literature. Having already won the prestigious Epstein Award for an

original short story, Cronenberg went on to win the Gertrude Lawler
Scholarship for finishing first at University College. In 1965 he inter-
rupted his studies in favour of European travel, returning the next year.
He graduated from the University of Toronto with a General BA in
1967.

There are many words you could use to describe my parents, and they all
don't fit! Intellectual. Cultured. None of them quite work because in
some ways they were very normal and very middle class. Very cosy. At
the same time, there were walls in my house that were literally composed
of books; corridors that I used to walk along as a child and didn't realize
were not real walls at all. There was no other place to put them in the
small house I grew up in.

My father was a rabid bibliophile. He was a journalist primarily,
although he tried his hand at fiction once in a while, writing short stories
for a Canadian magazine called *True Detective*, I think. He was always
writing for magazines, *Reader's Digest* or one of those things. He was a
philatelist and wrote a stamp column for the *Toronto Telegram* newspaper for almost thirty years. My mother was a pianist. She wasn't a solo
performer, but accompanied choirs and dancers, and used to play for
Nureyev and Erik Bruhn when they came to town for their exercise
classes. So there was always classical music at home. Live music. That's
the kind of house I grew up in.

Odd, because we lived at College Street and Crawford in Toronto
which was, and still is, an immigrant street. Whatever the latest wave of
immigration is, that's where people go. In those days the Jews were
starting to move out to the suburbs and to Forest Hill, an expensive
section of town which is predominantly Jewish, as opposed to Rosedale
which is very WASP. So on that street were Turks, a lot of Italians, some
Jews and some Irish Catholics. Quite a mix. And I was always amazed
when I went into their houses that there was no music and no books! I
didn't understand it. It seemed wrong somehow.

I wouldn't say that I felt an outsider consciously. It's true I had a
girlfriend when I was about five years old, and spent my time with her
rather than play baseball or football and that kind of thing. But I guess
there must have been some imprint of being slightly 'outsiders' in the
society. Not to the extent that it hurt me; I didn't feel the insecurity and
paranoia that some kids obviously felt. I was totally not directed by my
parents. I recognize their technique now, being a parent myself. It was a
natural one for them, not planned. They were just totally supportive and

enthusiastic for whatever it was I wanted. When I was interested in things scientific, my father would immediately bring out twenty books on microbiology. When I suddenly decided I was going to be a lepidopterist, then those books would come out. And when I got interested in classical guitar, my mother would swing into action. I played classical guitar for eleven years. When I realized that being a concert guitarist was not what I was meant to be, there was some sadness on my mother's part, but I was never made to feel guilty. It was a very wonderful childhood.

I think what I got at home was an unshakeable, totally realistic faith in my own abilities, and a confidence in being able to do what I wanted to do. We communicated a lot, and very well. I was never frustrated because I couldn't talk to my parents, or any of those things that are common conflicts. I could talk to them about everything.

I only realized later that they invented their own version of a lot of things. I think of myself as being resolutely middle class, and yet when I see what true middle-class values are, they're not mine. My parents really invented their own version of what it is to be middle class. They also invented their own version of what it is to be Jewish.

I went to Harbord Collegiate high school, which was almost totally Jewish at the time – they'd shut down for Jewish holidays because only five kids would show up. That's where I learnt about Jewishness, not from my family. That's where I got to understand all the North American Jewish stereotypes, the overtly possessive, suffocating Jewish mother. All that kind of stuff. But I haven't met anyone else who's got the same version of Jewishness I had at home. We didn't have Channukah, we had Christmas. We had a tree, presents under the tree, and I wrote to Santa Claus. It had nothing to do with Christ at all. So I feel mildly but definitely like an outsider in any Jewish function or celebration. I don't know what's going on. And yet if you say 'Are you Jewish?' I'd say 'Yes.'

Both my parents were anti-religious, but not in a proselytizing way. Particularly my mother. Yet she found some of the traditions – like the Passover meal, but without the Bible stuff – comforting. My father rejected it for himself as a young child. They would tell me what they thought – also what other people thought who didn't agree with them – and let me form my own opinion. Of course, what your parents think when you're a child has great weight. But I never grew up with a disdain or hatred of any particular religion, or Judaism itself. I just don't feel part of it.

Later, when my father died, I did feel haunted. I really understood what haunting is all about. I would hear phrases and words that he would use and it felt that if I just turned around he would be there. I would wake up in the morning and feel that I was him. I sat up in bed the way he did. It was very eerie. I was standing or sitting in the way he would. It was partly my attempt to deny he was dead, to become him. In a psychological sense, I obtained an insight into the beliefs of reincarnation and possession.

He started to die physically, but not mentally. The body went, but the mind didn't. It was a very non-specific disease. It started with colitis and became a very bizarre inability of his body to process calcium. His bones started to become brittle. He would turn over in bed and break ribs. It was quite horrible.

People ask me, 'Why horror movies?' Well, this is the serious part of it, which I'm not pushing on anyone. The real question has never been the existence of God. If God is a totally abstract force in the universe with no understanding for human beings, then it really doesn't matter. It's only if God is interested in the affairs of man and cares what you morally do that it makes any difference.

I thought I would grow up to be a veterinarian, like just about every other kid in North America! Just because of a love of animals, an identification with animals, and a desire to help them. Then, when I realized what the reality of being a veterinarian was, I realized I was totally uninterested in helping farmers fertilize cows and things like that; that the animal world – as it interfaces with the human one – is rougher than one imagines. I didn't want to deal with it. But, beyond that, it was always writing. I aspired to write very early. I was interested in underground novels – William Burroughs, Henry Miller and some of the people that T. S. Eliot introduced to North America. I always wrote. I can't remember not writing. I can't remember not expressing myself. I wrote my first novel when I was ten years old. It was three pages long. As far as I was concerned, that was a novel. So that was very natural to me.

I wrote stories and sent them to magazines. I tried short-story writing as a first attempt to get something published. I used to read *Writer's Digest* and various magazines that focused on the professional writer. When I was sixteen I got a nice letter from the editor of the *Magazine of Fantasy and Science-Fiction*, telling me that this story I'd written came close to being published.[1] Please send us more. As it turned out, I don't think I ever wrote another short story after that until I got to university, and I certainly never sent any off for publication. But I was very pleased that I'd gotten something back besides a rejection letter.

And then there was science. I was fascinated by the way that people dig around to discover how things work, and the way they codify and organize that knowledge. I interpreted that interest to mean that maybe I should be a scientist. By the time I left high school I saw a very schizophrenic future ahead of me: science and literature. That split. As a teenager I really admired Isaac Asimov, who seemed able to do those things. I thought that maybe that was what would happen: I would be a scientist who wrote fiction. There was almost a competition between teachers for my soul. I had a great English teacher and a great science teacher. Both thought I was wonderful and were very excited by what I could do. Both fought hard in subtle ways for me to go into their disciplines at university.

I went into science to begin with because I thought you couldn't be taught how to write, but you needed to be taught science. It only took a short period of time at the University of Toronto in Honours Science to realize I was spending all my time at the arts end of the campus. There was a medical/engineering/science end, and the arts/literature end. It was very polarized. Physically. I was always at the arts end. That's where I took comfort during those long winters, when you're trying desperately to study and you're having some terrible affair with some girl. I was not being fed by the techno-science end of the campus. I found no solace there at all: not in the people, not in the women (there were very few), and so I dropped out before the year's end.

Once again, coming face to face with reality – of what it was to be a scientist this time – I realized I was not meant to be that either. What we studied excited me tremendously, but the way it was taught suffocated me. I really do blame the system. The way a child discovers the world constantly replicates the way science began. You start to notice what's around you, and you get very curious about how things work. How things interrelate. It's as simple as seeing a bug that intrigues you. You want to know where it goes at night; who its friends are; what it eats. But the way science was presented at university then was very dry and alien to me: a classic version of what scientists are supposed to be – detached, distracted and passionless.

I think the best scientists are as mad, creative and eccentric as writers and artists of any kind. I feel a lot of empathy for doctors and scientists. I often feel that they are my persona in my films. Although they may be tragic and demented, I don't subscribe to the view that they are playing with things that shouldn't be played with. You have to believe in God before you can say there are things that man was not meant to know. I don't think there's anything man wasn't meant to know. There are just

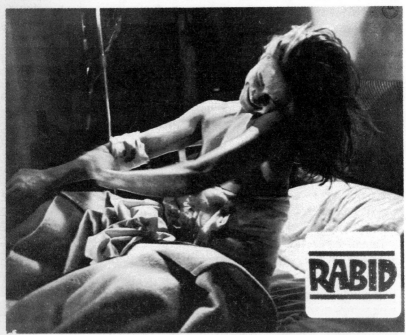

5 Victims of experimental treatment: a patient in *Stereo* . . .
6 . . . Marilyn Chambers in *Rabid*.

some stupid things that people shouldn't do. In another way, everybody's a mad scientist, and life is their lab. We're all trying to experiment to find a way to live, to solve problems, to fend off madness and chaos. So, to me, those characters in my films represent people in general, who somehow have to figure out what they're doing, what their worth means, what their relationship to society is, how to use their creative energy and how to deal with their destructive energy.

Our teachers at university were eccentric enough. We had a physics professor who would start his class whether there was anyone there or not. You could be the first to arrive and half the board was already covered with figures and he was talking. No one in the class. He was going to start at ten after the hour and that was that. But what he was teaching was very disconnected and dry. It all came down to statistics, figures, drawings and diagrams. Sad. What I needed was a feeling of excitement, discovery, creativity; the infinite possibility that you get with the study of literature, and which you should get with the study of science.

There are scientists who have managed to work within the structures they have to, and yet are able to give expression to their inventiveness and their madness. But it wasn't going to happen for me. I could see that. I can invent a science mentor who is fabulous. I'm sure they exist: people who can really teach this stuff in a way that doesn't kill the excitement. It was like having to murder an amazing creature in order to dissect it. Unfortunately, when you've dissected it, it's dead. All its colours fade. All the things that attracted you to it in the first place are gone.

All stereotypes turn out to be true. This is a horrifying thing about life. All those things you fought against as a youth: you begin to realize that they're stereotypes because they're true! I was in this particular chemistry class where everybody was doing things on long desks with sinks and Bunsen burners. There were only two women in this class. One of them was very attractive. She was going around with one of the science guys. I remember looking at them and saying to myself, 'I could be looking at Martians. I can't imagine what the basis of their relationship is. I see them together. They kind of hold hands. They nuzzle. But I don't know what they say to each other. I can't imagine how they relate. I really don't know what's going on at all.'

It was like studying weird specimens from outer space. And that was bad. It meant that at that point I was truly an outsider. I couldn't get in. I didn't know what they were doing. I didn't know what anyone's motives were for doing anything. I didn't have any friends among my classmates, only acquaintances. I just was not one of them. It was very much like *Invasion of the Body Snatchers*.² So that was it for science. Again, my parents supported me totally. I think they understood that I wasn't just being whimsical, that I hadn't totally lost my way and had no excitements left. That would have shaken them. They could see that I was still discovering myself.

The kids in *Dead Ringers* are partly modelled after me. I did wear glasses as a kid, I was interested in science and I was precocious. I'm still ambivalent about it all, because I loved it. I resent and regret having lost it. What I was studying nourished me. What you saw through the microscope was fantastic. But when you looked up from the microscope, you were lost. So in a way I completely identify with those two little monsters.

If I had stayed the course, I would have been in biochemistry. I was never interested in the hardware sciences. Chemistry was more interesting because it related to the body; not just the human body, but the planet's body. I loved botany. I loved the interchange of fluids and plants; the chemistry of plants. All that stuff. So it was biochemistry in a broader sense, because there's biochemistry in the brain, getting at the physical basis of human thought and imagination. I think it was natural that I should try to draw those parts of myself together and integrate them, finally, in film-making.

Still at that point I thought I would be a writer. A novelist. The next year I re-enrolled in the English Honours course, which was a very beautifully structured English–philosophy–history course. It was like you were a blotter, and the ink – which was blood – would just soak into you. Everybody there was crazy, passionate, well-read, excited about all the things I was excited about. It was fantastic. It's terrible to be a cliché, it really is. And it's inevitable.

Notes

1 This short story apparently concerned a disfigured handyman who lives in a boiler room. He is able to project himself into his one treasured possession: a painting of a scene in a Parisian café.

2 *Invasion of the Body Snatchers* (Don Siegel, 1956) is a classic example of the Cold-War science-fiction movie, concerning the takeover of human bodies by a visiting intelligence. The film works equally well as a critique of America's Communist paranoia or as the perfect expression of the fear of 'Reds under the bed'.

7 Return to childhood: Cronenberg directs *Dead Ringers*.

CHAPTER 2

Transfer: From Big Science to
Little Films

Not long after Cronenberg had successfully situated his mind and body at the most conducive end of the University campus and curriculum, his creative juices instigated yet another of their unforeseen flows. They began tentatively to investigate an alternative to the notion of being an author. This alternative was film-making.

These juices were all but uncontaminated by the condition known as cinephilia. Cronenberg was therefore not haunted by the spectres of great directors and classic movies – the inevitable inheritance of a generation of film-makers nurtured by the institution of film school. His intimidating influences were literary as opposed to cinematic. This initial, relatively pure 'reaction' to cinema is important to Cronenberg, considering his desire that his films should constitute their own genre.

There were no film courses at the University of Toronto in the early 1960s. They had courses for poetry, painting, dance, but not for film. At that point it wasn't a legitimate art or science. It was just entertainment – and you didn't have courses on TV or vaudeville. That's why it's hard now to reproduce the stunning effect that a film made by a fellow student had on me.

His name was David Secter. He had somehow hustled together a feature film called *Winter Kept Us Warm*, which is a quote from *The Wasteland*. I heard he was making a film, and that was intriguing because it was completely unprecedented. And then the film appeared, and I was stunned. Shocked. Exhilarated. It was an unbelievable experience. This movie, which was a very sweet film, had my friends in it as actors. And it was in Toronto, at the University, and there were scenes and places that I walked past every day. It was thrilling. That won't happen to kids now, because they've got video cameras at home and everybody has made twelve films by the time they've reached puberty. But then it was unprecedented. I said, 'I've got to try this!' That was the beginning of my awareness of film as something that I could do, something that I had access to. I had shot 8mm footage of car races – another of my many obsessions as a kid – but it never occurred to me to make a fiction film or anything like that.

As a child I had been a regular moviegoer, because there was no television in the late 1940s/early 1950s, and we were very late in getting a set. My father, being a book man who had owned a bookstore in the Depression (The Professor's Bookshop), was also very resistant to television. I had to go to friends to watch *Howdy Doody*. Then every Saturday afternoon there would be a migration down the streets, like a stream of lemmings, going towards the College Moviehouse or the Pylon. We would go every weekend. And my parents would take me to see movies during the week. But it was just like the air you breathed. Nothing special.

Eventually I became aware of European film and saw that here was something different. But I was never a film enthusiast or a cinephile. I had friends who belonged to various film societies. They would drag me off to see those movies and they would be terrific – Fellini, Bergman, all those. But they were film-maniacs. I was just going along with them. That was never my 'in' to film-making. It really was this one moment when I saw *Winter Kept Us Warm* that did it for me.

It was the access. I had certainly seen movies that had affected me, but the same goes for books. I'd been driving in cars that had affected me. Someone takes you for a ride in a Ferrari, and your whole understanding of what a car can be changes. It doesn't mean you immediately feel you must become a car designer. The same with movies. It just didn't occur to me that you could make a movie. They came from somewhere else. Just like cars. I didn't realize that in England at that time, for example, people did build cars. Like the Lotus. Many wonderful cars started that way. But in Canada you didn't build cars and you didn't make movies. You didn't know anyone in the movie business. You might know someone whose father ran a used-car lot.

So now I was no longer just a consumer of movies. It was now grist for the mill. All those things I'd seen were now learning experiences in terms of making my own film. My approach to film-making was very pragmatic. I like to take things apart. So my first approach was very mechanical, to understand the technology. I looked in the *Encyclopaedia Britannica* under 'Lens', 'Film', 'Camera' and 'F. Stop'. Things like that. I bought copies of *American Cinematographer* magazine. I couldn't understand the articles, but the ads showed pictures of stuff and I gradually began to get the idea: how you get the sound on to the film, how you edit both of them together. I didn't understand any of that.

The essence of creating anything is control and shaping, and you can't get control if you don't know how things work. That's how I felt about cars. You can't really drive them well unless you know what's going on. I've always found that fascinating. To take a car apart is to look into the brain of the people who designed it, and into the culture it came from. Ways of doing things and ways of dealing with the realities of metallurgy, combustion. For me it's immediately a philosophical enterprise to take something apart. It's not just monkey stuff.

I started to hang out with cameramen. There was a camera-rental place, Canadian Motion Picture Equipment Company. A woman called Janet Good owned it; a very fiesty, foul-mouthed (in a most delightful way) Scottish babe, who would just sit behind her desk and tell you where the world was at. Cameramen would come in, they'd all drink gin together, take cameras apart, and they'd show me how to load an Arriflex. They would tell me stuff. Finally, when I was ready, I went out and shot my first film. I did everything. I recorded the sound, held the microphone and shot at the same time.

It didn't take long before I dropped the techno part of it, though I still read the latest car magazines avidly to see what the latest developments are in cylinder combustion techniques. I'm not interested in the latest camera development. I'm very anti-techno. I've never shot in CinemaScope. I'm not interested. But I can't understand a director who doesn't really understand what different lenses do. I've got to tell my cameraman what lens I want. He can't tell me. If you don't have some technological understanding of why that looks that way, you'll never understand that it can be different.

I could see what was going on with Stanley Kubrick at a certain point: an obsession with technology. I thought, 'Why is there so much Steadicam[1] in *The Shining*?' It didn't surprise me when I heard that the guy had been hired to do one day and stayed for nine months! It was a new toy. In *Barry Lyndon* it was the emphasis on being able to shoot candlelit scenes by true candlelight, and modifying stills camera lenses for use on a movie camera. But why? The illusion is fine! It's the illusion I want. The reality is totally irrelevant.

Yet, inevitably, when you do special effects it's always an invention. It's always a new experiment, because the context is always different. Even in *Dead Ringers* I was breaking some new ground in small ways with motion control. Not because I wanted to, but because I had to, and wanted to survive the experience.

When he felt confident enough technically, Cronenberg began work on his first short film, Transfer. *Made in 1966, it cost approximately Can.$300, with Cronenberg as writer, director, cameraman and editor. Two friends, Margaret Hindson and Stephen Nosko, were the sound recordists. His second short,* From the Drain, *followed the next year and cost approximately Can.$500. Again Cronenberg fulfilled all technical roles. Both films were two-handers, performed by friends Stephen Nosko, Mort Ritts and Rafe Macpherson.*

It was very natural for me to write a script. By that time it was business as usual. The easy part. To realize the films was the hard part, the learning part. I've tried to suppress those films for many years. I guess they have an academic interest, but artistically they're so bad. I haven't seen them for twenty years. The last time I looked at them everything was wrong: the rhythms; the editing. I had no desire to re-edit them. They must stand as what they are.

Transfer was about a psychiatrist who is pursued by his patient wherever he goes, because the patient feels that their relationship is the only one he's ever had that meant anything to him. It's arty in that I tried visual dislocation. Most of it takes place in a snowy field, and they're eating on a table set up out in the field without any logical or realistic attempt to explain why. There is a surrealistic element, which didn't quite match with the psychological humour. Technically it was pretty lumpy.

From the Drain is definitely more like a Samuel Beckett sketch. There are two guys sitting in an empty bathtub with their clothes on. They begin to talk, and the first line is 'Do you come here often?' As they talk, you begin to realize that they're veterans of some bizarre war that you don't know anything about. It involves biological and chemical warfare. Finally, a plant comes out through the drain and strangles one of them. The other takes his shoes and throws them in a closet that is full of other people's shoes. So it's obvious that somewhere along the line there is a plot to get rid of all the veterans of that particular war so they won't talk about what they know. It was an evolution in the sense that I was becoming a little bit more technically adept and finding my way around the technology and the rhythms of editing.

It was tremendously exciting making them at the time. And then it becomes tremendously frustrating, because you're not able to get what you want. You don't have the facility. But then the impulse drives you on to the point where you can say that what's on screen is what you want to be there.

8 Cronenberg shoots *From the Drain* (1967).

At the time there was great excitement about New York underground films. You didn't have to go to Hollywood; you didn't have to carry someone else's cans around for twenty years; you could just go out and make a fucking film. And what's more, the culture of the times was set up so that you could go further than that. There was Jonas Mekas[2] and the Film Co-op of New York. Bob Fothergill, Iain Ewing, Ivan Reitman[3] and I started the Toronto Film Co-op. We said, 'We'll by-pass the structures; we'll make our own film catalogue; we'll put our films in it; we'll rent the films to people who will pay nothing (or something, depending). Somehow we'll survive and we'll continue to make films. But we know the main thing is that we want these films to be seen.'

It was different in Canada, as always. We wanted to by-pass the Hollywood system because it wasn't ours. We didn't have access to it. It wasn't because we hated it, but because we didn't have an equivalent, and we didn't have the thing itself. We didn't know people who distributed films; we didn't see Canadian films in the cinemas. Just as we didn't hear Canadian rock and roll on the radio in those days. I can still remember the first: The Ugly Ducklings. It was stunning to recognize yourself. Like any minority.

If we had accepted that we must play the system before making a film, we were saying, in essence, that we couldn't make films. Ironically enough, it was America that gave us a way round that: 'Go do your own thing, man.' And being the 1960s, there was a lot of fluidity; a lot of film-makers from New York and LA would come through for those screenings. You'd sit and watch underground movies, which were whacky and stupid and bad and dumb, and great to watch. I remember summer nights you'd stroll through various sections of town that were hippiefied and you'd find people screening films on sheets strung up on store fronts, and people sitting on the sidewalk watching. It was very exciting. Your film could be one of those, and you were part of it.

We based ourselves in Cinecity at Film Canada, which was Willem Poolman's brainchild, and which had a very long and profound influence on us. It connected us with very arty films and also with New York underground films. Poolman was a crazed Dutch lawyer who fell in love with movies, took over a post office and turned it into a cinema called Cinecity. Across the street, above a bank, he had the offices of his company, Film Canada. The really exciting stuff for me was all the Hungarian, Polish, Czech films; people like Miklos Jancso. And I'd go to Cinecity, where they had screenings of films that Poolman was looking at to see whether or not he was interested in distributing them for Film

Canada. It made us all feel like insiders as opposed to outsiders. And when you start to feel that you are an insider, it helps your sense of power. You feel you can actually do something rather than be just a spectator.

Poolman was very gay and gathered around him a lot of young male film-makers. We got to use his beautiful little theatre and had some wonderful screenings there. I particularly remember the Cinethon: an all-night marathon screening of underground films. You'd come out at three in the morning and have croissants and coffee – it was the beginning of the croissant attack – go back in and see a few more and stumble out in the dawn. And then you'd go back in and see another five hours' worth. It was fabulous. *Transfer* was among them.

I felt very much part of a community then. The 'otherness' had solely to do with the specifics of what I wanted to do creatively, in that I wanted isolation. So at that point you're talking about your own uniqueness; you need that alienness. You want the community – you don't want the pain of feeling outside – but you are threatened by acceptance because it dulls the edge. It dulls the anger. So it's very schizophrenic. Film-making is not collaborative totally, but it is collaborative. Kafka could write his stories in the context that he was in his time. He couldn't have made films. To die unpublished is something you can't do in film-making. Perhaps Kafka would have been destroyed by being successful; his sensibility was driven by paranoia, loneliness and despair. You can only have so much of that and make films at the same time. Because it involves other people, you need to have social skills. I don't know if Kafka had any social skills; he was an alien, alien, alien. He was a Jew and a German-speaker in a Czech city. He was just wrong.

By this time I'd done one year of Honours English, stood second in the entire university and first in my college. I'd proved that I was able to do that after the débâcle of the science assault! So I eased off and went to Europe for a year.

I lived primarily in Copenhagen, but did spend some time in London. The Carnaby Street era. I came back with shoulder-length hair and a paisley shirt, which was very shocking at the University of Toronto. When you see my 1967 graduation photo, I look like an ugly girl! I grew my hair in Copenhagen because the girls all thought that if you spoke English you were a Rolling Stone. So it was very necessary to have long hair.

When I came back to Canada I did two years of a general BA with an emphasis on English, graduated, and then didn't know what I was going to do. That's when I really discovered film-making, when I began thinking that maybe I really only wanted to do that. It was during my MA make-up year (I had opted to resume my studies) that I started to do *Stereo* and *Crimes of the Future*. By the end of *Stereo* I knew there was no point in doing an MA. I wanted to do film.

Notes

1 Steadicam is the trade name for a camera rig, worn by an operator. The device stabilizes camera movement, allowing complex, moving takes to be performed while walking, without camera shake.
2 Jonas Mekas (1922–   ) was born in Lithuania and emigrated to the USA in 1950. He organized the all-important Film-makers Co-operative in New York, which distributed influential 16mm experimental work in the 1960s. As a film theoretician he also edited the magazine *Film Culture*, and was a contributing film journalist to the *Village Voice*. Mekas was also an avant-garde film-maker in his own right, directing films such as *The Brig* (1964), Diaries Notes and Sketches (1969) and *Reminiscences of a Journey to Lithuania* (1972).
3 Subsequent to the Toronto Film Co-op, and his role as Cronenberg's producer on *Shivers* and *Rabid*, Ivan Reitman (1946–   ) went on to direct many highly successful Hollywood movies, including *Ghostbusters* (1984), *Twins* (1988) and *Kindergarten Cop* (1991).

CHAPTER 3

Crimes of the Future: Obsessions and Avant-Garde Films

Discussion and critical appraisal of David Cronenberg's work have tended to pivot on auteurist *principles. This particular strain of cinematic analysis was virulent in the 1960s in the most progressive film journals and journalism. It dissected films primarily to demonstrate the recurring thematic concerns and obsessions of the director – often at the expense of discussing mere* mise-en-scène. *It was progressive because it assisted in the re-examination of the work of certain American directors, and denied the oppositional equations of high versus low culture; art versus cinema; European versus American film-making.*

However, auteurism *lost its credibility as the cutting edge of film theory and criticism. No sooner had it passed into every newspaper film column as a basic review tool than it was usurped by more politically motivated forms of analysis: ideology; semiology; psychoanalysis. Regimes of all kinds. Auteurism had served its function. It became a reactionary rather than a progressive position.*

As a result, Cronenberg has suffered somewhat from being the subject of a criticism politically out of step with film theory. In practice he is, of course, a classic auteur, *a writer/director who, it seems from the very first films, had concerns and obsessions that he has continued to worry away at. Cronenberg's one-time cinematographer Mark Irwin once observed that his director had been making the same film all his life: 'Probably the sum total of his works will be more impressive than any single film.'*

If at first some progressive critics, knowledgeable audiences and producers with a good eye were delighted to see an intelligence at work in the exploitation/horror genre, Cronenberg's compulsion to replay the same hand again and again in order to finish the game most satisfactorily – win or lose – is a strength that seems to see him through cinema's ever changing critical and industrial landscape.

Certainly Cronenberg is likely to be unsympathetic to the notion that the auteurist *discourse is redundant merely because it construes thematic consistency as solely personal, and in no meaningful way societal.*

At a certain point I realized that what I liked about the classic film-makers of the 1960s and 1970s, like Bergman and Fellini, was that you entered a world of their own creation when you went to see their films. That world was consistent from film to film. There was a tone, a feeling and dynamics that were consistently at work. It wasn't really conscious on my part that I should do the same, but I started to notice that what I was doing was also creating a world that had its own very specific dynamic. That's scary, because on the one hand I could say, 'Well, that's what a serious film-maker should do,' but on the other hand it worries you because if it comes to be expected of you it can be a trap. You worry that a film will be rejected, or won't fit the pattern.

It's not unlike a child. I see it in how obsessive children become. When a kid's turned into a cat, if you try to relate to him as your son – disaster. Emotional psychic disaster. You've crossed the line. You've done wrong. Don't underestimate the seriousness of play; the necessity to have that fantasy. For me, it's the reason for returning again and again to certain themes. The thing that would not die, you know: disintegration, ageing, death, separation, the meaning of life. All that stuff.

Part of the pressure to be creative is pressure to be meditative and philosophical. Everybody has it. It's a cliché in movies: you get a minor character, like a cab driver, who tells you his philosophy of life in thirty-eight seconds. Even if it's bitter and negative and nihilistic, at least it's a philosophy. Masha tells Max Renn that Videodrome is dangerous because it has something he doesn't: a philosophy. Someone without a philosophy is weak, confused and fumbling by comparison. So there is a pressure to have that. Then it doesn't matter what your discourse is on: male/female relationships; life and death.

Someone said to Lawrence Durrell, 'I've read your latest set of books, but they're awfully like *The Alexandria Quartet*, don't you find?' He said, 'Well, they're written by the same person. We're all dealt one hand of cards in life, and we just play it continually.' Another way of explaining what Durrell had in mind when he said that is that he meant aesthetics, sensibility and one's life experience. That wall socket. There is a universe of sockets, but we all have different plugs. We can't all plug into the same socket. The art is to get other people to plug into your socket. The art is that for the time you're reading *The Alexandria Quartet*, you are Durrell. What he found significant and striking, you also find significant and striking. That's what I want to do. That's where you start to be able to define the difference between hack work and any art form. It has to do with getting other people to plug into your socket.

It makes things better, because you have the need to do it. If that need is frustrated – as when the sexual impulse goes wrong – you get rape, murder, war. You get pathology. If it's not frustrated, it brings peace. I think it's peace that one seeks. There are books you read because they're a diversion, and there are books you read when you're in spiritual trouble. They are soul food; they really do balm the soul. I want my movies to do that, get to the soul.

It's spreading the load, the stress. Like race-car frames. You spread the stress through the entire chassis, rather than let it hit at one point because that bends and breaks the frame. That's part of it: to share, because these things need to be constantly said. I don't want to have unfettered access to the brains, nervous systems and sensibilities of my audience. I want them to have unfettered access to mine. Then they can reject it, absorb it, be affected by it or misinterpret it.

When you're in the muck you can only see muck. If you somehow manage to float above it, you still see the muck but you see it from a different perspective. And you see other things too. That's the consolation of philosophy. The ideal is that on your deathbed you smile and say, 'Ah, yes of course,' and then die with a smile on your face. That's what I'd like. To deny the muck is no consolation; it's a false philosophy. The reason my films can be so dark is that I have a real compulsion to make optimism real, to have it based in reality, however tough. To tell a child, 'Don't worry about death, because you'll go to heaven and we'll all be there and you'll meet all your friends' – that's a hideous thing to say if you don't believe it. And I don't. That's not optimism or a positive approach to life and death; that's pure fakery. That's useless. If I can still find beauty and grace in tears, that starts to be more real. That's something I can use, build a philosophy on.

I think it's also the desire to see things naked. That's *Naked Lunch* really. Burroughs calls it the frozen moment, when everyone sees what's on the end of every fork. For real.

Cronenberg regards his two featurettes Stereo *and* Crimes of the Future, *started while still at University, as his first 'finished, complete and autonomous' films. Avoiding the obvious solution for the independent film-maker – shooting on 16mm – he went straight to 35mm, with a deferred rental on a 35mm Arriflex from Janet Good of Canadian Motion Picture Equipment Rental Company. Constituting a one-man crew, Cronenberg shot* Stereo *(1969) in black and white, and* Crimes *(1970) in colour, both without synchronized sound. This gambit was in part to avoid the*

9 Cronenberg shoots *Stereo* (1969) in 35mm.

noisiness of the Arriflex camera. Voice-overs – representing the thoughts and unspoken communications of his characters, and bare narrative details – were added later.

Dubbed Cronenberg's avant-garde movies, the films are nonetheless thematic blueprints for many of the cinematic adventures that were to come, well-formed embryos or prototypes for the subsequent experiments in Visceral Vision. Unlike the commercial features, however, they were able strikingly to demonstrate a concern for architecture, and for tonal, almost abstract, composition. The uncluttered, pure images, combined with a separate soundtrack clotted with convincing scientific mumbo-jumbo and philosophical musings, marked these early experiments as unique. Both films are credited to Cronenberg's production entity, humorously entitled Emergent Films, after a specific evolutionary theory.

My conceit was that my films would be, in the world of film-making, these emergent creatures that would be unprecedented and not able to have been predicted. You never did anything casually in those days!

Stereo was financed by Film House. I wrote to the Canada Council for a grant to make a film: to live on, if not to finance it. They didn't have a film category, even in the late 1960s. I had to do it as a writer. So I invented this whole Nabokovian novel that I was going to write, did a specimen chapter plus a plot outline, and got three notables to back me. Eventually I received Can.$3,500 which was a fortune to me at the time, to write this novel. So I immediately started to make *Stereo*. The next year, the Canada Council started a cinema category. They were very responsive. I used their money to establish credit at Film House and then got seriously into debt and couldn't pay them until about fifteen years later. But I did pay them! Ivan Reitman had been in the same situation, but paid them sooner! He was more successful.

Crimes of the Future (1970) was financially supported by the Canadian Film Development Corporation (CFDC) to the tune of about Can.$15,000. It was maybe the first and last experimental film they put money into. They were looking for their own mandate, and were supposed to help develop the Canadian film industry. But nobody knew what that meant. So I slipped in under the wire. I was knocking on the door before there was a door.

My general background as a would-be writer made me isolationist. I suppose it's a very Canadian thing to do. But I felt very private about the work I was doing, and the projects I was thinking of were just not communicable to anyone else. It never occurred to me to get help other than from a few friends; the actors were also friends and acquaintances. They were not professional actors.

There was something about the medium of film that just fitted my temperament like a glove. I'd made several attempts at writing novels, and was just beginning to feel that I didn't have the proper temperament to do it; the long isolation and obsessive introspection. And, when I did write, I was possessed by Nabokov and Burroughs. One of the things I had trouble with as a writer was getting out of their clutches. I couldn't find my own voice. But when I wrote for film, I was totally liberated.

I had no influences whatsoever. I don't mean that in an arrogant way, but in a very tangible way for me. I didn't feel the hand of someone on my shoulder, like Hitchcock's on Brian De Palma. There was not one film-maker who was so almost me that I couldn't get to the real me. An important element in my decision to go into film was because it did come relatively easily. I'm sure that was one of the reasons I wrote 'Orgy of the Blood Parasites' (*Shivers*). It just sprang up. There was some other momentum there, when I was writing for the screen, that wasn't there in the novel. That was exhilarating.

Interestingly, both *Crimes of the Future* and *Stereo* were influenced by Ron Mlodzik, a very elegant gay scholar, an intellectual who was studying at Massey College. He played the lead character in both of them. When I showed *Stereo* in Montreal, after a screening a young man came up to me and started to proposition me. I told him I was flattered that he should want me to go to bed with him just because he liked my movie, but I wasn't gay. He was shocked. He was sure after seeing *Stereo* that I was. I attributed that to the translation of Ron Mlodzik's presence in *Stereo* and *Crimes of the Future*. How that translates to the other films I'm not sure. It's still very illuminating about my own sensibility though, simply because I chose to use Ron as lead player in those films. How directly that connects with my own sexuality or not, it certainly connects very directly to my aesthetic sense of his space, and his medieval gay sensibility, which I like a lot. His Catholicism was very medieval, and so was his sense of style.

Both films, in particular Stereo, *are visually characterized by their long static, panning or moving shots in which characters wander as if in a dream. Many of these languorous, lucid takes are arrested further by use of stop-frame slow motion.* Stereo, *filmed entirely on a modernist university campus during the summer vacation, sees Cronenberg producing*

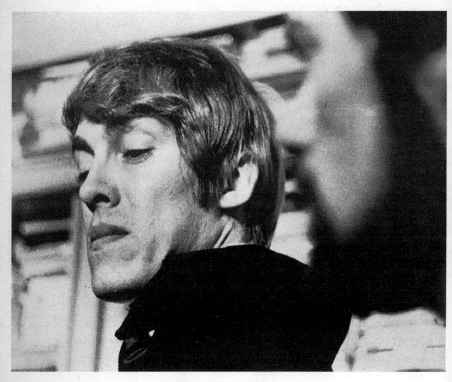

· 10 Ron Mlodzik in *Stereo*.

highly composed shots of linear and tonal frame dissection, 'irritated' by the somnambulistic wanderings of his casebook subjects.

One of the things you have to deal with when you're directing is space; how you show what, when, and how much of it. That translates technically into what size of lens you use, and what kind of camera move you employ, how far back you are, and what size close-ups you use. Since I was a very pure film-maker at the time, I suppose that was one reason those considerations were more strikingly apparent in those films. It is pure film-making in that sense: concerned with space and time and images and rhythm and how they relate to certain kinds of sounds and silences, which is something that you're totally afraid to do in commercial films. You would never have a completely dead soundtrack. But I had no fear at the time.

Toronto in the 1950s had a certain kind of stifling order. This was the Eisenhower era, which masked something very delicious, which turned out to be partially chaos but also just raw energy. There was a lot of sexual energy being repressed in society then. The massive architecture suggests order and calm and eternity, when in fact the poor human beings who have to live inside that society are inflicted with many things that don't have much to do with those concepts. I think I was trying to come to terms with the balance between the two.

I tend to view chaos as a private rather than social endeavour. That's undoubtedly because I was born and raised in Canada. The chaos that most appeals to me is very private and very personal. You have these little pockets of private and personal chaos brewing in the interstices in the structure of society, which likes to stress its order and control, and that's the collision you see.

I'm not particularly insecure or paranoid, but I always thought I would much more likely be put in jail for my art than for my Jewishness. A friend who saw *Videodrome* said he really liked it and added, 'You know, someday they're going to lock you up,' and walked away. That did not help. I suppose underneath I always had a feeling that my existence as a member of standing of the community was in grave jeopardy for whatever reason. It's as though society had suddenly discovered what I really am, what is really going on inside, and wants to destroy it.

My role in *Stereo* was as Dr Luther Stringfellow, the absentee scientist who actually set up the experiment, because, in a sense, I had set up an experiment. In *Crimes of the Future* I am Antoine Rouge, the absentee mentor who has died and who is reincarnated as a little girl.

Having decided to shoot Stereo *on 35mm, and at 65 minutes, Cronenberg was in a good position to attempt exposure at film festivals. After successful self-financed screenings of the film at both Adelaide and Edinburgh, a moneyed transportation tycoon advanced $10,000 for distribution rights via his own International Archives in New York. This led to further screenings at New York's Museum of Modern Art, press coverage and additional finance for the next experiment:* Crimes of the Future.

I used sound to make the experience of the films more like something you're watching and hearing. In *Crimes* I used a second soundtrack other than the voice-over, made up of deep-sea creatures, dolphins, shrimp. The sound of water is very much present. In a sense the soundtrack was meant to be Darwin's voyage of the *Beagle*. I thought of it as an underwater ballet. I wanted to create the feeling that you were watching aliens from another planet. There is a science-fiction element, but not as explicit as the genre demands.

There's a lot of satirical, academic stuff in both films, partly because I was still at university. I loved the academic life; film screwed that all up. I didn't write a script for *Stereo*; it was being invented as it was made. The voice-over was written afterwards. It was partly my own strange feelings about the academic life and the life of psychology. I never studied it, but I had friends who did; that attempt to somehow control, by understanding, very subtle and complex things. Maybe impossible, and also funny, but worthwhile trying. And sociology: the way it tries to trap phenomena with words.

One of the things you want to do with any kind of art is to find out what you're thinking about, what is important to you, what disturbs you. Some people go to confession or talk to close friends on the phone to do the same thing. And of course, your dreams are important. I've never approached mine in any methodological or psychoanalytic way, but I recognize that they're interesting – a version of my own reality. I have to pay attention to that. That's another way you let yourself know what you're thinking about. You have to subvert your psyche sometimes to know what's really going on.

I think of both *Stereo* and *Crimes of the Future* as perhaps happening underwater. There is definitely a sense of looking into an aquarium. At certain times in *Stereo*, the motion becomes stop-motion, not slow motion – it's multiple-frame printing with each frame printed five times – and then you get that jerky slow motion. At these times, the voice-over is neutral and announcerish as it reports on what is observed. The two always come together, as if someone were observing something under a microscope and had deliberately lowered the temperature so that whatever creature was there would move more slowly and be more amenable to observation.

I wanted to create a novel mode of interrelation. There is no speech, but we know there is a kind of speech in gesture. Every community has a whole unspoken dictionary, and I wanted to invent one of my own. I had seriously thought of having the people in the film speak a tongue I had invented, but it's very tricky to avoid making it ridiculous. I tried to get the alienness of culture involved in the film in subtle ways. One of them was to have that balletic sense of movement.

I also needed the correct fish for my aquarium. Hence Ron Mlodzik. He is capable of portraying an incredibly exotic, strange creature who is not quite earthly and, in terms of the gesture and the sexuality he projects, disquieting to an audience. He's the odd man out. He is the one who, in strange ways, goes underground; the one who may dabble in guerrilla warfare, but even there is not quite engaged.

In both films there is this idea of a man-made, man-controlled environment short-circuiting the concept of evolution. Survival of the fittest doesn't work any more. But the institutions aren't evil. They are almost noble in that they are an attempt by human beings, however crazy, to try and structure and control their own fate. On the other hand, they may be the cause of their own destruction.

I still wasn't thinking in career terms. *Stereo* and *Crimes of the Future* are not films one builds a career on, not in the sense of being a professional who earns a living making films. And making films that way was kind of lonely. But I really did start to feel that I had something to offer. I thought, 'There's something here and I'm really going to explore this.' At that point, everything else became irrelevant. I ceased to do university and I ceased to think in terms of writing fiction. I was making longer films – about 65 minutes – so I was edging towards the mainstream.

A French critic for *Le Monde* saw those films and wrote some very nice things about them. He was shocked to meet me in Paris years later to review *Scanners* and said, 'I was convinced after you made those films that you would never make another.' And he was right, in that they were a complete little pair of films – one was in a sense a sequel to the other. For me there was nowhere to go from there. I had to experiment and try that approach in order to grow. But they proved to be a dead end for me.

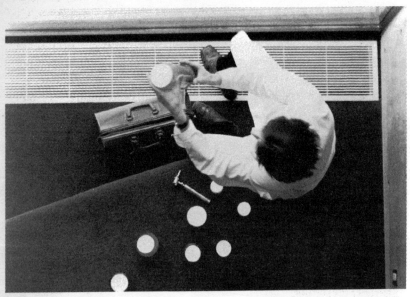

11 *Stereo.*
12 *Crimes of the Future* (1970).

Both Stereo *and* Crimes of the Future *take place in and around strange-sounding institutions. Events and experiments are initiated by even stranger-sounding committees and renegade groups. We hear of the Canadian Academy of Erotic Inquiry, the Institute of Neo-Veneral Disease, the Oceanic Podiatry Group and The House of Skin. Cronenberg remains fascinated by the machinations of institutions, and over the years has given us the Keloid Clinic* (Rabid), *the Somafree Institute* (The Brood), Consec (Scanners) *and Spectacular Optical* (Videodrome).

I often wonder what it's like to be a cell in a body. Just one cell in skin or in a brain or an eye. What is the experience of that cell? It has an independent existence, and yet it seems to be part of something that doesn't depend on it, and that has an existence quite separate from it. When you think of colonies of ants or bees, they aren't physically joined the way an organism made up of cells is, but it's the same thing. They have an independent existence, an independent history. But they are part of a whole that is composed of them.

That's what fascinates me about institutions. An institution is really like an organism, a multi-celled animal in which the people are the cells. The very word 'corporation' means body. An incorporation of people into one body. That's how the Romans thought of it. Five people would incorporate and become a sixth body, subject to the same laws as they would as individuals. I connect this with the concept of a human body, in which the cells change regularly. They live and die their own lives, and yet the overall flow of the existence of the body as an individual seems to be consistent. How does that work? It's very mysterious.

People are fascinated by little sections of the CIA, which might be said to develop independent of the body of the CIA. It's like a tumour or a liver or a spleen that decides it will have its own independent existence. It still needs to share the common blood that flows through all the organs, but the spleen wants to go off and do a few things. It'll come back. It has to. But it wants to have its own adventures. That's fascinating to me. I don't think of it as a threat. It's only a real threat if all your organs decide to go off in different directions. At a certain point the chaos equals destruction. But at the same time the potential for adventure and creative difference is exciting.

Stereo *and* Crimes of the Future *signposted yet another fascination for Cronenberg which continues to revisit his work with increasing intensity:*

13 Institution in distress: the House of Skin in *Crimes of the Future*.
14 Institution in action: Consec in *Scanners*.

male/female separation. Some critics and audiences have viewed develop-
ments here with mounting distaste, culminating with the difficult and
confrontational Dead Ringers. *One significant difference between these*
early films and what followed is indeed sexual difference. Whatever the
intention, Stereo *and* Crimes of the Future *seem more open to – and*
playful with – notions of 'omnisexuality' as a realizable alternative mode
of social/sexual reorganization. This early fascination – perhaps some-
what determined by a 1960s hippy idealism and milieu – has become a
compulsion continually to provoke audiences to comprehend the nature
and meaning of accepted sexual difference. Subsequent experiments have
gone on to yield darker results.

In *Crimes of the Future* I talk about a world in which there are no
women. Men have to absorb the femaleness that is gone from the planet.
It can't just cease to exist because women aren't around. It starts to bring
out their own femaleness more, because that duality and balance is
necessary. The ultimate version would be that a man should die and
re-emerge as a woman and be completely aware of his former life as a
man. In a strange way this would be a very physical fusion of those two
halves of himself. That's what *Crimes of the Future* is about. Ivan
Reitman once told me it could have been a great commercial success if I'd
done the movie straight.

William Burroughs doesn't just say that men and women are different
species, he says they're different species with different wills and purposes.
That's where you arrive at the struggle between the sexes. I think Burroughs really touches a nerve there. The attempt to make men and
women not different – little girls and boys are exactly the same, it's only
social pressure, influence and environmental factors that makes them go
separate ways – just doesn't work. Anyone who has kids knows that.
There is a femaleness and a maleness. We each partake of both in
different proportions. But Burroughs is talking about something else: will
and purpose.

If you think of a female will, a universal will, and a male will and
purpose in life, that's beyond the bisexual question. A man can be
bisexual, but he's still a man. The same for a woman. They still have
different wills that knock against each other, are perhaps in conflict. If we
inhabited different planets, we would see the female planet go entirely
one way and the male another. Maybe that's why we're on the same
planet, because either extreme might be worse. I think Burroughs's
comments are illuminating. Maybe they're a bit too cosmic to deal with

in daily life, but you hear it reflected in all the hideous clichés of songs: 'you can't live with 'em, and you can't live without 'em'.

Burroughs was fascinated when I told him about a species of butterfly where the male and female are so different it took forty years before lepidopterists realized. They couldn't find the male of one species and the female of another. But they were the same species. One was huge and brightly coloured and the other was tiny and black. They didn't look like they belonged together. When Burroughs talks about men and women being different species, it does have some resonance in other forms of life. But there are also hermaphrodite versions of this butterfly. They are totally bizarre. One half is huge and bright and the other half – split right down the middle of the body – is small and dark. I can't imagine it being able to fly. There's no balance whatsoever.

15 Male/female split: Roy Scheider as Dr Benway emerges from Fadela's body in *Naked Lunch* . . .

16 . . . Antoine Rouge is reincarnated as a little girl in *Crimes of the Future*.

CHAPTER 4

Body Talk: The Cinepix Years

After Stereo *and* Crimes of the Future, *the way forward was not obvious to Cronenberg. Having contracted the film bug and worked through an avant-garde phase, he took a year off. Spending much of that time in Tourettes-sur-Loup in southern France (a small village frequented by, among others, André Bazin,[1] Terry Southern[2] and Ted Kotcheff[3]), he shot some small 'fillers' for Canadian television (CBC):* Tourettes, Letter from Michelangelo *and* Jim Ritchie Sculptor.

A filler is a little impressionistic documentary, two or three minutes long, which you could make some money on. Very free-form, so you could do what you liked. I bought a 16mm camera with another Canada Council grant and got the film stock I wanted from Marseilles. At that point, I was also trying to write a novel again. I wrote a lot of pages, which I've since thrown out. I obviously hadn't totally given up the possibility. I wasn't really sure where I was going.

I was also interested in sculpture, and made one of my own which I called *Surgical Instrument for Operating on Mutants*. It was cast in aluminium at a foundry in Nice and handworked afterwards. Part of the sculpture was the organ to be operated on, and part was the instrument itself. All this emerged later, of course, in *Dead Ringers*. I don't have that sculpture either.

The Cannes Film Festival was on at the time and so I forced myself to go. There was the Carlton Hotel with the three-storey cut-out of James Bond on it. The incredible hype, and the Rolls-Royces, and the hustles. I had turned into a medieval country bumpkin who couldn't deal with the traffic, the people and the noise. The CFDC let me sleep on the couch in their offices in the Carlton. But I was really appalled by the festival and fled back to Tourettes. I licked my psychic wounds there for a while and then said to myself: 'If you're going to do real movies, you're going to have to deal on some level with what the Cannes Festival represents. Maybe if you don't take it so seriously, it'll feel better.' So I went down again and just laughed for a week.

That was a crucial moment for me, because that's when I made a decision. I knew I couldn't make movies like *Stereo* and *Crimes* and consider myself a professional film-maker. I also really wanted a broader audience. I really wanted to get my hands dirty and try. So I went back to Toronto and wrote the script for *Shivers* (which I then called 'Orgy of the Blood Parasites').

After his return to Canada, Cronenberg also continued to shoot fillers for the Canadian Broadcasting Corporation. In June 1972, he also directed Secret Weapons *for them, from a script by friend and colleague Norman Snider, for the CBC's* Programme X *series. Cronenberg has often referred to* Secret Weapons, *the last made by his company Emergent Films, as his 'suppressed' film. Although it has therefore rarely been seen, its function as the perfect conduit between the avant-garde films and the commercial features to come is all too apparent. Its story of a monolithic pharmaceutical company putting pressure on an ex-research scientist experimenting with aggression stimulants during an unspecified civil war has resonances of Cronenberg's second short* From the Drain, *passing through the concerns of* Stereo *and* Crimes of the Future, *as well as prefiguring aspects of* Scanners.

By this time I had my first child, my daughter Cassandra. I could see what a lot of my colleagues and former mates in the film-making underground were doing. A lot of them were floundering; a lot of them had gone into the CBC. We were now in a sort of half-life, the afterglow of the 1960s. Charles Manson and Woodstock had happened. Bobby Kennedy had been shot. It was another era. It was well and truly getting to be the 1970s. I knew that despite the fact I now had a family to support, I didn't want to do any of that other stuff.

I looked around to see what kind of film industry there was in Canada, and there really wasn't one! Even at the National Film Board, film-makers had to pretend they were doing a documentary and then sneak a feature out of it. It was all the heavy hand of John Grierson,[4] whose influence I began to realize was as suffocating to me as it was liberating for people who wanted to make documentaries – the idea that a real movie is a document of real people (meaning normal people), who work the land, who are fishermen; the Eskimos, the Arctic. That was film-making. Even when features got made, like *The Drylanders*, they were basically fictionalized documentaries about how hard it is to work the prairies and all that stuff.

So Canada was really one-legged at that point. There was no film-making of the imagination. When I looked around for it, the closest I could come up with was Cinepix, a little company operating out of Montreal. They had primarily been sleazy distributors, and I say that with great affection – my kind of people. They distributed softcore porno films from Europe, although porno is not really the right word. Much of what they did was in French because of Quebec, and they didn't get widely distributed in English Canada. But they made a film directed by Denis Héroux called *Valerie*. In it, this guy with a black leather jacket rides up on his Harley to a convent, literally rides through the halls, sweeps up Valerie, the convent girl – who is dying to get out – and blasts out into the street. And then they do stuff – have sex, ride bikes, do great bad stuff – all to the accompaniment of this wonderful French-Canadian melodramatic rock and roll.

By the time I contacted Cinepix, they had made a couple of other films too: very sweet, gentle, lush softcore films with a lot of tits – great tits actually. Their films were being shown in cinemas to paying audiences; records that were spin-offs of the soundtracks were being played on Quebec radio. All this was unheard of in English Canada. This was really my introduction to the fierce nationalism of Quebec, and how well it worked in terms of a very enclosed culture that could excite itself. It was very hard for English-Canadian culture to excite English Canadians. They were excited by Americana. But, because of the language and the strange isolated culture that became Quebec when it was abandoned by France, their own language and their own relationship to the Catholic Church was still very vibrant. The convent stuff in *Valerie* was no joke; it was very serious. It was very exciting to me to connect with Quebec film-making.

Cinepix was just André Link, a European Jew who spoke French, and John Dunning, who was totally WASP. For me to say they represented French-Canadian film-making is very ironic, but they did. They were the Roger Corman of Canada, and there were no alternatives. I was aware of Corman,[5] and didn't go to Cinepix out of a fierce sense of nationalism. I just thought that I should be able to make films in Canada. I knew that Norman Jewison,[6] Ted Kotcheff and other expatriate directors felt they had to go first to England and then to Hollywood to have a career. I just didn't.

I remember seeing one of Kotcheff's first movies, *Tiara Tahiti* because there were naked tits on Toronto cinema screens for the first time. Boy, I loved it. I thought it was great, very exciting and very hard to come by. As a kid I used to go with my parents to New York (I had an aunt and uncle who lived there) so I could see Brigitte Bardot movies. I loved Brigitte Bardot. You weren't allowed to see her films in Toronto. So the cinema for me always meant sex, among other things. It meant fantasy. It was luscious, erotic, wonderful. Toronto in the 1950s was none of those things. It was very Eisenhower, very repressive. Rock and roll was also luscious and sexy. I remember hearing Little Richard and Fats Domino for the first time; I didn't even know these guys were black, because in Canada there were no black American people.

So here were Cinepix making movies which maybe would have induced contempt in other serious film-makers. But for me these were real movies, no question about it. These were movies that started to do stuff that I wouldn't mind doing, though maybe not in the same way. So I showed them *Stereo* and *Crimes of the Future* with some trepidation. I'll never forget what John Dunning said. He liked the films, to my shock and relief, and said, 'We know you've got a sexual sensibility there, we're just not sure what kind it is!' This was important, because I was auditioning to direct one of their softcore movies. That's what he was looking for: can this kid, who has never directed a real movie in which actors get paid, come across with the goods? He was very gentle and sweet and very encouraging.

I actually shot a screen test in which I got another founding member of the Film Co-op – Iain Ewing – to audition for the lead role in a movie they were getting together called *Loving and Laughing* – an important movie in my psychic history. I directed a sequence on a swing in a studio – the first time I'd ever seen one. Iain and this lady took their clothes off in this scene where they're on a garden swing together and end up fucking. We didn't go that far in the studio, but we did a little dialogue. I was lying on the ground under the swing with the camera to get these angles, and of course it was the wrong thing to do! I didn't get the job, and neither did Iain. But we had made some contact with Cinepix, who were desperately looking for something that would break them into the American market.

I wrote *Shivers*, and John Dunning loved it. It was exactly what he was looking for. It was a natural thing for me to write, and wasn't the slightest bit calculated. It fitted right in with the kind of writing I'd been doing my whole life, but it was a horror film. Dunning and Link were astute enough to see that you could get a foothold in America with

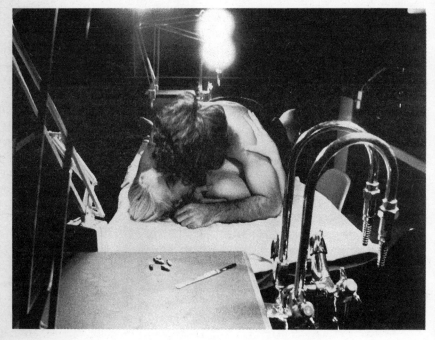

17 'What kind of sexual sensibility is it?': *Stereo*.

low-budget movie-making, which was the only kind they could do. It's old hat now that a young film-maker with little experience can be somewhat encouraged and protected by the genre, but this had never happened in Canada. As far as I know, there had never been a serious horror film made in Canada before *Shivers*.

Dunning and Link went to the CFDC with the script (*Crimes of the Future* had been part-funded by them) and it was greeted with absolute revulsion and confusion. It had since been decided that it was more appropriate for the Canada Council to fund experimental films, and that the CFDC should only do movies that could get a commercial release and make a profit. That was their mandate. But *Shivers* did not fit: it was disgusting, awful, horrific, perverse. It took three years for Cinepix to get them to finally agree to put money into it.

The two or three years that I had to wait between writing the script of *Shivers* and getting the movie made were very hard years emotionally – frustration every waking and sleeping moment. I do remember having these horrible moments of waking up and thinking that it was all just a dream. It was like some fantasy; I was really someone else entirely. I was an accountant who had this absurd film fantasy and woke up to realize that now he's not a film-maker at all. It was bad. It required a lot of endurance to not go do something else.

During that time I thought maybe Canada wasn't going to work for me. So I went to LA with Norman Snider, my friend from University. That was my first time there. It was late February, when the weather was absolutely dismal in Toronto. We got off the plane and, my God, the sun was shining, and there were palm trees! We rented a Mustang convertible, listened to the Beach Boys and drove on the Santa Monica freeway with the wind in our hair and the music in our ears. We thought, 'This is really it!'

I made the rounds of all the low-budget horror producing companies, including Corman's New World. I didn't get to meet him, although I did see him; he was on the way to the dentist. He said, 'Hello.' I think he was having a root canal done, so he couldn't talk to me. I also spoke to John Davidson along the lines of 'Is this insane? They're saying in Canada that what I want to do is nuts. They're saying I can't do it for this much money because of the special effects, and secondly – even if I could – why would I want to?' I was really beginning to doubt my sanity at this time. What I mainly got from Corman's outfit and other people was interest and excitement and acceptance of this as just business as usual. And that's really what I needed.

I was prepared to move to LA to get *Shivers* made when I met Jonathan Demme there. He was renting Barbara Steele's beach house.[7] We were sitting on the beach and Demme says, 'I've read your script.' I said, 'You've read my script!?' He said 'Yes, this guy from Cinepix came down and asked me if I wanted to direct it.' I just went insane. Cinepix desperately wanted the script, but they didn't want me to direct, for obvious reasons. To come 3,000 miles to discover this betrayal! So I went back to Toronto really angry. But, when I arrived, there was a message waiting for me saying that Cinepix had finally gotten agreement from the CFDC to put money into *Shivers*. So that was the beginning of my career as a movie-maker, and the end of my career as a film-maker.

I don't know for sure what made the CFDC change their mind. I did have a lot of access to Michael Spencer, the first head of the CFDC. He had a good sense of humour and a good sense of irony. He did say to me once, 'There are a lot of people who say that a guy like you should spend ten years carrying around Julian Roffman's film cans' (Roffman was a producer). But he and I both knew I wasn't going to do that. I believe he certainly was a champion of mine at some level. And, of course, the CFDC finally helped finance *Shivers* and their worst fears were totally realized by the results.

On the basis of the script, the CFDC may have been aware of the probable impact of Shivers, *but innocent audiences worldwide were not. At its most obvious level – the raw, startling and shocking imagery – the film has never been bettered, not even by the director. It is at this level of outrageous imagery that the film first assaults any viewer. One experiences a tremulous sensation that suggests one might have witnessed the end of the unconscious. There it seems to be, thrown up on the screen in all its truly perverse and initially repulsive splendour, unmasked and unashamed.* Shivers *was beyond one's worse fears of repressed forces, desires and twisted sexual fantasies. It was then, and remains, an unforgettable experience. It inevitably opened the floodgates of disgust and outrage – purely at the image level.*

I don't think of my films as being radical. They're often received that way, or are perceived with horror of a different kind by censors and by people who feel they must protect the common will. Because of that I look at them and say, 'I suppose if I were in their shoes, and my understanding of human endeavour were theirs, then these are radical.' But I don't think someone in a country that banned one of my films would say it was because the film was politically dangerous. I don't think 'political' would be the right word in this context. I think it's because of the imagery, not the philosophical suggestions behind the imagery. It's the imagery that strikes them first, and then the general disturbing quality of the films.

If it were just a question of mutilating bodies the way that hack-and-slash movies often do, I wouldn't find extreme imagery interesting. People often say to me, 'Why don't you do it the way Hitchcock did and just suggest things?' First of all I say, 'Have you seen *Frenzy*?', which has a couple of very nasty scenes. The man did them – he wanted to, no one was forcing him. I think that Hitchcock's reticence to show stuff had more to do with the temper and censorship of the times than it did his own demons. I have to show things because I'm showing things that people could not imagine. If I had done them off-screen, they would not exist. If you're talking about shooting someone, or cutting throats, you could do that off-screen and the audience would have some idea of what was going on. But if you imagine Max Renn in *Videodrome* and the slit in his stomach ... If I'd done that off-screen, what would the audience think was going on? It simply wouldn't work.

I'm presenting audiences with imagery and with possibilities that have to be shown. There is no other way to do it. It's not done for shock value. I haven't made a single film that hasn't surprised me in terms of audience response; they have been moved, shocked or touched by things that I thought wouldn't nudge them one inch. For me, it's really a question of conceptual imagery. It's not just 'Let's show someone killing a pig on screen and we'll get a good reaction.' You would. So what?

I don't know where these extreme images come from. It seems very straightforward and natural and obvious to me as it happens. Often they come from the philosophical imperative of a narrative and therefore lead me to certain things that are demanded by the film. I don't impose them. The film or the script itself demands a certain image, a certain moment in the film, dramatically. And it emerges. It's like the philosophy of Emergent Evolution, which says that certain unpredictable peaks emerge from the natural flow of things and carry you forward to another stage. I guess each film has its own version of Emergent Evolution. It's just like plugging into a wall socket. You look around for the plug point and, when you find it, the electricity is there – assuming that the powerhouse is still working. That's as close to describing the process as I can get.

Each film really does have its own balance, its own equilibrium. Things

18 Allan Migicovsky and Joe Silver: *Shivers*.
19 Barbara Leigh Hunt: *Frenzy*.

that seemed appropriate for *Videodrome* did not, for example, seem appropriate for *The Dead Zone*. At the beginning, when a film is just a kind of nymph, it's hard to anticipate what its dynamics really are. So often you start with things that are very extreme. I do. Then I cut back to something that works from beginning to end. It depends what the genesis of the film is. If it begins with a book, as *The Dead Zone* did, or with a short story and a film, as *The Fly* did, it might work the other way. You might start with something very narrow, then gradually it begins to show jagged peaks and edges.

There are a lot of underground films that are very sexual and very violent and could never be shown. Certainly symbolic violence was everywhere in underground films, partially I think because the people who felt they were undergrounders had a certain rage and anger. I mean, Kenneth Anger's name is no mistake.

Shivers did start with a dream I had about a spider that emerged from a woman's mouth at night while she slept. The dream was very casual. It wasn't a horrific dream at all. It was just 'Oh yeah, the spider that lives in her mouth'. It seemed that the creature just lived there, inside her. It would come out at night, go round the house and go back into her mouth. Back into her body. During the day she knew nothing about it. Afterwards, on reflection, I thought, 'My God, that image is really giving a physical presence to the idea that things go on within us which are strange and disturbing.' Also, it seemed the spider in some way gave her life when she was awake. Embodying that in an insect or creature was really the unique thing about the dream. That was really the crystal at the centre of what became *Shivers*.

The very purpose was to show the unshowable, to speak the unspeakable. I was creating certain things that there was no way of suggesting because it was not common currency of the imagination. It had to be shown or else not done. I like to say, during the course of the film, 'I'm going to show you something that you're not able to believe, because it'll be so outrageous or ridiculous or bizarre. But I'm going to make it real for you. I'm going to show you this is for real!'

I do believe there's a point past which you start losing vast segments of your audience by being too extreme, but one of the reasons people like to see my movies is because they expect that I will go further than they would. Anyway, an artist is meant to be extreme.

No less outrageous than the imagery of Shivers *was the film's budget: approximately Can.$180,000. In true guerrilla film-making style, the*

film commenced shooting in Montreal in August 1974, on an improbable
production schedule for a major special-effects piece.

I remember one moment with crystal clarity: finally sitting in the first
meeting, with Ivan Reitman – who was going to produce – John Dunning
and André Link, and a couple of other people. Everyone was very
excited: talking detail, planning the schedule and budget, working out
this and that. You'd think it would be one of the most exhilarating
moments of your life: this is really going to happen. In fact, I was stricken
with the most profound melancholy. It only lasted a few minutes, but it
was overwhelming and incredibly potent. I didn't realize at the time that
it was an incredible sense of loss: this was no longer mine. It was
everybody's, a shared event. It was goodbye to a certain kind of film-
making, where you do everything, if you can get a couple of friends to
help.

Suddenly, I had fifteen days to learn how to make a movie. I didn't
know how to make movies, just films. My first production meeting was a
model of bluff. I sat there nodding and didn't know what the fuck was
going on. I didn't know who anyone was: I didn't know what an
assistant director did; what a production manager did; what an art
director did. I could sort of figure out costume, but then what was a
dresser? It was odd to suddenly have a cameraman, and not know what a
focus puller was.

Casting was a totally new experience – just the possibilities for humiliation, degradation and weirdness right there. We had open auditions,
and I mean open. We had a sign on the street saying, 'Anybody who
wants to be in this movie . . .', with a little office upstairs. The strange
people that just came in! But Cinepix realized that Ivan was a very
capable director in his own right, with a very commercial eye. Their
technique – given that they were forced to accept me as the director – was
to surround me with people with much more experience. It worked. Ivan
was invaluable; he'd been the low-budget route and knew what we had
to do, knew the craziness. And he was very forceful. He was nothing but
astonishing, and always knew what he wanted. I wavered at a certain
point. He never did. He knew entertainment, commercial film-making.

So there I was shooting this movie, and it was difficult, visually.
Suddenly, instead of having the incredible feeling of fluidity and ease I
had shooting my own stuff, I felt awkward and clumsy. Everybody was
in the way; the close-ups were the wrong size; the height of the camera
was wrong relative to the faces; dolly shots were a big deal. I just wasn't

getting what I wanted; I could feel it on the set.

I'll never forget the first day's rushes. Fortunately we saw the first three days' rushes all together, because for some reason we couldn't screen them each day. When day one came up, my heart just sank! Nothing I wanted to be there was there. Nothing. It looked wrong, it sounded wrong, everything was wrong. It was the first and only time that it occurred to me, 'Maybe I can't really do this.' It had never occurred to me before. The moment of truth. Fortunately, it only lasted twenty minutes, because then the next day's rushes came on. They were better. And then the next day's, and I started to see some shots I thought were right.

So I was spared the agony of having to go to the set feeling that I couldn't do it. I was learning to use the crew machine, the big movie machine. I'm still learning that one. And it was incredibly hectic. It was 'OK, we shoot the guard, rape the girl and crash the car in the morning. In the afternoon we get into the bug effects: the bug comes out of the mouth, the stomach bursts open, the thing jumps on the face.' The schedule was unbelievable!

There are more effects in *Shivers* than in *The Exorcist*. And some of them are really good. Dick Smith, who had developed the bladder technique for making things move under the skin, was really stunned when he saw the movie; it was one of those moments of simultaneous invention because Joe Blasco invented it for us at the same time. We had to go to LA for effects, because there was nobody in Toronto to do this stuff. It had never been done before. I didn't have much to do with that; that's where having experienced people with good instincts around you comes in. How do you find a guy who's cheap, who can really do it, and will come to Montreal with his pack and his guys?

Blasco used to do Lawrence Welk's make-up.[8] He said that's where he got his training in horror make-up! His work on *Shivers* was world class; he was totally ingenious and brilliant. State of the art, and cheap. We just used balloons to make the fake chest of Allan Migicovsky writhe. I don't think we even used condoms then (now common) – just balloons set in sequence, blown up one after the other so that it looked as though the bugs in his stomach were moving, wriggling around. Dead simple and brilliant. Those effects were based on my understanding of human-body reality; fantastic, but not so fantastic. There's always a sexual element but also a very real element. I've seen people's stomachs move, knots in their stomachs because they're tense. It looks like that, like something's trying to get out. That's very sexual; something living is inside you.

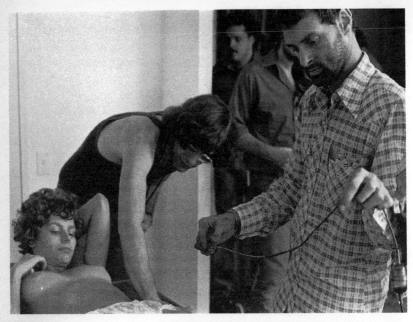

20 and 21 Joe Blasco works on *Shivers*.

Special effects is fiddly, silly stuff. It's like magic; an illusion. They have taken on an almost hallowed, revered status now, but on set it's all 'Fuck! The balloon broke' or 'The cable snapped, oh God ...' You have to forget everything outside the frame, because it's only what's in frame that is real, in your movie. Joe was the master of fiddly, conceptual stuff, and he certainly knew his chemistry: you don't smear KY jelly on that foam because it will eat it away. All that. Conceptually he was wonderful too, and also very funny and intense. An unsung hero as far as I'm concerned.

In conception, the effects were a little more pure than *The Exorcist*. *Shivers* is a very pure film, pure and naïve. I wrote it the way I wanted to see it, and my technique is still the same. I just don't worry about how much it's going to cost and how we're going to do it. Maybe you have to change something because you don't have the money or you can't figure out a way to do it. But on the first draft I write what I want to see and forget everything else. So those images came right from my imagination to the screen uncensored, partly because John Dunning really understood me. He loved what I did; he had a wonderful, twisted sense of cinema. I was lucky to reach him. Even producers in Hollywood who would do a horror film didn't really get *Shivers*. Sam Arkoff might have made it, but he wouldn't have understood it.

We moved the entire production into Nuns' Island high-rises. This was going to be Starliner Towers, where the film takes place. The only way we could afford for me to live there too was that my apartment doubled as the special-effects workroom. I slept in a bed slimy with fake blood, and there were parasites and chests taped to my windows. I had leeches in the fridge, because for a while we were thinking of using real leeches for the parasite close-up stuff. I used to feed them raw meat. One day the crew turned the fridge up to cool their beer and my leeches were frozen solid.

The parasite bugs came out of my childhood fascination with the microscopic, and with insects. When I grew up, most other kids weren't into watching praying mantises eating grasshoppers. To me, there was definitely more than just a little beauty in that, just as visually and intellectually there are things which you see under a microscope that are satisfying. A lot of people don't understand that response.

I went to a medical artist and showed her what I had in mind for the bugs, and Blasco translated the leeches and medical drawings into a sculpture. They were made of foam latex with a spring inside to give them elasticity. Often they were manipulated by mono-filament fishing line – nothing very elaborate. Most of the effects were done by cutting and the simplest possible techniques. When the bug is sniffing around in the bathtub drain, that was assistant director Danny Goldberg manipulating it underneath the plug – basically a finger puppet.

We had no money for sets, so we put notices in the elevators for people to give us their apartments to shoot the movie in. We would look at them and say, yes, this character could live here. We were totally dependent on luck to find homes for our characters. Some of them altered because we got a different kind of apartment. So the line between the reality of living at Nuns' Island, and the fantasy of the movie became a very thin line, especially at night. Living on your own set is odd.

I did learn a lot about editing because we didn't have a lot of footage. The mandate was: dialogue scenes get short shift because the effects are where this movie is at, and they're going to take the time. So you set up a dialogue scene so it's easy to shoot: not too fancy with the camera moves and stuff, and you don't do too many takes. Later, it hurts when people criticize you because you can't direct actors, as though you don't know what's wrong.

The lead actress, Sue Helen Petrie, had been in a couple of the Cinepix porno films. In fact, she was in almost every Canadian film being made then. She was very voluptuous but very pretty, and not a bad actress. Funny and very bright. We're on set and we're doing this scene, and she has to cry. She really has to cry a lot in the movie because her husband is weird right from the start. She says, 'David, I've got a confession. I can't cry on screen. I've never been able to do it.' I said, 'You've got to!' She says, 'That's why I wanted to do this role – to show that I can cry. But I can't.' I said, 'Oh my God, what are we going to do now?' So she says, 'I'm going to grate onions and put them in my eyes, and then you're going to slap me across the face, and then I'll go in front of the cameras and do it.' She wasn't kidding; this was another kind of desperation I was having to deal with.

So I say to the crew, 'OK, you're going to roll and we're not going to be on set, and then Sue's going to run in. So just keep rolling.' We go around the corner of the kitchen (we were shooting in a very small apartment), and she rubs the onions in her eyes. It doesn't look like she's crying. She said, 'Hit me,' so I gave her a little tap. 'That's not hard enough, you've really got to hit me.' So I hit her, really hard. Then she said, 'OK, now do it ten more times.' So, five on each cheek. My hands were burning. She shrieks. Shriek, whack, whack, shriek. Then she ran out and we shot immediately.

Then Barbara Steele arrives, and the first scene she has to do with Sue

22 Barbara Steele consoles Sue Helen Petrie in *Shivers*.

is when she gives her a parasite kiss. So it's pretty tricky; low-budget stuff throws you into that because you have no time for niceties. So Barbara is sitting there, and everybody on the crew is now completely blasé about our technique for making Sue cry. The make-up lady comes to me and says, 'She's on the verge of bruising now and I won't be able to cover it. You better take that into consideration.' But it's business as usual. We roll the camera. Barbara's all ready, but I don't say 'Action'. Sue and I go into the kitchen. Barbara's wondering what the fuck's going on. So it's smack, smack, smack; shriek, shriek, shriek. Sue comes out sobbing. Great. Barbara is horrified; there's a look of total shock and anger on her face. I say, 'Action, action. Do it, do it!'

When it's 'Cut', Barbara stands up (she's real big, and she was in high heels) and literally grabs me by the lapels and lifts me up. She says, 'You bastard! I've worked with some of the best directors in the world. I've worked with Fellini. I've never, in my life, seen a director treat an actress like that. You bastard!' She was going to punch me out. I said, 'No, Barbara, don't hit me. She made me. I hate doing it. I'm afraid to do take two . . .' 'Really?' she says. 'Yes, really.' Barbara lets me go. 'How hard were you hitting her?' she asks, 'show me.' She holds out her forearm and I hit it hard. 'That hard?' 'Yes,' I say. 'Hmm,' says Barbara. A pause, and then her eyes fix on me. 'Do I have any scenes where I cry?' That was my introduction to the world of actresses. People who see *Shivers* and think that I didn't deal with acting and actors are completely wrong.

Each of my films has a little demon in the corner that you don't see, but it's there. The demon in *Shivers* is that people vicariously enjoy the scenes where guys kick down doors and do whatever they want to the people inside. They love the scenes where people are running, screaming, naked through the halls. But they might just hate themselves for liking them. This is no new process; it's obvious that there is a vicarious thrill involved in seeing the forbidden.

French critics really saw *Shivers* as being an attack on the bourgeois life, and bourgeois ideas of morality and sexuality. They sensed the glee with which we were tearing them apart. Living on Nuns' Island we all wanted to rip that place apart and run, naked, screaming through the halls.

The standard way of looking at *Shivers* is as a tragedy, but there's a paradox in it that also extends to the way society looks at me. Here's a man who walks around and is sweet: he likes people, he's warm, friendly, articulate and he makes these horrible, diseased, grotesque, disgusting movies. Now, what's real? Those things are both real for the person standing outside. For me, those two parts of myself are inextricably bound together. The reason I'm secure is because I'm crazy. The reason I'm stable is because I'm nuts. It's palpable to me.

The older you get, the more children you have, the more accepted you become in your society and the more a part of the establishment you become, the more tenuous the grip on your 'insideness' is. Your awareness of yourself is driven deeper because the layers or veneer of civilization become thicker and thicker, but inside you know. I'm just much more in disguise. There's a strength to be taken from that. There's also a certain sadness at the same time.

Prior to the release of Shivers, *Cronenberg was lucky to be asked by John Hirsch – a Hungarian-Jewish theatre producer and director recently appointed by the CBC – to join a video training course he was establishing there. In Studio 7, Cronenberg got his first experience of monitors, buttons, switches and multi-camera set-ups for shooting drama on two-inch video tape. This led to his being invited to contribute to the CBC's Peep Show series, for which he directed* The Victim *and* The Lie Chair, *in August and October 1975 respectively.*

The Victim, *blandly scripted by Ty Haller, does manage to generate some interest in its detailing of obscene phone-caller Donald's room (full of softcore porn pictures, nasty newspaper cuttings and a poster for the as-yet-unreleased* Shivers!), *but suffers from the wholly predictable 'sting' apparently so necessary to this teledrama genre.* The Lie Chair, *again predictably scripted (this time by David Cole), is devoid of any interest as a tale of the supernatural – a subject never of interest to Cronenberg in his feature work. Luckily, Cronenberg was not to pursue a career in television (perhaps still an option at this time); the release of* Shivers *in October 1975 was to prove an event in itself.*

It was the Canadian release that opened a nasty sore which continued to fester for some time after. Robert Fulford, under the pseudonym Marshal Delaney, wrote for the influential magazine Saturday Night. *Cronenberg had shown Fulford* Stereo, *and received an enthusiastic review. In a moment of alarming naïveté, he arranged a private screening for Fulford of* Shivers, *only to make the cover of the next issue.*

It said, 'Inside Marshal Delaney reviews the most perverse, disgusting, repulsive film he has ever seen.' He was basically saying that, if this was the kind of movie Canada had to make to have a film industry, we shouldn't have an industry. In addition, he made a big deal out of the fact that taxpayers' money had been put into this piece of filth. This blew the lid off the poor CFDC. This was the beginning of the realization of all our worse nightmares. Fulford was very influential, so I went to Michael Spencer and said, 'There are only a hundred people who read the magazine.' He said, 'Unfortunately, they're the wrong hundred.' The CFDC was part of the Secretary of State's ministry, so the buzz in Ottawa was 'What are we going to do about this guy Cronenberg?'

Accurate as it was, Cronenberg regarded his original title, 'Orgy of the Blood Parasites', as too reminiscent of 1950s' horror movies or, worse, of a pastiche. For the infamous Canadian release it was retitled The Parasite Murders. *The French-language version,* Frissons, *performed so well in Montreal that the English title was switched again to* Shivers, *under which it was sold throughout the world, apart from America. There, AIP predictably came up with their own perfect audience-catcher:* They Came from Within; *again resonant of 1950s' horror, but without the satiric overtone. This didn't prevent the American release from being a disappointment. Substandard prints and poor distribution only compounded problems, which began in the Classification and Ratings Administration of the Motion Picture Association of America (MPAA). In order to avoid the American X-rating (meaning completely uncut, and associated primarily with pornography), certain scenes from* Shivers *were 'trimmed': Allan Migicovsky pulling off the parasite bugs stuck to Joe Silver's face and greedily stuffing them back into his own mouth, for instance. As Cronenberg has said: 'He's not eating them. They're just his boys and he wants them back.'*

What Shivers *did achieve was distribution in forty countries, and a return of some $5 million for its low production cost of $180,000, making it the most successful movie the CFDC had ever been involved in: 'The taxpayers' money was paid back on that film; it filled the coffers, but the attitude was that they didn't want public coffers filled with filth. Huge pressure was put on the CFDC and the whole episode probably cost me a year.'*

I had full confidence that everything I was doing was great. I had to master the form, but what I was writing was what I really wanted to do. It was, and continues to be, something that challenges me from top to bottom. Vladimir Nabokov himself said that there's nothing so exhilarating as philistine vulgarity – with some irony, but not total sarcasm. He was saying it rather wistfully. He absolutely adored movies, went to see them all the time and talked about them. He understood the energy of movies, the narrative drive of movies and the collision of imagery. It's possible that he loved the movies whose literary equivalents he would have despised.

Cinepix were very pleased with *Shivers* and said, 'Let's do another one! Have you got any ideas?' I did have this thing called 'Mosquito' (later changed to *Rabid*), which I wrote out as a treatment for John Dunning. It was about a woman who is a strange kind of modern-day vampiress, a biologically correct vampiress – that's to say, nothing to do with the supernatural. It had more to do with modern plastic surgery done on her that goes wrong. (I watched a plastic surgeon at work for three hours in preparation for those scenes.) I developed it under the wing of Cinepix, which was quite different from what happened with *Shivers*. They were involved in working on the script.

It was difficult making that script work because it had so many characters and elements. It was much broader than *Shivers* because I was now showing an entire city in thrall to rabid maniacs: army trucks, martial law in Montreal and so on. It was on a much bigger scale. I remember Dunning letting me stay at his place in the country outside Montreal, and trying to write it. At one point I said, 'John, I just woke up this morning and realized that this is nuts. Do you know what this movie's about? This woman grows a cock thing in her armpit and sucks people's blood through it. It's ridiculous! I can't do this. It's not going to work.' You see, I'd lost the magic. It was like a child suddenly growing up and saying, 'Oh yes, that's not real. I can't turn into a dog.' But Dunning never wavered. He told the whole story back to me and said, 'There's something about it. It's compelling and weird. You haven't done a movie for a while, but you've got to jump back in. You can't stop now. You've only done one. You have to keep the momentum going.'

We always approached the material in a very realistic way. We all have lives that would be either high or low melodrama with a lot of symbolic overtones if they were put on screen, but not while you're living it. That's the level when you're working with actors; I've never met an actor who really wanted to deal with stuff on an interpretive level while making a film, because you can't do anything with that physically.

It had been some time since *Shivers*, because of the freeze at the CFDC, and this was my moment of loss of faith. Dunning brought me back from that. I wasn't thinking that *Rabid* was schlocky and that I should be doing something more classy. It was just that, on its own terms, I thought it would never work on screen and that people would laugh at it. When you do horror, you're always walking that line, because it's always on the verge of being ridiculous. You have to work hard to keep the magic going. You have to believe it yourself. You have to believe that the audience will believe it, or you're dead. So, with John and Ivan Reitman's help, I beat the script into shape.

It also took longer to get this second movie off the ground because of the CFDC problems. And you couldn't finance a movie in Canada without them, and Cinepix. Maybe we could have gone to the States, but I didn't want to. There was no way of doing an American production in Canada. I would have had to go there. Because *Shivers* had been made here, and worked here, and made money here and established me here, I don't think I even considered going to the States at that point.

Rabid finally went before the cameras in November 1976. However, in the meantime, Cronenberg had again returned to the CBC to make another 30-minute film, this time for their Teleplay *series. Shooting on 16mm, Cronenberg wrote and directed* The Italian Machine. *The film is a surprising delight, and by far the most successful venture into TV Cronenberg made in the 1970s. It fuses the director's obsession with racing machinery as art (the Italian machine of the title is a motorcycle lusted after by bike freaks who are thwarted by its purchase as an* objet d'art), *with some truly eccentric and sophisticated characters; memorable performances from actors who were to appear later in Cronenberg's features: Frank Moore* (Rabid), *Gary McKeehan* (The Brood) *and the unsettling Geza Kovaks* (Scanners, The Dead Zone). The Italian Machine *was also the first comic piece Cronenberg directed (and the last, because his 1980s' feature project 'Six Legs', also a comedy, failed to make it to the screen).*

The CFDC wouldn't put money into *Rabid* because of 'official' reaction to *Shivers*, and that kind of film. However, finally, to their and Michael Spencer's credit, they surreptitiously put finance into the film by cross-collateralizing it with another. I think it was a trucker movie called *Convoy*; that and *Rabid* would be put together so that technically they would put money into *Convoy*, but really into both. Then *Convoy* fell through and *Rabid* became my next Cinepix project. But the CFDC were very afraid.

Casting porno star Marilyn Chambers[9] as Rose was Ivan's idea again. You've got to go to the Cannes Film Festival and sell a film like this territory by territory – which Cinepix were brilliant at doing – with 2,000 other films in a market, most of them absolute shit. Why does a distributor from Spain (say) want to see *Rabid*? He'll go see it if Marilyn Chambers is in it. He might just do that.

23 The Cronenberg choice: Sissy Spacek in *Badlands*.
24 The Reitman choice: Marilyn Chambers in *Rabid*.

I wanted Sissy Spacek. I'd seen her in *Badlands* with Martin Sheen and thought she was fantastic. John Dunning said no, because she had too many freckles and he didn't like her Texas accent. We really needed an actress with a name, which Sissy Spacek didn't have at that time. Then she came out with *Carrie* before we finished shooting *Rabid*, and suddenly she was a big star.

Ivan had heard that Rip Torn and Marilyn Chambers were going to do a straight movie together, so here was our chance. Ivan just said, 'It would be really great for us if you like Marilyn Chambers for this movie, because her name means something, we can afford her and she wants to do a straight movie. But if you think she's bad, we'll forget it.' I think what she had to sell was the girl next door, who fucks eight guys at once. She's the cheerleader; she's the one everybody wanted to fuck at high school. And she does it, right there on screen. I've never to this day seen one of her hardcore movies, but I saw a softcore movie she did and she was incredibly sweet and unspoiled.

When I met her she was a lot harder than I had hoped. She had plucked eyebrows and her hair was very pre-Farrah Fawcett. She had been doing Las Vegas. Chuck Traynor, her husband/manager, was not my favourite kind of guy. Very tough. They were both into trading gold-plated revolvers with Sammy Davis Junior, that kind of thing. It's a world totally foreign to me; not one I think I'll ever get to know too well. But Chuck was protective of Marilyn, and supportive of the movie. And Marilyn herself was very shrewd and sharp, and worked really hard. She'd obviously had some rough times since that first little movie that I saw of hers. But she was a real trouper, and invented her own version of Method acting. When she had to cry it wasn't a problem, because Chuck would say, 'Remember when Fluffy died' – that was her cat – and then she'd cry. I thought she really had talent, and expected her to go on and do other straight movies. But she went back. I don't know whether it was Chuck, or that the industry still wouldn't accept her.

Rabid managed to be released and responded to just as a normal picture within the horror genre. It made money and got the usual complement of good and bad reviews, and also some feminist stirrings. There were the first glimmers of that as far as my pictures were concerned. I remember being totally bemused by the complaint that I was portraying female sexuality as predatory. With *Shivers* I had been attacked for showing women as sexually passive. So I was beginning to realize that this was a no-win situation. Unless all the women in your movie are absolutely done by the feminist book – and, of course, it depends which feminist book – you are not going to escape. Someone who writes an anti-sexist tract is not going to write a great anything.

As horror films are so primal, and deal with such primal issues – particularly death and therefore also sexuality – they are automatically in the arena that has become the feminist arena. It's a natural genre for the discussion of those issues. It's fitting that a horror film should be attacked or defended by various feminist groups. It makes a lot of sense to me. In a way, it pleased me – and still does – not to be seen as adhering to anyone's party line. That suits me temperamentally. I thought I was suitably nasty to everybody at one point or another in *Rabid*: male, female, homosexual, child, everybody gets it. If you're going to accuse me of something, you might as well accuse me of being misanthropic. I don't feel I'm that either.

Cronenberg's tendency to cut to the bone during editing (see his comments on Videodrome *later) did produce some confusion for the audience in* Rabid. *How exactly did Marilyn Chambers develop that blood-sucking penis in her armpit? A short dialogue scene between radical plastic surgeon Dan Keloid and his patient had been removed because Cronenberg felt it broke the tension of the scene. In it, Keloid explained how he intended her new tissue implant to grow and produce the new intestines she needed to survive after her motorcycle accident. But instead the tissue itself had decided to do something completely different. 'That was a mistake. It would have provided a simple rationale for people to understand. Even those who like the movie have asked "But what was that thing?"'*

Despite this confusion, Rabid *continued Cronenberg's success in the marketplace. On its modest budget of Can.$530,000 it went on to make $7 million on its release in 1977 – with the help of Cinepix's expertise in the 'exploitation' arena. This made Cronenberg the most bankable director in Canada after only two movies. It also firmly established him as a director of horror.*

Cronenberg maintains that horror was not the genre he sought. With Shivers, *the aim was first to make a movie; it just emerged that way from the typewriter. Since then, the genre has offered mixed blessings to Cronenberg and those whose job it has been to market films which are part horror, part science-fiction, part psychological thrillers and, therefore, something else.* Videodrome *was the first real challenge in this respect, while the most recent work –* Dead Ringers *and* Naked Lunch *– seem as remotely connected to the horror genre as they are to anything else in the current cinematic landscape.*

There's a Latin quote that goes 'Timor mortis conturbat me,' which, roughly translated, means 'The fear of death disturbs me'. Death is the basis of all horror, and for me death is a very specific thing. It's very physical. That's where I become Cartesian. Descartes was obsessed with the schism between mind and body, and how one relates to the other.

The phrase 'biological horror' – often attached to my work – really refers to the fact that my films are very body-conscious. They're very conscious of physical existence as a living organism, rather than other horror films or science-fiction films which are very technologically oriented, or concerned with the supernatural, and in that sense are very disembodied.

I've never been religious in the sense that I felt there was a God, that there was an external structure, universal and cosmic, that was imposed on human beings. I always really did feel – at first not consciously and then quite consciously – that we have created our own universe. Therefore, what is wrong with it also comes from us. That isn't to say that we make all the rules, just that my worldview is human-centred as opposed to being centred outside humanity. I think that naturally leads you to the feeling that, if you're dealing with horror, it must also be human-centred. It comes from within man.

Jaws seemed to scare a lot of people. But the idea that you carry the seeds of your own destruction around with you, always, and that they can erupt at any time, is more scary. Because there is no defence against it; there is no escape from it. You need a certain self-awareness to appreciate the threat. A young child can understand a monster jumping out of the closet, but it takes a little more – not really beyond most children, in fact – to understand that there is an inner life to a human being that can be as dangerous as any animal in the forest. So my films are not a projection of childhood fears, as George Romero has said his films are.[10] It's not the long dark corridor. It's a little more sophisticated, in the sense that it needs understanding of what a human being is.

At the same time, I find that kids do respond to my films. Very young children often find them too scary. They're able to take the destruction of the universe, but they can't take what my films show until they've reached a degree of maturity and stability. But we're still talking ten, eleven, twelve years old. They do understand them. They do get them.

At the beginning of my career I encouraged labels like 'the reigning king of schlock horror'. It was a defence. To say that what you do is in some way artistic leaves you vulnerable. Andy Warhol stood on that defence himself. He said, 'Oh yeah, my stuff is trash. No question about it.' It's very hard for people to attack you when you say that. Plus the fact that my acceptance of that crown connected me with AIP and Roger Corman, which wasn't such a bad thing.

When I looked at Corman's and other people's films I thought, OK, these guys make mistakes. But the genre has enough power and clarity to help carry them through that. When the stuff they were doing suddenly did click it had enough momentum to make the film worth seeing. The field has a lot of flexibility to it. You can do terrific stuff. But schlock means inferior goods. My films by this time are just as technically good as any film being made. So I resist that label now.

My films are *sui generis*. It would be nice if they could form their own genre, or subgenre. It's the need to sell films that causes this kind of categorization. And, of course, there's always a critical impulse to categorize and label. But people seem to think that it's necessary to categorize before they can understand. My films really do exist on their own. There is no need to do that to experience them properly.

Most people have a certain understanding of what a horror film is, namely, that it is emotionally juvenile, ignorant, supremely non-intellectual and dumb. Basically stupid. But I think of horror films as art, as films of confrontation. Films that make you confront aspects of your own life that are different to face. Just because you're making a horror film doesn't mean you can't make an artful film. Tell me the difference between someone's favourite horror film and someone else's favourite art film. There really isn't any. Emotions, imagery, intellect, your own sense of self.

It really is a matter of endurance. You have to be prepared to endure, even as William Burroughs did. He had some champions of *Naked Lunch*, but most people were able to dismiss his early work as sensationalist, disgusting and perverse. I had an easier time of it. I didn't need the critics to take my films seriously to survive, because the *aficionados* of horror were always willing to see these films. They understood that there was something unique about them. Then it's just a question of surviving to the point where you've outlived a lot of your critics and your existence has become accepted through time. It's like, 'Well, he's still doing that. He's still doing it the same way. Maybe we'll look at it again.' Those who criticized my films as being sensationalist trash now say that at least they might be thoughtful trash.

They not only don't expect to see sophistication in horror, they don't want to. The other side of the genre coin – especially when you're doing low-budget films to begin with – is that they want to see bad acting, bad technique and ludicrous dialogue because that's part of the pleasure of low-budget film-watching. Unless it's an art film with a capital A. I was getting critics who would say that the acting in my films was bad when it obviously wasn't.

But the horror genre is very kind if you are wild and want to be outrageous. It forgives a lot of faults and it encourages madness of a certain kind. I'm not too worried about staying within it because it encourages exactly those things that I value most about art. Picasso's *Guernica* is a horror work of art. If he'd only done those things, and been classified as a horror artist, would that mean that *Guernica* was any less a masterpiece and a political statement? That's the double-edged sword. The very things that nurture you in the horror genre are also the things that can suppress an understanding of what you're trying to do.

The appeal of horror is beyond politics. It's accessible to political criticism, but the appeal is very direct – right into the viscera, before it gets to the brain. And you don't have politics in the viscera. It only eventually filters from the stomach to the head, and then you can talk about politics. That's why I try to short-circuit discussions like 'Why are there so many horror films now?' In the last fifteen years there hasn't been a year when someone hasn't said, 'Why are horror films so potent, so omnipresent, have such a hold on public imagination?' They're looking for answers like 'Because of the political uncertainty of the times/the oil crisis/the atomic bomb'. I don't think any of them is relevant. It's always beyond that; it deals with things much more primordial – those old standbys, death and separation.

Other issues produce anxieties that affect the surface texture of horror. One of the things that I did in my own small way was to be part of bringing horror into the twentieth century. At the time I started to make *Shivers*, there was already *Night of the Living Dead*. But for the most part horror was gothic, distant, not here. Maybe science-fiction was. I was certainly influenced, in the style of what I was doing, by the tenor of those particular times. But the basic appeal remains very deep. Only the surface currents, the ripples, change.

Directors like George Romero and Tobe Hooper,[11] who started out as independent, low-budget film-makers, are now accepted by the Hollywood establishment as potential money-makers and therefore substantial people. That can be good, and it can be bad, because it would then require you – if you wanted to take advantage of that – to try and do the same thing you've been doing independently within the studio system, and that's a whole other game. It's a different dance you have to do there.

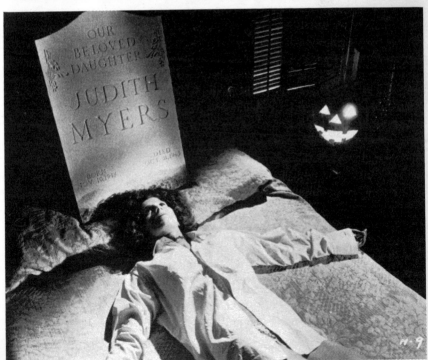

25 Contemporary horror: George A. Romero's *Night of the Living Dead* ...
26 ... John Carpenter's *Halloween*.

That's one of the reasons Romero has declined to do that, and Hooper is now getting to be much more mainstream.

Major studios have been willing to finance and back – with all the distribution power they have – films which fifteen years ago they wouldn't have touched, that they would have given to a subsidiary if they had been interested at all. I remember with *The Brood* trying to get distribution from some people like Universal Studios and they were not in the slightest bit interested. It wasn't long after that that *Halloween* and *Friday the Thirteenth* made them take a second look. It was really an élitist question. They thought these films were beneath them. At first they had to learn to like them because of the money involved; you could make a film that was not very expensive and make a lot of money. Then gradually their aesthetic sense changed to the point where they understood that some of these films can be quite good; they have nothing to be ashamed of by distributing them.[12]

Notes

1 André Bazin (1918–58) was the most influential film critic and theorist of his generation in France. Bazin started his own film periodical, *Le Revue du Cinéma*, in 1947. In 1951, he co-founded Europe's most important film publication, *Cahiers du Cinéma*, with Jacques Doniol-Valcroze. His writings, particularly on the *politique des auteurs* (the *auteur* theory), greatly influenced the French New Wave, most of whom wrote for *Cahiers du Cinéma* before becoming film-makers in their own right (Godard, Truffaut, Rivette, Chabrol). Bazin's writings about the cinema were first assembled after his death in the four-volume work *Qu'est-ce que le cinéma?* (*What is Cinema?*), published in 1967.

2 Terry Southern, a novelist and screenwriter who wrote various movies, including *Dr Strangelove* (1964), *The Cincinnati Kid* (1965), *Barbarella* (1968), *Easy Rider* (co-script), *The Magic Christian* (1970) and *The Telephone* (1980).

3 Toronto-born Ted Kotcheff (1931–   ) started work in Canadian television before moving to Britain in 1957, where he directed a number of TV productions, plays and films. Most known for his highly successful *The Apprenticeship of Duddy Kravitz* (1974), *First Blood* (1982) and *Uncommon Valour* (1983).

4 John Grierson (1898–1972) is the man credited with first coining the expression 'documentary' (from the French *documentaire*, meaning travelogue). Grierson became a leading figure in the development of the form, primarily as a driving force, producer and theoretician. In Britain he founded the Empire Marketing Board (EMB) in 1928 and the influential GPO Film Unit in 1933, and was appointed Film Commissioner for the Canadian Government in 1939. It was in this capacity that he founded the National Film Board of Canada.

5 Roger Corman (1926–   ) is undisputed king of 'exploitation' cinema, who produced and directed some forty-five low-budget features between 1955 and 1970, many for the independent company American International Pictures. Tackling almost every genre, or

popular 'cycle', his prolific output included the famous, more expensive Edgar Allan Poe series. Nearly all, with the notable exception of the more personal and campaigning *The Intruder* (1962), were major box-office successes. Responsible for giving many major American directors their first films (Martin Scorsese, Francis Ford Coppola, Jonathan Demme, Monte Hellman, etc.), Corman abandoned directing for producing in the 1970s (for his own companies New World Pictures and then New Horizon), finally returning to direct *Frankenstein Unbound* (1990).

6 Norman Jewison (1926–   ) was born in Toronto, and after a short spell with BBC Television in London and Canadian TV moved to the USA. Since 1963 he has directed a number of movies for Hollywood, including *The Cincinnati Kid* (1965), *In the Heat of the Night* (1967), *Rollerball* (1975), *Agnes of God* (1985) and *Moonstruck* (1987).

7 Barbara Steele (1938–   ) is an English-born actress who became best known for her various vampire-like incarnations in predominantly Italian 1960s' horror movies. Films include *Sapphire* (1959), *The Pit and the Pendulum* (1961), *Castle of Blood* (1964), *The She Beast* (1966), *Terror-Creatures from the Grave* (1966) and *Caged Heat* (1974).

8 Lawrence Welk, the American MOR band-leader, very popular on Canadian TV in the 1960s. It is reputed that, as Welk grew older, he looked younger and younger.

9 Marilyn Chambers, one of the great female names of soft- and hardcore pornography. Productions in which she appeared were characterized by their relatively high production values, and an interesting 'classy' veneer beyond the requirements of mere coupling (bare narrative, acting, more inventive/imaginative situations). Movies marketed on her name include *Behind the Green Door* (1972), *Insatiable* (1982) and *Insatiable II* (1984).

10 Pittsburgh-born George A. Romero (1939–   ) became an influential horror director in the 1970s/1980s with a series of low-budget independent productions, most notably his darkly humorous and increasingly visceral 'Zombie Trilogy' (*Night of the Living Dead, Dawn of the Dead* and *Day of the Dead*). He also directed the impressive *Martin* (1978) and *Monkey Shines* (1988).

11 Tobe Hooper (1943–   ) burst on to cinema screens in 1976 with the infamous and influential *Texas Chainsaw Massacre*. Since then, he has directed a number of movies, the most interesting being *Poltergeist* (for Steven Spielberg in 1982) and *Lifeforce* (1985).

12 Although the American horror movie has always constituted one of the most popular if disreputable genres, it experienced a renaissance in the 1970s with a number of mainstream successes (most crucially *The Exorcist, The Omen, Carrie*, etc.), as well as low-budget and cross-over productions (*Halloween, It's Alive, The Hills Have Eyes, Night of the Living Dead*, etc.). In contrast to the genre's regular cycle of box-office popularity, the 1970s/1980s were marked by their ability and readiness to spawn the sequel or the series from an individually successful movie. They also tended to locate horror within the family/society. This financial reincarnation of the horror movie was paralleled almost exactly with a reawakening of interest in science-fiction and faraway places (courtesy of George Lucas and the *Star Wars* cycle). At the end of the 1970s, many of the decade's most successful movies were from the horror and sci-fi genres.

CHAPTER 5

New Flesh for Old:
The Tax-Shelter Experiments

On the basis of Shivers and Rabid alone, David Cronenberg had become
a force and a talent in cinema to recognize, if perhaps also to abhor.
Within the context of North American independent film-making, he had
successfully transformed his work, concerns and particular vision from
the avant-garde or underground arena into commercial movie-making.
Intriguingly, the concerns – if not the style – had remained intact. The
'vision', in the process of making this perilous journey, had been transformed in the process into something more extreme. This particularly
sturdy strain of venereal horror, which emerged unexpectedly from a
country at best in the twilight zone of film-consciousness, was also a
conspicuous financial success. Few film-makers had made the transition
from cinémathèque to cinema, underground to overground, so assuredly.

Audience response to the Cinepix movies was clear. They were either
exhilarated or repulsed by them – possibly in equal measure – with few
shades of opinion in between. Box-office receipts at least testified to their
interest. However, the reactions of cinema theorists, critics and cinephiles
were appropriately more complex, contradictory and sometimes confused. Their primary concerns were for the function and operation of film
– issues of ideology and representation – and in Cronenberg's chosen
area, the specifics of horror.

Part of the necessary process of redeeming horror from the 'low
culture' dustbin had been textual analyses stressing the subversive
potential of the genre. The Monster, an embodiment of our most unacceptable, repressed desires – twisted into ugliness by its imprisonment in
the unconscious – was traditionally the centre of sympathy in classics of
the genre (as in Frankenstein). It was with ambivalent regret that the
audience accepted its necessary destruction, so that repressive order
could be reinstated. Identification with the Monster, and the excitement
derived from its disruptive function, enhanced the genre's subversive
tendencies.

However, some critics found it hard to identify with Shivers's

*phallic/faecal and faceless parasites. The sheer visceral repulsiveness of
the overthrow in* Shivers *and – to a greater extent – the vision of a
disease-driven apocalyptic revolution in* Rabid *led them to certain con-
clusions: Cronenberg obviously bemoaned the passing of the status quo,
greatly feared repressed forces and evinced a degree of sexual disgust.*

Sexuality is one of those very basic issues. Life and death and sexuality
are interlinked. You can't discuss one without in some way discussing the
others. Since my films are concerned very much with death and the
human body, sexuality is automatically discussed. And in this area we are
not fully evolved – culturally, physically or in any other way. The films
are an attempt to try and perceive what, having said that, a fully evolved
human being might look like.

Separate sexuality from the function of childbearing and then what is
it? What could it become? What should it become? That was happening a
lot in the 1960s; I don't claim any originality for the exploration. I had
read Norman O. Brown's *Life against Death*, that kind of thing, in which
he would discuss the Freudian theory of polymorphous perversity, the
kind of sexuality that a child has. Completely non-genital, not focused.
Just in everything. A sort of suffusing sexuality, or sensuality. Even old
Norm had some trouble when he tried to figure out how that kind of
Dionysian consciousness would function in a society where you had to
cross the street and not get hit by a car. How does that all-enveloping
sexuality work when you're just walking down the street? It's tricky!

I think it's a classic situation. Even political revolution often ends up
this way. You tear down something that's ugly and repressive, and you
create something that's even more ugly and repressive. That doesn't
mean you have to stop. It's a given of human existence that you just don't
stop. You never stop. What seems revolting at the time is later incorporated into the mainstream of cultural flow. The strength of the middle
class is that it's like an amoeba. It can absorb anything. The way it
defends itself against what seems radical and threatening is not to put a
shell around itself that can be cracked and broken, but to absorb whatever it is and assimilate it.

Take a simple thing like long hair on men. In the 1960s people would
spit on you in the street if you had shoulder-length hair. I remember that
happened to me in Yugoslavia, because it was also a political statement.
Here was the decadent West right in the town of Lubljana. Then lawyers
and accountants started wearing long hair. If you felt politically separate
from them you had to shave your head. Now it's not a question at all. But

it was revolting to some people early on. And it was sexually confusing, sexually threatening. Then it developed its own aesthetic. Then it was beautiful. Then very acceptable. When something comes along that is enduring, and really represents a basic change, it will take root and establish itself. Its period of being ugly and revolting will pass. It will not have to change. I think that's what will happen ultimately: true revolution will cease to be revolting and ugly and become beautiful. Our perception of it will make it so. Being middle class, that's what I'm doing – protecting myself. Making films about it. That's my trick.

One aspect of horror, and certainly my films, is revulsion. I have to tell people that some of the things they think are repulsive in my films are meant to be repulsive, yes, but there's a beautiful aspect to them as well. There's true beauty in some things that others find repulsive. That's the way I feel, and sometimes it's very difficult to convey that.

Adverse analytical reaction to Cronenberg's cinema also regarded his vision of societal upheaval and destruction as offering no positive political alternatives, merely contagion and death. Some critics preferred the 'walking dead' revolutions of George Romero's Zombie series, perceiving these movies to be a radical political commentary on consumer society run riot (people return from the grave to eat those who are still 'alive'). The glimmer of political hope in Romero – that society is forced to find alternative ways to restructure and reorganize itself post-zombie apocalypse – was viewed as a more positive subtext and a more subversive criticism of existing structures. In short, their reading of the genre was that there were progressive film-makers working subversively within the conventions of the horror film, and that there were film-makers – Cronenberg among them – who represented the reactionary tendencies of the genre. The considered critical analyses of Cronenberg's work that began to appear after Rabid were the stirrings of what has emerged as a continuing ideological confrontation.

People who say 'Revolution now' and aren't worried by it are foolish. The lesson of history – early, middle, late – is that revolution brings with it death, pain, anguish and disease: often nothing positive to replace what was destroyed. Also, revolutions are always betrayed. To be so intent only on the event itself, and not to have any thought to what happens after, means you're not being a serious, pragmatic revolutionary. You are being that most hideous of things, a poseur, driven primarily by private anguish rather than social vision. There aren't many people who have achieved it: Castro, yes; Che Guevara, no. I don't agree with arguments that say to admit to any kind of weakness or doubt is to betray the cause. By that time, you've lost me.

You have to live a life that balances between safety and disaster. On the other hand, I don't personally want to live in the midst of chaos and disaster. I don't want either, and therefore it means that you're constantly balancing.

I don't believe that anybody is in control. That's what McLuhan was talking about when he said the reason we have to understand media is because if we don't it's going to control us. We don't have to anthropomorphize the media and say it will control us. The media does not have a brain; it's just technology. What it means is that things are out of control. Nobody's in control. There is only the appearance of control. I feel disorder is very close, which is one of the reasons I suppose I feel like an outsider, simply because I think I'm more conscious of the presence and closeness of chaos.

We are condemned to be free. We have to continue to try and wrest control from the world, from the universe, from reality, even though it might be hopeless. I think the more inventive and extreme we are, the better off we are. I know that is a dangerous route to take, so I am also exploring the dangers of going that particular route.

You can interpret anything in the light of a particularly dogmatic stance, whether it's Freudian or Marxist or whatever. You can rigorously apply these standards to any work or person or thing or newspaper or article, and then judge the artefact as wanting or not wanting. But is that really the function of criticism? I don't think so.

Why should I be beaten over the head by what was written about me in *The American Nightmare*. What Robin Wood says is 'these are good film-makers who are on the side of progressiveness, and these are bad film-makers who are reactionary'.[1] I don't think that is what art's about, or what criticism is about. I don't think that films have to be positive or uplifting to be valid experiences. A film can be depressing and still be exhilarating.

The critics I have admired the most are a lot less schematically inclined because I don't base my life's value and work's value in any ideology. There is a very strident moral imperative being broadcast from Robin's work that is really saying that, despite the fact this piece of film by Larry Cohen is awful, it is admirable and should be seen because it proposes what I think it right for human beings to do in society. Now that is very twisted.

One of the things Robin Wood dislikes about my films is that he believes there is this real affection for middle-class normality, and that there's a certain sadness in giving that up. I say 'Yes' to that. That's true. However, I'm surprised sometimes that he doesn't realize that I have ambivalent feelings about that, which are very obvious in the films. I'm not prepared to totally throw out middle-class America. There are some things that are very valuable in the middle class. I'm not a revolutionary in the sense that I believe that everything must be dismantled, destroyed and torn down and we must start from scratch. If that makes me a reactionary, then I plead guilty.

I'm sending out my films as integral, organic living things. The people who are my audience receive them that way. The people who are not my audience dissect them, looking for the gall bladder to see whether it's diseased or not. If you walk into a room and someone is looking at you as a potential model, they don't see you as a whole person. They see you as a model who will sell a particular product. That's obviously not the way you hope most people will respond to you. You want people to respond to a total entity. Dissecting my films to look for one little thing is killing them in the process. That's what I resent. That's what special-interest groups do: cut them apart. You hope that people will respond on many levels. If one level offends them and touches a political nerve, they have to be aware that if they focus on that – one element of the film to the exclusion of everything else – they'll have a very lopsided response to the film.

Take *The Big Chill*. A lot of people liked the movie, but they hated it politically. They hate the politics of the film because it suggests that all the hippies of the 1960s who were revolutionaries have sold out, except for the guy who died. They think this is suggesting something which they resent politically, even though on another level they enjoyed the film. That's a very schizophrenic response. They don't accept it on its own terms.

At this time, tax-shelter incentives were introduced in Canada to encourage private investment in an indigenous film industry. This system, later perceived as a hideous loophole and consequently stopped, allowed anyone with money to burn to promise investment in a specific production. At that point, the investor could write off tax owed on a much larger sum, actually contributing a much smaller amount to the making of a movie. Promissory notes to provide the remaining finance further down the line – should it be needed – were security enough.

Given Canada's fiscal year, this meant that in October potential investors panicked and looked around for film productions in which to invest their profits. The film industry consequently began to starve for eight months of the year, prior to new, feverish activity which began to occur in November/December. As any such production had to be certified Canadian – complying with a strict points system with regard to Canadian content on all levels – this often led to a shortage of available technicians and talent during four months of crazed activity. This accounts for the lack of summer scenes in what became known as 'the tax-shelter production'.

If a lawyer's client said, 'Jesus, what am I going to do, what kind of tax shelters are there available?', the lawer would say, 'Well, you can invest in MURBs – Multiple Urban Residential buildings.' But then there was movies. So it was 'What would you rather have your money in? Because you can visit the film set, bring your kids, see Donald Sutherland in action.' That really worked.

I was a hot property in this context. I had a track record, and there weren't many other Canadian directors around. People were desperately looking up lists of foreign Canadians. It was 'John Ireland is a Canadian? Glenn Ford is a Canadian? My God! Does he still have his passport?' It was like 'Who is the secret Canadian?' Here was a very real, sound financial reason for ferreting out hidden Canadians. You could say, 'We've got Glenn Ford in our movie,' and it didn't count against you. A points system. You had to be certified Canadian.

It affected me in terms of 'Sorry, you can't have that actor, because he's not Canadian, and you've used up your quota of foreigners,' so you had to know about that stuff in self-defence. You had to know that you could only have one foreign actor, and who was your cameraman and was he Canadian? In those days, you could fight for a second actor, as long as the foreigner didn't get more money. That's where we were later with *Videodrome*: you could have two foreigners as long as the second didn't get more money than the first Canadian. Ludicrous stuff. Other than that, I tried not to know too much about it.

However, once the movie was made and everybody got their cut, whether it got distribution was not so important. The money guys were not Cinepix. Cinepix were movie people: their living was making and distributing movies. But this was a whole other era of lawyers and brokers suddenly becoming producers overnight because they could raise the money. They knew the tax-shelter laws. I had some strange meeting at some brokers' firms with these guys who yesterday were selling bonds and today were talking about 'Can we get Bobby de Niro?' All the abuses people remember that era for were real. People would get their two hundred grand for getting the money together, and didn't care after that. They didn't know enough about the film business to even make the movie successful commercially so they could make more money.

The first feature Cronenberg was offered under the new tax-shelter regime was Fast Company. *This has been perceived as his aberrant movie by determined auteurists. As it is neither a horror movie nor based on an original Cronenberg script, it simply doesn't seem to fit. The usual textual obsessions are absent. Yet it is connected with one of the director's private passions: motor racing.*

Strange as it may seem, I don't think I was getting offered anything at that time! So I was interested. It was a drag-race movie. I like motor racing of all kinds, and was interested in working out of Toronto, although we ended up shooting in Alberta. It doesn't seem to fit with the rest of my work now, but it does. It has to fit; it's all coming from me. It was a labour of love; it wasn't a hack job. True, I had less control over it than any other movie, but visually I was honing my style. And technically. I thought it could have done well. It was a good solid B-movie actioner, as they say, with some interesting elements. But unfortunately it was the tax-shelter era. *Fast Company* got caught up in that. We ended up with a distributor in the States who immediately went belly up and the picture got involved in litigation because it was an asset, and died. Disappeared. It was barely shown anywhere.

I worked with the writer on *Fast Company*, Phil Savath, and did enough to ultimately deserve my co-writing credit. This happened because we were in the position where we were shooting a movie and the script wasn't there. When we went to Edmonton to do pre-production, I spent a lot of time with the drag racers and realized that they had this very rich verbal and visual idiom, and none of this was in the script. So I'd get up at five o'clock in the morning, write pages until seven, then go to the set and see if I could find a way to make it happen. A bit inventorish. I don't do my best work under those conditions.

At this point I'd never been on anyone else's set. I didn't know how other directors did it. I was then, and still am, always fascinated to hear the atrocities that other directors commit; of course I love that best. What now feels to me like the normal way of directing – I wouldn't say

27 Cronenberg on location for *Fast Company*.
28 Man and machine: *Fast Company* (1979).

the only one – is something that I've invented myself. I hear from actors – John Saxon on *Fast Company* for instance – 'You're awfully good-natured for a director, David.' Through feedback and other crew members I get a mirror image of myself as a director. I think it was Godard who said that he invented or reinvented the cinema. I suppose I feel the same way. I invented my version of making cinema.

I had to struggle with other people's concepts of what this movie was going to be. Michael Lebowitz had never produced a movie before, and he had a very strong idea of what the western mythology should be. I didn't think it had anything to do with the way this movie had to be made. I had to deal with all this mythology of movie-making, rather than dealing with the reality of it. We had arguments and discussions of a kind I had never had before. I just thought they were doing their movie wrong.

Fast Company proved to be a very important movie for me. I met Mark Irwin (cinematographer), Carol Spier (production designer), Bryan Day (sound recordist) and Ron Sanders (editor) on that picture – people who would become important to my film-making later. And I enjoyed making the movie and working with Bill Smith and Claudia Jennings and all those B-movie actors. I'd never had that lust, love and total devotion to B-movie stars that guys like Scorsese had. I liked them, I just never mythologized them as much.

Scorsese talks about how he's amazed Michael Powell can quote from books, and that he feels he's from a newer tradition: movie literacy. I must come from the older tradition because I don't refer to movies. I have no impulse to do it. Many of the best books written are full of literary allusion, references and resonance. You might say for a movie-maker the equivalent would be these references to other movies. The question is, where is the real life of your movie coming from? Does your film have its own life, or is it only a parasitic thing? My films were never parasitic. They just had their own life. They had inner reference for me, but I felt I was coming to grips with the stuff of life itself. Dealing with real demons, the nitty-gritty. It was no longer a question of style or context. It was me and it. If those films have their fierce life, that's where it comes from: I wasn't fooling around. It was serious stuff to me, despite the humour. It was a serious endeavour. If it started to go wrong or feel as though I couldn't bring it off, it was heartbreaking. That's the best phrase I can use. My heart was being broken. It wasn't an ego thing; it wasn't a power struggle. It would break my heart to see this thing destroyed or wrecked, because then it wouldn't be the nitty-gritty. It wouldn't be real. Those were, and still are, my references. Maybe *Fast Company* is the least successful like that.

What I like most about the movie came out of my appreciation and understanding of race cars and racing machinery, which I get very metaphysical and boring about. Secondly, it really did spring out of me. I knew about racers and raced myself. I got the drag racers' particular version, which is very much a beer-drinking, wet T-shirt thing. They even had T-shirts that said 'Suck my pipes': a great phrase. I made sure I got that in. Great stuff. Not my sensibility, but definitely theirs. I was doing a bit of documentary film-making with that movie. I was reading those Hot Rod magazines and was ready to build myself a hot Camaro. So I wouldn't disown one frame. It was also the first movie I did that had rock music in it, and the first that I had an original score composed for.

One of the things I wanted to do was make the John Saxon character a woman. Lebowitz said that there were no women in drag racing; they were all wet T-shirt girls. It's a male-dominated sport, with the myth of the west and all that stuff. He was totally against the idea. Later he saw *Heart Like a Wheel*[2] and to his credit said, 'You were right. You could have made something much more interesting and special if I'd listened.' But it didn't break my heart.

With film activity in Canada now irrigated by private investment, it was inevitable that Cronenberg should begin to find himself in demand. His next film, The Brood, *was shot almost back to back with* Fast Company *as a consequence. It represented a return to more personal work, indeed perhaps too personal for comfort. However, Cronenberg has always been a staunch believer in the theory of catharsis – a position viewed by most censors as a discredited justification for morally reprehensible behaviour.*

Catharsis is the basis of all art. This is particularly true of horror films, because horror is so close to what's primal. We all prepare ourselves for challenges that we can anticipate. It's only when cultural imperatives require that we avoid the discussion of things like death and ageing that the impulse is suppressed. Humans naturally prepare themselves to meet those kind of challenges. Certainly ageing and death are two of those things. One of the ways man has always done this is through art. The cinema is one way we can do that. We confront things in a relatively safe context.

You can see this with kids. In their games and in their play they anticipate stuff like their own sexuality, violence, social difficulties, etc. They are rehearsing, in the same way that tigers do a play version of hunting and killing and mating. It's a built-in need that we rehearse the difficult things of life, so they don't come as a complete surprise and don't overwhelm us.

Why do actors love death scenes? Partly because they know the scene's going to get them some attention. But part of it is mastery over death; to be able to die, come back to life, and refine it. 'Let me try that again.' They're trying out what's aesthetically and philosophically pleasing. Same for me. 'Here's Martin Sheen committing suicide in *The Dead Zone*. Should he put the gun in his mouth? No. Clichéd. How about under the chin? He's a guy who'd go out with his chin up.' You can't help thinking, when you hear the gun click, 'Would I have the guts to do that? Would it ever be worth doing that?' You're deciding the moment and style of your death. I thought at the time it was a defeat when Hemingway shot himself. Since then I've come to feel it was a very courageous act. He said the only things that meant anything to him were fucking, fishing and writing, and he couldn't do any of them worth a damn any more. He lived by his word.

This sounds very dreary and serious and very involved. Of course, it's not like that at all. It's much more like play. That's really the way I think of film. It's the adult version of tigers' play. There is an exhilarating, youthful and entertaining element that must be involved. I don't think of myself as the professor or the doctor leading my flock through difficult times. I don't look upon it as a responsibility. It's really my own need to do that, and to do it in a public way. This leads to an audience being involved too. And audiences want that. They want you to overwhelm them. They want you to do things to them that have not been done to them before. And they don't appreciate it if you can't. That's the challenge, the real pact. They're saying 'OK, go ahead. I'm here. I'm ready. Do it.' And I try.

Why is it not much consolation that a hundred billion people have gone through death before us? You'd think by now we could say, 'Well, Alexander the Great died, so what am I complaining about?' Does it help? No. The fact that it's so common doesn't diminish its potency on a personal level. That's why it's endlessly being discussed. There is a moment when you have to tell your kids that they're not going to live for ever. It's a stunning moment. Up until that moment they had no reason to think otherwise. The sooner you tell them the better.

I'm not a big fan of the therapy theory of art, in the psychotherapeutic use of art, because it's devalued. It's like Freud psychoanalysing Shakespeare by looking at *Hamlet*. But I think on a very straightforward level it's true that any artist is trying to take control of life by organizing it and shaping it and recreating it. Because he knows very well that the real version of life is beyond his control. It's one of the main reasons people create: to have some control over the universe. To me, that's when a movie becomes part of the process of life rather than a hole into which you disappear for six months and emerge into real life.

How about some of these films being a rehearsal for a life after death, or a transmuted life – a life that is transformed into something else?

Vision 4, one of many companies inspired into existence by the potential offered by tax-shelter finance, had approached Cronenberg in search of projects. Headed primarily by Victor Solnicki and Dick Schouten – in association with producer Pierre David – they agreed to proceed with an idea that had been in Cronenberg's head for ten years. Tentatively entitled 'The Sensitives', it was, in essence, Stereo *revisited: a story of troubled telepaths with extraordinary power. However, as Cronenberg began to work on the script, it gave way to an altogether more personal and cathartic story:* The Brood.

I had bought a house with some of the money I had from *Rabid*. I remember writing *The Brood* with gloves on, because it was unheated upstairs. It was winter, and freezing. I cut the fingers off the gloves so I could type. I couldn't write the script I was supposed to because *The Brood* kept coming. It was a compelling script; it insisted on getting written. It pushed its way right up through the typewriter. It pushed 'The Sensitives' aside completely. I really don't think I had any choice. It was like automatic writing (the automatic part was pulling it, not writing it). It's my most autobiographical script, and I was very compulsive about writing it. I remember walking into Victor Solnicki's office when I had a first draft and saying, 'Here's the script. It isn't the one we talked about, it's another one you know nothing about.' This was the one I wanted to make. I just had to do this. And because it was those tax-shelter days, and it didn't matter what you had, everything was right.

The Brood was a very finished script. It took a while to get it made, because tax-shelter financing was a whole new ball game for Pierre, Victor and Claude. One of the good parts of waiting was that the script got very tight, and was shot very close to the way it was written. They were also very serious about distributing *The Brood*; they were not tax-shelter rip-off types, so they wanted names. It was 'Who will do this movie, strange as it is, and whose name will bring the distributors? Who can we afford who is a legitimate movie name?' The Samantha Eggar role of Nola Carveth was a tricky one to play. I had a lot of difficulty getting anyone to play that, even Canadian. I can't remember how we fixed on Samantha, but she looked a little like my ex-wife; that was a personal little weirdness. And the husband looks a little like me, too. They were a reasonable movie facsimile.

Samantha really understood the movie; she said that it reminded her of her own childhood. To me that meant she was seeing past the horror-fantasy elements to the psychological elements, which were really the basic underpinning of the movie. I've said this *ad nauseam*, but *The Brood* was my version of *Kramer Vs Kramer*.[3] I was really trying to get to the reality, with a capital R, which is why I have disdain for *Kramer*. I think it's false, fake, candy. There are unbelievable, ridiculous moments in it that to me are emotionally completely false, if you've ever gone through anything like that.

The Brood got to the real nightmare, horrific, unbelievable inner life of that situation. I'm not being facetious when I say I think it's more realistic, even more naturalistic, than *Kramer*. I felt that bad. It was that horrible, that damaging. That's why it had to be made then; it wanted to be made full blast. Getting philosophical and mellow, you make another movie. The reality needed to be expressed in what, if you're a critic, are symbolic terms. I can't remember if I tried a more obviously naturalistic version of it, but that wouldn't have satisfied me. It wouldn't have been cathartic enough. *Kramer Vs Kramer* also had a kind of happy ending. Not my version of that situation.

At the time I was fighting for custody of my daughter Cassandra by my first marriage. I got a call from my ex-wife saying she had decided for religious reasons to go and live with these nice people in California and was going to take Cass with her. I'd get to see her at Christmas and stuff, and she was leaving tomorrow. I said, 'OK, that's nice, great, good luck.' I put the phone down, told Carolyn (I was now remarried) and went to the school and kidnapped my daughter. It wasn't really kidnapping, but we were still sharing custody. I got a court order which prevented her from taking Cass. And then she left. After swearing that she would never leave her daughter, she signed her over to me so that she could go. And that's where she's been ever since.

I wanted her to go because it was tearing my daughter apart. It's giving the devil his due. It's why the Romans used to follow the bridal pair as they were being married, cursing them. It's saying, if you give the devil his due, and you admit to the possibilities of the most horrific things, then

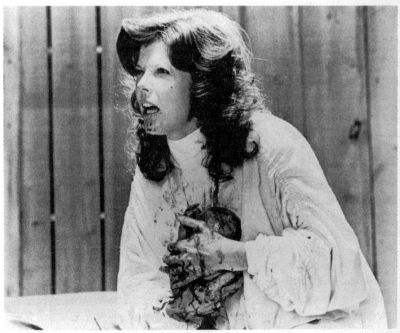

29 Motherhood: Meryl Streep in *Kramer Vs Kramer* . . .
30 . . . Samantha Eggar in *The Brood* (1979).

maybe they won't happen. It's what I do when I make movies. You're hoping it's going to stay on the screen and not come into your life. That's little understood by critics. It's as though they think you want those things to happen. You can glamorize war and make it attractive and undercut your saying it's an anti-war movie, but the mere fact you portray war on screen doesn't mean you support it. By that token you wipe out most of the great art that's ever been done.

The Brood is the most classic horror film I've done: the circular structure, generation unto generation; the idea that you think it's over and then suddenly you realize that it's just starting again. That's classic horror-movie structure. But it was difficult to script; the autobiographical stuff got in the way. It took me a long time to get through that. There's a terrible compulsion to put down exactly what happened; you want the character to say this particular line, because the character in your life said that. There are some lines in the movie that are like tape-recorded versions, real lines, or impressions of real monologues. I couldn't get the script to work until I abandoned all that. I had to say, 'OK, let's stop sweating. Back off a little. This is the movie and here you are coming in objectively. Why doesn't this work? Throw that out. Get rid of that character. Make that character do this instead.'

It's a commonplace concept really, but not ever properly understood; everything you do is autobiographical in the sense that it's filtered through your experiences and sensibilities, especially if you write your own stuff. Unless you're doing a real hack job. The core of The Brood is the most melodramatic, the most soap-operatic, the most obvious of my movies. It could have been a disease-of-the-week movie. Maybe that gave it a more accessible, more obvious shape and form and power. Because The Fly is just as autobiographical, it's just more subtle. Dead Ringers even more so. If you know me, you'd say there's nothing in Dead Ringers that's me, but deep within my nervous system I can totally relate to that movie; it is autobiographical. It's so misleading to say that because it gets jumped on: 'Oh yes, you're a misogynist, you hate women, you like to dissect them.' But it's so subtle.

People do feel the power and the potency if it's working properly. It comes through everything: the way you move the camera; the way you deal with actors; the dialogue. The Brood was more obvious; people can relate to that situation. I was a little more distant from Scanners, and from Shivers and Rabid – which is why they're a little funnier in some ways. But I don't think that's a legitimate measure. There was a time critically when the approach that a man's personal life should be examined in tandem with his work was considered an abomination. Just not a legitimate approach to art at all. Things are completely reversed now. That's one of the reasons I'm defensive about my private life. I could have shut up about *The Brood* and not said it had anything to do with my private life, but I obviously felt the need to mention that it did. So the consequences are there. But it's a failure of the imagination if you can only imagine those characters who are real to you in your own life. *The Brood* ended up nowhere near autobiography in strict terms, because I refuse to have invention taken away from me.

Often cited as the earliest example of a mature, perfectly realized Cronenberg movie, The Brood *does articulate many of his obsessions most ingeniously and effectively. The featured quasi-scientific/therapeutic practice of Psychoplasmics enables patients to manifest repressed fears and aggressions as physical evidence on the body, in order that they might be cured. In the all-too-believable practice of Dr Hal Raglan, Cronenberg had found the perfect metaphor for his own severe case of Cartesian doubt. The bogus textbook explaining Raglan's theories and methods –* The Shape of Rage *– is also a perfect, self-reflexive description of Cronenberg's own work up to that point and beyond.*

Many of the peaks of philosophical thought revolve around the impossible duality of mind and body. Whether the mind aspect is expressed as soul or spirit, it's still the old Cartesian absolute split between the two. There seems to be a point at which they should fuse and it should be apparent to everyone. But it's not. It really isn't. The basis of horror – and difficulty in life in general – is that we cannot comprehend how we can die. Why should a healthy mind die, just because the body is not healthy? How can a man die a complete physical wreck, when his mind is absolutely sharp and clear? There seems to be something wrong with that. It's very easy to see why many philosophers detach the mind from the body and say, 'The answer is that after the body dies the mind continues to work somehow.' But I don't believe that. All cultures try to come to some kind of accord with this reality. But I don't think anybody's really successfully done it to the extent that men walk around completely integrated.

Perhaps it all means that we are just beginning a very important phase of our evolution, which I think will primarily be a physical one. And I suspect that the way we are changing the earth – which seems very destructive to us right now – might be very much involved. I don't think natural selection, as Darwin understood it, is really at work any more as far as human evolution is concerned. I think something more along the lines of nuclear disaster is perhaps a natural part of our evolution. It may be a strange philosophy, I'm not sure. But my instincts seem to suggest that we were meant to tamper with everything – and have done – and that this will reflect back on us and change us.

I'd love to write *The Shape of Rage*! I'm sure it would be a big bestseller. I've always said that, if I don't make it in the film business, I can always open a Psychoplasmics clinic north of Los Angeles. The basic idea for Psychoplasmics was that people do get rashes when they're stressed out; muscles do tighten up. I deal with that again in *The Fly*. The idea of a creative cancer; something that you would normally see as a disease now goes to another level of creativity and starts sculpting with your own body.

Attitudes to the flesh, and disease, are crucial to the understanding – and misunderstanding – of Cronenberg's Project, not least of all because the happy conduit between the two is often explicitly sexual. It is the pungent mixture of horror, sexuality and diseased, treacherous flesh that has led many critics to the conclusion that the real subject-matter of the films is sexual disgust.

I don't think that the flesh is necessarily treacherous, evil, bad. It is cantankerous, and it is independent. The idea of independence is the key. It really is like colonialism. The colonies suddenly decide that they can and should exist with their own personality and should detach from the control of the mother country. At first the colony is perceived as being treacherous. It's a betrayal. Ultimately, it can be seen as the separation of a partner that could be very valuable as an equal rather than as something you dominate. I think that the flesh in my films is like that. I notice that my characters talk about the flesh undergoing revolution at times. I think to myself: 'That's what it is: the independence of the body, relative to the mind, and the difficulty of the mind accepting what that revolution might entail.'

The most accessible version of the 'New Flesh' in *Videodrome* would be that you can actually change what it means to be a human being in a physical way. We've certainly changed in a psychological way since the beginning of mankind. In fact, we have changed in a physical way as well. We are physically different from our forefathers, partly because of what we take into our bodies, and partly because of things like glasses

31 Art Hindle and Oliver Reed: *The Brood.*

and surgery. But there is a further step that could happen, which would be that you could grow another arm, that you could actually physically change the way you look – mutate.

Human beings could swop sexual organs, or do without sexual organs as sexual organs *per se*, for procreation. We're free to develop different kinds of organs that would give pleasure, and that have nothing to do with sex. The distinction between male and female would diminish, and perhaps we would become less polarized and more integrated creatures.

I'm not talking about transsexual operations. I'm talking about the possibility that human beings would be able to physically mutate at will, even if it took five years to complete that mutation. Sheer force of will would allow you to change your physical self.

To understand physical process on earth requires a revision of the theory that we're all God's creatures – all that Victorian sentiment. It should certainly be extended to encompass disease, viruses and bacteria. Why not? A virus is only doing its job. It's trying to live its life. The fact that it's destroying you by doing so is not its fault. It's about trying to understand interrelationships among organisms, even those we perceive as disease. To understand it from the disease's point of view, it's just a matter of life. It has nothing to do with disease. I think most diseases would be very shocked to be considered diseases at all. It's a very negative connotation. For them, it's very positive when they take over your body and destroy you. It's a triumph. It's all part of trying to reverse the normal understanding of what goes on physically, psychologically and biologically to us.

The characters in *Shivers* experience horror because they are still standard, straightforward members of the middle-class high-rise genera-tion. I identify with them after they're infected. I identify with the parasites, basically. Of course they're going to react with horror on a conscious level. They're bound to resist. They're going to be dragged kicking and screaming into this new experience. But, underneath, there is something else, and that's what we see at the end of the film. They look beautiful at the end. They don't look diseased or awful.

Why not look at the processes of ageing and dying, for example, as a transformation? This is what I did in *The Fly*. It's necessary to be tough though. You look at it and it's ugly, it's nasty, it's not pretty. It's very hard to alter our aesthetic sense to accommodate ageing, never mind disease. We say, 'That's a fine-looking old man; sure he smells a bit, and he's got funny patches on his face.' But we do that. There is an impulse to try and accommodate ageing into our aesthetic. You might do the same

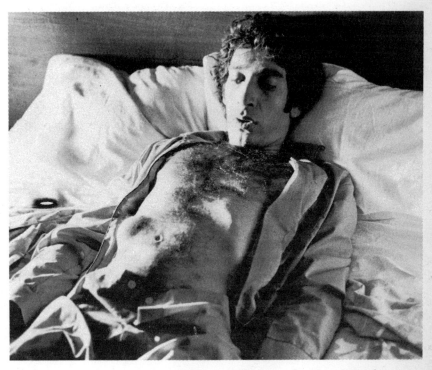

32 Parasites in *Shivers*.

for disease: 'That's a fine, cancer-ridden young man.' It's hard, and you might say 'Why bother?' Well, because the man still exists. He has to look at himself.

That's why it seems very natural for me to be sympathetic to disease. It doesn't mean that I want to get any. But that's one of the reasons I try to deal with that, because I know it's inevitable that I will get some. We could talk about the tobacco mosaic virus but that wouldn't interest us much, not being tobacco plants ourselves. Naturally we're interested in human diseases. But how does the disease perceive us? That illuminates what we are.

The Brood was certainly a very interesting and potent experience. It really was cathartically satisfying in a very direct way. Some of the violence in that movie was very cathartic for me to get on screen. Screaming and yelling. I don't usually have lots of screaming and yelling, but there's a fair amount in that movie. I don't do much screaming and yelling; I don't have it in my life. I don't like it much. But that was good stuff. It really worked. I certainly felt poised and in control during filming; it insisted on being made in a very personal way. It's as close to literal autobiography as I've ever come. I hope I don't come that close again. I can't tell you how satisfying the climax is. I wanted to strangle my ex-wife.

I ran into Samantha Eggar ten years later at the Sitges Film Festival where she sat in the audience to watch *Dead Ringers*. She said, 'The Brood* was the strangest and most repulsive film I've ever done.' I had to remind her that she told me it related to her own life. Maybe she forgot that. I was very lucky to get her. She was only there three days, but it's a role in which she never moves. She just sits in the same place. The most she does is rise from sitting to her knees; a strange, immobilized character. Very bizarre, intense and weird.

My general feeling was that the kind of rage Nola had was an all-purpose one – genderless. Her rage goes beyond certain moral categories, so the resulting creatures were primal, nearly foetal, nearly formless. Just pure anger. I hadn't realized the film had a similar premise to *Forbidden Planet* until I picked the name for the school (the Krell School). Then I made the connection: creatures from the unconscious, making the mental physical. That's what *The Brood* and *Forbidden Planet* are really about. I was knocked out by that film as a kid. The creatures are, in fact, embodiments of my own rage, my anger, guilt and disappointment. You can look at the film as an allegory and it becomes very realistic.

The visual image for the climactic scene crystallized for me in a sort of waking dream. It didn't come from sleep. It came from whatever unconscious place these images arise. I had a long and loving close-up of Samantha licking the foetus that was quite fantastic. I really regret that it's not in any final version of the film. The ironic thing is that when the censors, those animals, cut it out, the result was that a lot of people thought she was eating her baby. That's much worse than I was suggesting. What we're talking about here is an image that's not sexual, not violent, just gooey – gooey and disturbing. It's a bitch licking her pups. Why cut it out? Here's a woman who's nurturing her rage as personified by these creatures, and the fact that they should be grotesque children is even better. It fucks the whole movie as far as I'm concerned. I could kill the censors for their stupidity and narrow-mindedness. Talk about rage!

Released in 1979, The Brood was a major development for its director in all respects. Its budget, at $1.5 million, was his largest to date. It featured two respectable stars – Oliver Reed and Samantha Eggar. The performances throughout were more even and better realized. Its mise-en-scène was more sophisticated, and its extreme imagery more spare and controlled – if no less disturbing. Already the proud-to-appear-schlocky tendency of Shivers *and* Rabid *had mutated into an altogether more mature, dark and serious purpose.*

Not surprisingly, Cronenberg was disappointed by the way New World Pictures opted to sell the film in America. Predictably blind to the movie's ambitions, they deployed an unsophisticated exploitation campaign aimed at their traditional drive-in market. Consigning The Brood *to B-horror film, they cheated the movie of the broader audience it deserved. The horror genre and its well-established modes of distribution and exhibition, so convenient to both* Shivers *and* Rabid, *began – with* The Brood *– to work against the maturing Cronenberg Project.*

With the unexpected death of Dick Schouten, Vision 4 had been dissolved. It now regrouped and became Filmplan International Inc. Victor Solnicki joined forces with both The Brood's *executive producer Pierre David and producer Claude Héroux. Despite AIP's approach to releasing the film in the States, it was a success, and remains the Cronenberg picture Solnicki is most proud of ('It's our Disney family picture!'). All were anxious to repeat the experience. In a classic case of the 'return of the repressed', the next film was already there in the form of forgotten 'Sensitives'.*

Scanners, as the film was renamed, had existed in many forms since the early 1970s. Cronenberg had written a script called 'Telepathy 2000',

which featured artificially created telepaths and an underground group
spearheaded by a charismatic leader. A friend had showed it to Roger
Corman at the time: 'Nothing happened with it, though Corman's Death
Race 2000 *did come out after that.' Now, Filmplan International, with*
tax-shelter financing, were able to offer Cronenberg a budget in excess of
$4 million to make his first picture ever to top the US box-office charts –
albeit briefly.

Scanners was a whole other thing. It was 'OK, we're forming this
company; we like each other so much and it's such a nice balance of these
three guys' – and it was, they were all good at different things – 'It's
called Filmplan and we're going to do film packages. Three films, and
cross-collateralize them.' And they did. *Scanners* supported the package,
I hasten to add, because the other two died completely and my film ended
up supporting them. 'So, what have you got?' 'What about "The Sensitives"? Why don't we do that?' 'Great. Two weeks and we're shooting.'
There were literally two weeks pre-production on what became *Scanners*.
Two weeks. Without a script.

The excitement was that the money was there before anything else.
Before the project. Fantastic opportunity. As a result, *Scanners* had the
longest post-production of any film I've ever done. It was maybe nine
months of editing, shooting some new scenes, trying to make stuff work.
It's one thing shooting on location in Little Italy; you know the tone of
the stuff, it's all there and you're just shooting in the streets. What you're
improvising there are the characters and the plot. With *Scanners* you're
improvising the design of a whole invented world, suggesting a futuristic
world without really saying it's futuristic. You're having to invent conference rooms and computer rooms, because you have to blow them up.
You're not going to walk down the street and find a great location. It all
had to be made. So it was very hard on poor Carol Spier, who did an
incredible job.

Inevitably the first day was the most disastrous shooting day I've ever
had. We went out, and there was nothing to shoot. Nothing was there:
we didn't have the truck; we didn't have the insignia on the building; we
didn't have the costume for Stephen Lack. We were shooting along the
expressway, and the traffic was jamming up. A guy in a truck was
watching us shooting by the side of the road and didn't notice that
everyone in front of him had stopped. I turned round in time to see his
truck climb up on top of this little Toyota. Our grips had to jump the
fence and drag these two women out of their car and lay them on the

verge. Dead. It was hideous. Everybody was just shocked and depressed. We weren't responsible, but if we hadn't been there, it wouldn't have happened. It was just a total wipe-out. All because we had to start shooting. That's all.

It kept on being that difficult. Patrick McGoohan was part of the reason. He's a brilliant actor: the voice, the charisma, the presence, the face. Phenomenal. And he was ageing so well; he looked so great in that beard. But he was so angry. His self-hatred came out as anger against everybody and everything. He said to me, 'If I didn't drink I'd be afraid I'd kill someone.' He looks at you that way and you just say, 'Keep drinking.' It's all self-destructive, because it's all self-hating. That's my theory. He was also terrified. The second before we went to shoot he said, 'I'm scared.' I wasn't shocked; Olivier said that he was terrified each time he had to go on stage. With Patrick, though, it was just so raw and so scary – full of anger and potent. But he was sensing the disorganization; the script wasn't there, so he was right to worry about it. He didn't know me. He didn't know whether I could bring it off or not. We parted from the film not on very good terms ultimately.

Also, without telling me, my producers sent Jennifer O'Neill a script in which all the violence had been removed because they'd heard that she wouldn't want it. When she saw the real script, she started to sob and cry in the trailer and was really disturbed and upset and didn't want to be a part of this movie. So let's talk about it. It's like Geneviève Bujold in *Dead Ringers*: 'I'm not going to have the camera looking up your snatch in the gynaecological scenes.' You can't tell that from the script because I don't say where the camera is. I told her I wouldn't do that, but I'm not going to tell her the script doesn't have a gynaecological examination in it.

There was a terrific pressure to lie to people about things. The desperation to get the fucking movie off the ground before the end of the year was huge. That was another bad thing about the tax-shelter era; these abnormal time pressures on everybody, not just the director, to do weird stuff to get it to happen in time. If the money wasn't spent, if the principle photography wasn't complete by the end of the year (31 December), then all these guys who were totally dependent on their tax-write-off from you didn't get it. So there was a lot of hanky-panky, doing two months of second-unit photography after the New Year, and so on. On the other hand, can you see *Scanners* shot in the lushness of summer? It was meant to be very deadly – a cold, harsh, nasty film. It was perfect. And for *The Brood* too. I loved it in the winter. The two things came together in a kind of kismet fashion. If I'd had to shoot in the summer I would have found a way to get that tone across anyway.

Scanners *is the closest Cronenberg has ever come to the science-fiction genre. Interestingly, the film is also unusually optimistic in its conclusion, compared to the endless cycles of disease and family trauma implied by the closing sequences of* Shivers, Rabid *and* The Brood. *In a scene which at once harks back to* Crimes of the Future *(the reincarnation of Antoine Rouge as a young girl), and forward to* Dead Ringers *(where twin brothers who share the same nervous system are trapped in separate bodies), estranged brothers Cameron Vale and Darryl Revok become as one, after a scanning battle to the death.*

Cameron Vale survives as a mixture of the good guy and the bad guy. I was suggesting that this new creature was a blending of the two brothers, that they had fused. We went with contact lenses and different hair colour and the voice lowered to be halfway between Stephen Lack (Vale) and Michael Ironside (Revok). Jennifer O'Neill's look at him is very tentative. But maybe I wasn't successful cinematically in selling that. We were shooting in the winter in Montreal in buildings that weren't heated or insulated. That just draws the energy out of you. And I was once again in the position of having to write the scene between five and seven in the morning and then seeing if there was a way to get it to work physically the rest of the day: can we get the set; can the actors learn the lines; can we shoot this stuff? And out of sequence.

I remember the scene which sets everything up, in the conference room of Consec where they discuss going to find the scanner to do this and that. I had to anticipate everything I hadn't written yet. How could I anticipate? I didn't know what the end of the movie was going to be. Wandering around with your crew and finding the movie is paradise if that's your temperament. Not for me. Also, you're still writing the script when you're editing because you can put in new dialogue. God knows, in *Scanners* you wouldn't believe the trickery. That was a new high in editing trickery for me.

Although Scanners *contains many of Cronenberg's trademark obsessions (making thought physical; the misguided scientist; an unexpected physical ability brought about by unorthodox medications), its emphasis is on action: car crashes, explosions, shoot-outs and scanning battles. The internal drama of* The Brood, *written at a time of pessimism and personal*

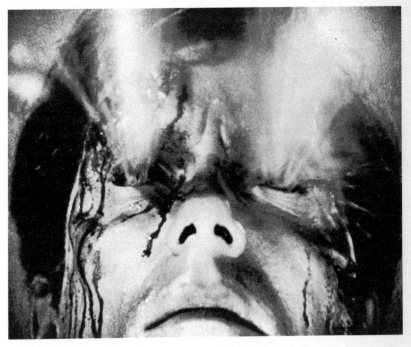

33 Stephen Lack as Cameron Vale in *Scanners*.

difficulty, is here vanquished in favour of thrills. 'I'd remarried; I'd had another kid, and was feeling much more optimistic about things in general. I was exploding heads just like any other young, normal North American boy.'

The infamous exploding head in Scanners *was created by Chris Walas, then in the employ of Lucasfilm Ltd. Walas went on to establish his own company, providing Cronenberg with the Academy Award-winning make-up effects for* The Fly, *and most recently some fifty creatures for* Naked Lunch. *The MPAA insisted the exploding-head scene, as shot by Cronenberg, be trimmed for an R-rating release. Cronenberg also re-edited the film after test screenings, moving the sequence further back in the narrative. It was originally intended as the picture's opening.*

The make-up guys really surprised me. I came back to my apartment one night, and there was this head sitting on the table. It was so life-like! It was soft to the touch and dented just like real flesh when you touched it. It was the most realistic head possible. I knew right then it was the one I wanted. For the scene, Gary Zeller was shooting from behind and at an upward angle. When the blast hits the head, the face goes inside out and sort of swings down under the neck. Then the body slumps down under the table. It's an incredible shot. Incredibly gruesome, but also quite beautiful. It's so surreal that it's also quite lovely in its own way. The producers were alarmed when they saw the rushes and wanted to film less graphic takes as insurance. I said 'Sure, go ahead.' They shot three more heads blowing up in various ways, but I wasn't there to watch them. I just went back to my Winnebago and took a nap. I wasn't interested. I had the one I wanted.

A complete film-maker should be able to appeal to all facets of human existence, the sensual as well as the cerebral. If you do get this mixture together properly, you have a perfect example of healing the Cartesian schism. You have something that appeals to the intellect and to the viscera. If you mix them together you get a whole movie. I don't particularly like cerebral movies. On the other hand, I don't like movies that are all viscera and no brains.

Determined that Scanners *should get a decent chance in the marketplace, Filmplan forged sounder distribution ties with major companies such as Avco Embassy. Avco had demonstrated with film-makers such as John Carpenter that they could reach a much broader-based horror-film audience with a more accomplished product.*

34 The exploding head in *Scanners*.

Scanners was a breakthrough film for me, because it was number one on the *Variety* chart when it came out. This was a big deal for a low-budget Canadian horror film, which was basically the way it was perceived. True, it was a slow week, but that doesn't ever count. If you're number one, you're number one. A lot of people in Hollywood started to notice me then. The picture did make a dent. The important thing about getting offers was that I didn't have a film lawyer or an agent. I did have a divorce lawyer for a short period. I remember when Pierre David called me to see if I was interested in being involved in *Scanners II*. I wasn't, but said, 'Am I going to get any money on the sequel based on my original characters and idea?' He said, 'No. You didn't have a lawyer then.'

Once you're represented by an agency and you have an agent in LA, and a lawyer, that really encourages people to send you stuff, because they know where to send it for one thing. Just a simple thing like an address for 'this Canadian guy up there ... I don't even know the city ... see if you can find him ... I can't.' At one time Scorsese tried to find me in Toronto and was told I didn't exist! It wasn't until after *Video-drome* that I started to get serious offers.

The success of Scanners *helped to establish the Cronenberg sensibility with a public beyond the drive-in/exploitation audience. The fact that 'Cronenbergesque' now signified something specific in a quality com-mercial horror context possibly contributed to the full page ad in* Variety *at this time which announced 'David Cronenberg's Franken-stein'. The director elaborated for* Cinéfantastique *in 1980: 'Pierre David came up to me one day and said, "Listen to this. Just listen, and tell me what you think.' And then he said, "David Cronenberg's Frankenstein." So I said, "Sounds good to me. What about poor Mary Shelley?"'*

Even with the early Frankenstein proposition, Cronenberg was clear about how his own sensibility would interact with such established material. 'It would be more a rethinking than a remake. For one thing, I'd try to retain Shelley's original concept of the creature being an intelligent, sensitive man. Not just a beast.' Apparently Cronenberg also intended to rescue Frankenstein from his period-piece trappings, and contemporize the story.

The project never materialized. The fusion or splicing of 'Cronenberg' with established material was eventually, and inevitably, to happen later with his filming of Jeffrey Boam's adaptation of Stephen King's The

Dead Zone, *his reworking of* The Fly *(part-written by Charles Edward Pogue) and, most recently and completely, the creation of his own version of William Burroughs's* Naked Lunch.

In the event, Videodrome *– a totally original work – was to be Cronenberg's next movie, his last under the Canadian tax-shelter system, and his third with the production grouping of Victor Solnicki, Pierre David and Claude Héroux – now called Filmplan II Inc. Less rushed than* Scanners, *it proved to be the director's most conceptually challenging work of the period. Never afraid to confront the uncomfortable aspects of an inner life, Cronenberg here turned the tables on his own film-making practice. Critics eager to spot his reactionary tendencies were rewarded with a story about the unpredictable and unpleasant effects of sexually violent imagery on Max Renn – a softcore sex-and-violence cable-station owner in Toronto. Perversely, Cronenberg had decided to investigate the very censorious notions to which his own work had fallen victim.*

Pierre David said, 'Listen, tax-shelter money is everywhere. It's getting to be November when the money comes in because they need the tax write-off. We want to do another movie. What have you got?' I remember I rode my motorcycle to Montreal to meet him, because a Russian satellite had come apart and they thought it might land in Canada. All flights had been cancelled. So I jumped on my bike, which Pierre thought was very eccentric. I said, 'I've got these two ideas,' and he chose *Videodrome*. It was just a concept, but he liked it. So I said, 'I'll work it up.' It sounded more like a thriller than anything else, and he liked what I said. But when I started writing it, and all of these other things started to leap out at me, I really thought Filmplan would reject it. It was so much more extreme than my premise had suggested. To my surprise, all three of them loved it. But Claude Héroux said that, if we shot it as it was written, it'd get a Triple X rating for sure. I told him that I'd written it in a more extreme fashion than I would want to see it on the screen *myself*.

It began life as something I'd written earlier, called 'Network of Blood'. It was a very straightforward melodrama about a man who discovers a strange signal on television. That came from a lot of my own late-night television watching as a kid, and suddenly seeing signals come through. This was long before cable, when you had the old antenna that you could rotate. As certain strong stations went off the air, you got weaker signals that had been formerly masked coming through. Sometimes they were very strange and evocative; sometimes you were projecting your own meanings on them because you couldn't hear the sound properly. It was that experience that led me to posit a man who picks up a signal that's very bizarre, very extreme, very violent, very dangerous. He becomes obsessed with it, because of its content, tries to track it down, and gets involved in a whole mystery.

I was finding it difficult to write at home – because of kids and stuff – and rented a room in the same building downtown where my editor Ron Sanders had his. I just had a chair, a table and a typewriter. When I started to write that story, it suddenly started to shift. Max began to hallucinate, and impossible physical things started to happen to him. It went even further than in the movie; at a certain point he began to find that his life was not as he had thought: he was not who he'd thought he'd been. I had to pull back finally because it got so extreme it was too much for one film. The writing really did surprise me.

If you're going to do art, you have to explore certain aspects of your life without regard to a political position or stance. With *Videodrome* I wanted to posit the possibility that a man exposed to violent imagery would begin to hallucinate. I wanted to see what it would be like, in fact, if what the censors were saying would happen, did happen. What would it feel like? What would it lead to? But there is the suggestion that the technology involved in *Videodrome* is specifically designed to create violence in a person; we know that by the use of electrodes in certain areas of the brain you can trigger off a violent, fearful response without regard to other stimulants.

Cronenberg tried something new with Videodrome *that he has since reformulated for* Naked Lunch: *a movie which slips, unannounced, into the protagonist's hallucinations. However, unlike his fusion with Burroughs,* Videodrome *all but abandons a complex and fascinating conspiratorial plot some 40 minutes in, for a relentlessly first-person point of view – never to return. As Max begins to lose any sense of reality or the ability to control his situation, so the movie wilfully disintegrates along with its confused protagonist.*

Our own personal perception of reality is the only one we'll accept. Even if you're going mad, it's still your reality. But the same thing, seen from an outside perspective, is a person acting insane. The two ideas clicked together.

Something that's unresolved in *Videodrome* is Max's take on life; I feel it, but I'm not sure that everybody gets it. He hasn't reached a point in his

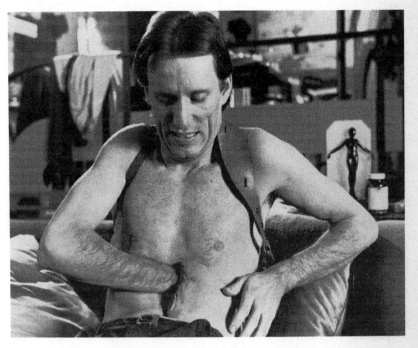

35 James Woods in *Videodrome* (1982).

life where he actually connects with melancholia. But I think it's there –
down the line. Max never makes it that far in life; he's still at the stage
where he's confident, glib and full of energy. The essence of him was that
he is glib but is being forced to come to terms with some strange, difficult
stuff that he's not prepared to deal with in a real way, a real emotional
way. It has to get twisted into hallucination and strangeness for him even
to begin to come to grips with it.

At the same time, I feel that Max ultimately manages to manipulate this
new reality he finds himself in to seek his own equilibrium again. I think
that's what would happen. People in prison camps, or people subjected to
all kinds of psychological and physical torture are constantly trying to
rebalance themselves. There is an innate balance that wants to be
expressed.

Even though we don't look alike, Jimmy Woods's presence on the screen
began to feel like a projection of me. It was exciting to find an actor who
was my cinematic equal. I'd never really considered that as a possibility
before. I'm very verbal and there are few American actors known for being
verbal. It was nice to hear Jimmy do dialogue that I had written.

There's an undertone I intend to be there that implies he's not really sure
of his own relationship to what he shows on television, how he relates to
his own sexuality, and so on. Being a human being who's as sensitive to
himself as anybody else, I suppose I have similarities to Max at that point,
but then we start to diverge. That isn't to say that I haven't noticed that I'm
attracted to images of sexual violence, and wonder what that means about
myself, but I'm not Max.

Videodrome was different from *Scanners* because it was so strange.
Scanners had a fairly straightforward sci-fi action plot – two rival groups
and so on – but with *Videodrome* I was really breaking some new ground;
I hadn't seen anything like it myself. I don't remember there being the same
kind of pressure I had with *Scanners*. If we started shooting in November,
then there were pressures. But if we started in September or October,
probably there weren't. I don't remember and don't want to blame the
tax-shelter rush again. But when we started to shoot, things started to
change. I hadn't quite gotten the ending that I wanted. I'm happy with the
ending we have, but there were other possibilities. It wasn't the kind of film
where you just know when you've got it. It was slippery.

The first extreme draft of Videodrome *had been enough to attract Oscar-
winning (for* American Werewolf in London) *special-effects wizard Rick
Baker. However, production began with a toned-down second draft, only*

two months' preparation time for Baker (he wanted six), fewer effects and a reduced budget with which to achieve them – around Can.$500,000. Originally, the script contained scenes such as Max's and Nicki's faces melting in the passion of a kiss, dribbling down and across the floor, and up the leg of an onlooker, melting him.

Alterations to the second draft were to continue throughout production until the last day of shooting, and beyond that into post-production. One alternative ending was a mutated transsexual orgy in the Videodrome chamber. After Max shoots himself (the last image in the final version), we might have seen Bianca O'Blivion (Sonja Smits), Max (James Woods) and Nicki Brand (Debbie Harry) sexually entwined, all in each other. 'A happy ending? Well, my version of a happy ending – Boy meets Girl, with a clay wall maybe covered with blood. Freudian rebirth imagery, pure and simple.' Max's imagined abdominal vagina was here to be matched by Nicki's and Bianca's newly found penises (à la Rabid). Male and female mutated sex-organ appliances were designed, but Cronenberg decided to drop the scene altogether. Constant references in Videodrome to 'the New Flesh' may have been clarified by this vision: another, more inventive, satisfying fleshy existence waiting just on the other side of death.

I ultimately felt that it wouldn't work. I'm pretty obstinate; I will not let go of the ending of a movie if I think it's right, just because of money. I would talk to the producers. This is the Canadian way. This is why we're different. Michael Cimino and I are the two sides of the North American coin. But I don't think it would have worked. It might have been laughable. Finally, I liked what we got; Max shooting himself was the right ending for the movie. And it's almost the same ending as *Dead Ringers*, *The Fly* and *The Dead Zone*. On each of those films there was a coda written that never ended up in the picture. I think *Videodrome* would have been exactly the same. It was not in the original script; it occurred to me as we were making the film.

It was an odd movie. The crew was really freaked out by it; most of them people I'd worked with many times. We had some ladies come in and take their clothes off, then we'd chain them to the Videodrome wall and beat them – not for real. One or two of them quite loved it. Most of them were extras, and had never had this kind of attention. But the weirdness of it actually excited a couple of them. One kept reappearing on set, very made-up, very dressed, and just floated around. It was strange; she was someone who'd been strangled and beaten in the scene.

So it was undeniably freaky being on that set. It makes sense that it was; it was supposed to be.

I had to make speeches to the crew every once in a while, because at a certain point we were in disarray. I was indecisive at certain junctures as we got closer to the end. We would set up in a place to shoot and then I'd take it apart and go somewhere else. I was feeling my way through a difficult film. Despite the fact that I talk about liking to have a script together, it's not because I think that means you've solved every problem or understood your film. I was beginning to understand more of what was going on in the movie, and that what I originally thought would work wasn't going to. At one point on the Videodrome chamber set, I actually told the crew what was going on and what I was thinking, to reassure them things were in hand. They were wondering if I was falling apart, or under pressure because of something they didn't know about. I suppose the immediate thing crews think of is 'Is this picture going to be cancelled tomorrow? Am I going to be out of work?'

A film like *Videodrome*, which deals specifically with sadomasochism, violence and torture, is naturally going to have a lot of nervous systems on edge. There was a woman politician in Canada who had pickets out on the streets of Ottawa. They finally got the picture removed from a theatre there because the owner just didn't want the hassle. That's fine. That's his right. But this woman was a politician, connected with a certain party in Canada, and had many particular axes to grind.

Adverse critical response to Videodrome *was not restricted to local politicians. Cronenberg's transgressions in the sexual-political arena have continued to antagonize certain audiences and critics. Nicki Brand, so named – presumably – because of her taste for burning her breast with lighted cigarettes, was merely the latest in a line of predominantly rapacious female creations. As with Cronenberg's obsession with the male/ female opposition – in which female 'difference' can slip imperceptibly into 'the other' (and, in* Naked Lunch, *into the 'non-human') – his determination and desire to be free of politicized constraints and considerations in imagining his women, and their sexuality, will continue to offend.*

I'm male, and my fantasies and my unconscious are male. I think I give reasonable expression to the female part of me, but I still think that I'm basically a heterosexual male. If I let loose the social bonds to see what my sexuality is at its darkest and its most insane and its most amoral –

not immoral – if I'm going to get into scenes of bondage and torture, I'll show a female instead of a male.

I've talked about admiring *Naked Lunch*. One of the barriers to my being totally 100 per cent with William Burroughs is that Burroughs's general sexuality is homosexual. It's very obvious in what he writes that his dark fantasies happen to be sodomizing young boys as they're hanging. I can actually relate to that to quite an extent. I really understand what's going on. But if I were to fantasize something similar, it would be more like the parasite coming up the drain, and it would be attacking a woman, not a man. To say that's sexist is politicizing something that is not political. It's sexual, not sexist – that's just my sexual orientation. I have no reason to think that I have to give equal time to all sexual fantasies whether they're my own or not. Let those people make their own movies – leave me alone to make mine. I feel censored in a strange way. I feel that meanings are being twisted and imposed on me. And more than meanings – value judgements.

As a creator of characters, I believe I have the freedom to create a character who is not meant to represent all characters. I can create a woman as a character who does not represent all women. If I depict a character as a middle-class dumbo, why does this have to mean that I think all women are middle-class dumbos? There are some women out there who are. Why can they not be characters in my film? If I show Debbie Harry as a character who burns her breast with a cigarette, does that mean that I'm suggesting that all women want to burn their breasts with cigarettes? That's juvenile. To give guidelines to the kind of characters you can create, and the kind of acts they can do . . . that's obscene, a Kafka hell.

It's very difficult to divine what's unconscious and what's conscious, but if you were to find by analysing my films, for example, that I'm afraid of women, unconsciously that is, I would say, 'OK, so what? What's wrong with that?' If I am an example of the North American male, and my films are showing that I'm afraid of women, then that's something which could perhaps be discussed, perhaps even decried. But where do you really go from there?

I would never censor myself. To censor myself, to censor my fantasies, to censor my unconscious would devalue myself as a film-maker. It's like telling a surrealist not to dream. The way I portray women is much more complex than any ideological approach is going to uncover. The advertisement says that the image of a woman sitting on top of the car in a bathing suit is what a woman should aspire to. This is more insidious. A twelve-year-old girl who sees *Videodrome* might be very disturbed because she is attracted and repelled by the sexuality – an image of a woman burning herself springs to mind – and by the imagery. But that's different. There's no clear message in the film that a twelve-year-old would absorb about how she is to behave when she is mature. That's not the purpose of art – to tell us how we should live.

To me politics does not mean sexual politics. Politics has to do with power struggles, and parties and revolutions. People use the term sexual revolution in a metaphorical way. It's a semantic thing.

Videodrome had attracted the interest of an American major studio at a very early stage, on the strength of its bizarre, provocative and contemporary themes. Its director had enjoyed some success with Scanners, *and the new movie was to feature Debbie Harry, as well as James Woods. With the help of Pierre David, a Cronenberg movie finally stood to benefit from the kind of distribution muscle only a Hollywood major studio can flex – assuming they could properly market such a unique film as* Videodrome.

Pierre had started to make connections in Hollywood, and *Videodrome* was his entrée into studio film-making. He was a classic French-Canadian entrepreneur, but so unusual. For four days or months, he was the Minister of Education for some bizarre African state that had just become independent. He was going into the religious life at one time, ended up being the Quebec Cardinal's right-hand man, went to Africa and suddenly they didn't have anyone who could handle the Ministry of Education. Before that he was a disc jockey. Then he had radio stations, and then he got into film. Now he's in LA. He always wanted Hollywood, and was talking to Tom Mount – one of the longest-surviving entities at Universal – who was there with Hitchcock in his decline. He was a real politician, who survived many administrations and did some interesting things; one of them was to talk to Ned Tanen about *Videodrome*. At a certain point, while we were shooting, it definitely became a Universal picture.

I was dealing with Tom Mount, and then Verna Field, when we were having troubles with finishing the film. Verna was editor on *Jaws*, then became a famous editor and then post-production overseer of everything at Universal. I think it's amazing that Universal Pictures went with *Videodrome*, produced it and distributed it. They approved the project on a one-page description and were co-investors; they didn't finance the entire film, so it's not technically my first studio film. But Pierre managed to find people who were receptive. In retrospect I realize how extra-ordinary and unusual it was: first, that they even partially financed it – they were one of the most conservative major studios – and second, that they allowed it to continue once they saw what it was becoming. And finally, that they should make good their word and release it with a fair amount of enthusiasm. Generally, the system destroys pictures like *Videodrome* before they get to the public.

I remember Sid Scheinberg saying that he felt it had been a mistake to release the film wide; that it should have been handled as an art film, and been given slow, deliberate promotion using critical response to promote it. He was right. But he liked the picture. This is a man much vilified for the non-release of *Brazil*. But he did seem to have an empathy for this movie even though, at one point, I heard that when he finally read the script he came running down the corridors saying, 'Is it too late to stop this picture?!' Once he saw it, I thought his response was sound and sympathetic.

We had a test screening in Boston. It was a disaster. This was one of my introductions to the way movies are made in Hollywood. The official test screening. I was suddenly locked into the machinery of Universal Pictures. So we're showing it at this particular theatre, and there were response cards. Scary, because I don't know what's going on; I know that there's politics in there somewhere, but I don't know how it works or who to talk to about it. Neither does Pierre.

When I cut, I'm very ruthless. I don't care how long it took to get a shot, it's just whether it works or not. I get bored with things, and tend to take out too much in my first cut. I think we went into that screening with a 75-minute version of *Videodrome* which was totally incom-prehensible, however incomprehensible one might think it is now. I knew everything; I forgot the audience doesn't know until it's told. Classic mistake.

There was a transit strike in Boston that day, so we got about half the audience we wanted. I remember being shocked to see black ladies coming with their two-year-old kids, because it was a free movie and they didn't have a babysitter. One baby screamed all the way through. I realized that I was in trouble. They saw the movie; it had no music and no temporary track – I didn't know about temporary tracks. So there were all these audio holes in the movie, which is disturbing to people who don't know how movies are made. Complete disaster. I don't know if there was one card that said anything nice. Basically it was 'You're fucked.' But everyone was very sweet. It was 'How can we help you make this better? Let's figure out what went wrong.' Tom Mount was very blunt: 'This is terrible and bad.' But he never said the picture was lost. And with all these cards on the floor: 'Listen to this one – "I hated your fucking film."' It was excruciating.

In a way, what you're asking for is the judgement of strangers when you make art of any kind. You're asking them to relate and respond to it. But the cards are brutal. I've always used them myself, ever since. So I went back to the editing room feeling bruised, and started putting stuff back in the picture to make it work. The politics are that the word of how the screening went will get back to the powers-that-be. If they think the film is going to be a disaster based on that, they'll cut back on their advertising budget and on the number of prints. I didn't realize the audience was going to kill me. Fortunately, it didn't break my heart. I got the chance to recut, and we never had another official screening, just lots of little ones.

They ended up releasing 900 prints, which is not massive: 1,100 or 1,200 were certainly not unknown then. But 900 was a lot for a movie like this. It played for a week and was gone. They spent the money on it, as much as they were supposed to. But it didn't reach anyone. It didn't reach the horror fans, and it didn't satisfy them when it did. It wasn't *Scanners*. Nor did it reach a more sophisticated audience that would be able to take the nastiness. And it didn't last long enough for any criticism to generate. It was just a down-the-middle strange campaign. *Scanners* had a very hardcore sell, which I wasn't crazy about, but I sure had to admit it worked. *Videodrome* wasn't an exploitation sell and it wasn't an art sell. I don't know what it was.

The formal adventurousness of Videodrome, *its narrative complexity and overt philosophical dimensions, and its graphic imagery perhaps all contributed – along with an over-optimistic release pattern – to the film's commercial failure. Luckily, Cronenberg had spent some time during* Videodrome's *post-production preparing his next movie,* The Dead Zone, *and was already shooting it when news of* Videodrome's *bad performance at the box office reached him. This may have helped a little to lessen the blow. Nonetheless, the director regarded* Videodrome *as his most powerful and ambitious achievement to date.*

I was devastated. It's almost like how do you deal with the inevitability of death. If death is inevitable, it means that everything that comes before is irrelevant and trivial and meaningless. Why should you be alive up to your death? You might as well die right now, or go to bed and eat ice cream. It's the same with having a film not reach the people you think might want to see it. It happens to everyone who makes more than one. When I hear that someone saw *Videodrome* on a bootleg tape in Cuba, I smile a big smile and say, 'That's one more.'

When I studied American literature, it really struck me how all the great American writers of the eighteenth, nineteenth and early twentieth century died in despair. Whitman, Melville, Hawthorne, Poe: all died thinking that their work meant nothing, that they had achieved nothing, and that it was all meaningless. It sounded inevitable, because, on a cosmic level, that's absolutely true. It means nothing. I believe that. But you can't live your life on that level. You can make yourself crazy thinking that you cannot reproduce a film from any print of that film. Its physical essence is very fragile and tenuous. I can make myself crazy thinking 'Where is the negative of *Videodrome* now?' I don't know.

So I guess it's the consolation of philosophy, ultimately. When you're face to face with someone who's seen the film and liked it and was affected by it, that's one you know. Maybe that's enough. That's the minimum. There's got to be one. I think it was the Eskimos, or some Indian tribe, who had One, Two and Many as their number system. 'How many enemy are coming?' 'Many!' It could have been three; it could have been fifty. It's dangerous creating art. Burroughs talks about how writing is dangerous. I know exactly what he means. So, you go on. Hopefully by the time your film is released, you're involved with the next one. Which is exactly what happened with *Videodrome*.

To this day, Cronenberg is outraged about certain cuts made in Videodrome, *requested not by the MPAA, but by Universal Pictures themselves. Head of production Bob Rehme took particular exception to the film's 'fake' piece of Japanese softcore pornography – 'Samurai Dreams' – in which a geisha lifts a doll to reveal a well-sculptured ebony dildo beneath. Because it was a studio picture, Filmplan were contractually obliged to ensure that* Videodrome *was passed for mainstream distribution. Cronenberg had already met with the MPAA's Richard Heffner to discuss various trims and dissolves, in order that the film be granted an R as opposed to X certificate, and reached amicable agreement. For Rehme to add his own cuts, particularly to scenes with which the MPAA had no problem, is regarded by the director as 'the worst betrayal. I wanted support from him. I wanted his help. I don't forgive him for that. I'm as*

36 Personal chaos and the end of the road in *Videodrome*.
37 Personal chaos and the end of the road in *Dead Ringers*.

anguished right now as I was then. It hasn't diminished with time.' The
scene was trimmed, resulting in the usual jarring cut.

Considering the nature of his practice, Cronenberg may appear to have
suffered remarkably little at the hands of the censors – The Brood and
Videodrome *being particular casualties. However, his rage at their inter-*
vention, on nearly every level, is part of a more considered campaigning
spirit against the entire notion of censorship as it is presently constituted
and carried out by those officially charged with such responsibility. On
anti-censorship issues Cronenberg has become united with his own critics,
and – as a self-confessed apolitical director – been driven to political action.

When I had to deal with the Toronto Censor Board over *The Brood*, the
experience was so unexpectedly personal and intimate, it really shocked
me; pain, anguish, the sense of humiliation, degradation, violation. Now I
do have a conditioned reflex! I can only explain the feeling by analogy.
You send your beautiful kid to school and he comes back with one hand
missing. Just a bandaged stump. You phone the school and they say that
they really thought, all things considered, the child would be more socially
acceptable without that hand, which was a rather naughty hand. Everyone
was better off with it removed. It was for everyone's good. That's exactly
how it felt to me.

Censors tend to do what only psychotics do: they confuse reality with
illusion. People worry about the effect on children of two thousand acts of
murder on TV every half hour. You have to point out that they have seen a
representation of murder. They have not seen murder. It's the real
stumbling-block.

Charles Manson found a message in a Beatles song that told him what he
must do and why he must kill. Suppressing everything one might think of
as potentially dangerous, explosive or provocative would not prevent a
true psychotic from finding something that will trigger his own particular
psychosis. For those of us who are normal, and who understand the
difference between reality and fantasy, play, illusion – as most children
readily do – there is enough distance and balance. It's innate.

Censors don't understand how human beings work, and they don't
understand the creative process. They don't even understand the social
function of art and expression through art. You might say they don't have
to and you could be right. If you believe that censorship is a noble office,
then you don't have to understand anything. You just have to understand
censorship.

It's an endless struggle between those who are basically fearful and mistrustful of human nature – and they have ample proof that their version of humanity is right – and those who feel that a truly free society is possible, somewhere. It's conceivable that in the near future there won't be anything approaching a free society anywhere. That's more than possible. Which is why I resist, in the small way I can, any attempts in Canada to increase censorship. I've had responses here, like one from Margaret Atwood, who said she felt that literature should be uncensored but that films should be. Given that she's a writer and not a film-maker, that did upset me. Of course, the reason is that film is more potent and more accessible. I find that very Canadian: what's regarded as impotent can be allowed freedom; what's potent must be harnessed and mutilated.

Videodrome's narrative about a man's exposure to violent imagery via video cassette and broadcast signals, and its effect on his sense of reality, could not have been more prophetic; in 1985, three years after its release, Britain introduced the Video Recordings Bill. Initially fuelled by the quality press's concern about certain 'unpleasant' films freely available only on video – particularly the then infamous Driller Killer, SS Experiment Camp and I Spit on Your Grave – the equally infamous, but undefined, 'video nasty' suddenly came into being. In reality, though usually violent, these were simply low-budget independent films, crossing many genres and coming from many countries. Some had been in existence for years. They were 'unleashed' en masse by virtue of home-video technology and new world markets made possible by its popularity, particularly in Britain (30 per cent of homes had video recorders at this time, compared to only 19 per cent in America).

The horror genre, which had witnessed a renaissance in the 1970s, now became almost illegitimate. Although the so-called 'video nasty' clearly observed no generic bounds, it was the horror movie which was to suffer most – flesh-eating zombies a particular target for potential prosecution. With the Video Recordings Bill, Britain became the first country to censor and classify videos for viewing in the home, on the broad justification that children could be watching.

Any person who is a control freak must certainly find video the most threatening technological development ever. There's freedom to record, to change, to edit, to freeze-frame and look again, to exchange tapes. The video cassette is freedom of the image. It doesn't surprise me at all that censors should shift their focus from the cinema to what's happening in the home, because it's where there should be no censorship whatsoever. You can read *Naked Lunch* to your children over breakfast if you like. It's a strange reversal of what you would think is appropriate. We are in a wave of reaction and fear; control of imagery and dialogue is a manifestation of that.

Having children has assured me that there is a built-in resistance to exposure to things which might actually be damaging. The only problem is when adults drag a kid to a movie and the kid can't get away and doesn't want to be exposed. But I've found with my own kids that they literally put their hands over their eyes in order not to see something they can't take. At the same time, they do have a definite desire to test themselves, to take themselves to the limit in terms of what's scary or disturbing. I think that's natural and normal. When things are left to evolve naturally and not interfered with by social structures, they work. Most of the studies on child psychology point out that the things that disturb children are often very different from the things that disturb adults. Adults sometimes don't even consider the things that scare children most, like scenes of separation of a child from its parents.

People really have to examine themselves and their attitude towards society. If you believe that an individual is a responsible human being – he has the right to vote, to join the army and kill – then you have to accept that that person is also likely to be able to raise a child. If you take the paternalistic, élitist view, which is that everybody is an idiot and a dangerous hooligan and must therefore be controlled, channelled, structured and imprisoned, that's a whole other thing. Then you say, 'We are the only ones who understand how things should be run. We are the only ones who are fit to protect the children of this country. Even their parents are not, and no amount of education will help that.' Then you start with bannings, censorings and restrictions.

Cronenberg is not always in agreement with his own critics in his censorship concerns. The feminist movement has understandably found some sympathy for what might otherwise be regarded simply as the censorious impulse, where it has been applied to films which seem to relish violence against women. However, as in the case of the documentary Not a Love Story – A Film About Pornography *(later changed in Britain to* A Film Against Pornography*), the women film-makers were unable to have their movie distributed uncut in Ontario; this despite the assertion by Mary Brown – then head of the Censor Board for Ontario – that she was a feminist. It is now commonplace for the British Board of Film Classification (which continues to censor as well as classify) to discuss its actions* *against certain films conveniently within a feminist discourse, somewhat belatedly appropriated.*

It becomes complex when it gets mixed up with the women's movement. You find great splits there between those who think censorship is necessary and those who still believe in total free expression. An image of a man whipping a woman, for instance. It must come out of a film, whether the movie is set up in such a way that the audience understands this is just play between two lovers who've been together for forty years and have twenty kids. That wouldn't matter. The image has to go. So censors become image police: they don't care what the context of the image is; it's only the image itself.

The belief is that an image can kill. Literally. It's like *Scanners*: if thoughts can kill, images can kill. So the very suggestion of sadomasochism, for instance, will somehow trigger off masses of psychotics out there to do things they would never have done had they not been exposed to that image. That's why film classification, as opposed to censorship, is legitimate; when it's a suggestion rather than a law. But then, no one is particularly more qualified to be a classifier than anyone else, which is the problem with censorship. How can someone who is my age, my contemporary, see a film and say that I cannot see the film? I don't understand that.

Notes

1 Film critic and theorist Robin Wood has, for some years, championed certain horror movies and directors, and decried others. His position was most concisely expressed in *The American Nightmare* – a small publication edited with Richard Lippe for the Festival of Festivals in Toronto in 1979. At that time, Wood's position asserted that horror movies functioned as collective nightmares: products of the shared structures of common ideology. A basic all-purpose formula could also be applied to them which would expose their ideological subtext, determining whether they belonged to the progressive or reactionary tendencies of the genre. This formula was based on a movie's depiction of (a) 'normality', (b) the Monster, which always disrupts normality, and, crucially, (c) the relationship between the two. Wood's writings are highly illuminating. It is, however, to Cronenberg's advantage that, as expressed at the time, Wood's critical approach reads as ruthlessly schematic and overly determined to incorporate (primarily) the theories of Marx and Freud: dominant ideology, bourgeois capitalism and sexual repression.

2 *Heart Like a Wheel*: directed by Corman protégé Jonathan Kaplan in 1983, and starring Beau Bridges and Bonnie Bedelia, the movie unconventionally told the story of a woman racing driver.

3 *Kramer Vs Kramer*: adapted from Avery Corman's novel, directed by Robert Benton in 1979, and starring Dustin Hoffman, Meryl Streep and Justin Henry, this Oscar-winner dealt with an advertising man's efforts to bring up his son after his wife leaves.

CHAPTER 6

Unrequited Life: From Dead Zones to Dead Ringers

On completing Scanners *in 1980, Cronenberg had acquired his first and only agent, Mike Marcus. Based in Los Angeles, Marcus was in Toronto at the time scouting for Canadian directors to represent. Having signed Cronenberg, he encouraged him to visit LA at that time to introduce himself to the film community there. It was during this first Hollywood industry 'coming out' period that Cronenberg met – among many others – Carol Baum, then working for Lorimar. She had much admired* The Brood *and* Scanners *and had a project at Lorimar, to be produced by Sydney Pollack, that she wanted Cronenberg to direct. It was Stephen King's* The Dead Zone.*

Not having read the book on which the movie was to be based, Cronenberg's discussions with Baum inevitably turned to more personally interesting material: the Marcus brothers. Real-life identical twins, both men had been gynaecologists and both had died in strange circumstances. This pet project, about which Cronenberg and Baum were passionate, was finally born years later as Dead Ringers. *Baum was to discover that director Stanley Donen was in line to direct* The Dead Zone, *and so their conversations were put on ice.*

In the meantime, it wasn't until Videodrome *was completed, and Cronenberg was being offered directing assignments for the first time, that* The Dead Zone *re-emerged as a potential Cronenberg movie.*

Videodrome was a very heavy experience. If you're used to comedy, *The Dead Zone* is a heavy picture. But if you're used to *Videodrome*, *The Dead Zone* is not. At that point I needed to do something based on somebody else's work, as relief. I was not ready to write another script. *Videodrome* was a turning-point; I had done the most of something that I wanted to do with that film. I couldn't take it much further. It happened that way with my two early films – *Stereo* and *Crimes of the Future*.

I had met John Landis[1] in Toronto and we'd become friends. I visited him in his studio office in LA, and Debra Hill was there. I'd never met her, but knew of her because of her work with John Carpenter. She said, 'I'm doing a movie with Dino De Laurentiis² and you might be interested in it. It's *The Dead Zone*. Would you be interested in directing it?' I immediately said, 'Yes.' I surprised myself. This was maybe three years on, but obviously it had gestated in my mind to the point where I just wanted to do it. That was the beginning of my Dino De Laurentiis adventures.

I was aware of the whole concept of me as a writer/director – an *auteur* in the French sense. I could have driven myself crazy wondering what the French critics would think of me doing something that I hadn't written myself, and based on someone else's novel. For some reason I said, 'Yes.' I was confident I could find a version of *The Dead Zone* that would completely satisfy me, challenge me, and that would be me.

Inevitably, there was some cynicism and disappointment about Cronenberg accepting the Dead Zone *assignment, not least from his admirers. A far cry from the conceptual ambition and ingenuity of* Videodrome, *it looked suspiciously like a director's move towards the mainstream, perhaps never to return. Also at this time the cinema machine was already clotted with unsatisfactory Stephen King adaptations, released or to come. Stanley Kubrick's* The Shining *had split critics;* Cujo *and* Christine *were disappointing efforts from interesting directors (Lewis Teague and John Carpenter respectively);* Firestarter, *directed by Mark Lester, was a none-too-interesting addition to the King cinema canon;* Children of the Corn *was stranded in a B-horror-movie twilight zone. None had been received as well as the first – Brian De Palma's* Carrie. *The name Stephen King above a movie title obviously did not guarantee the artistic and financial success of the novels. It was also beginning to sound too familiar. For whatever reasons, it had proved difficult to adapt his work successfully for the cinema screen.*

The Dead Zone wasn't a calculated attempt to get a bigger audience on my part. People who think it's a cynical film, in so far as I didn't follow my own instincts, are completely wrong. If you chase a mass audience you die. You don't reach one. Even Fellini had his hits! And Antonioni with *Blow Up*, accidentally. He hadn't had one before and he hasn't since. But it was a perfect Antonioni film. He didn't chase. If I had a huge hit, it would be by accident.

Any human being is more complex than any body of work. If I wanted to reach a larger audience, what would be required would be to focus on other aspects of myself, other imagery and other characters that I'm also interested in. You can see in Fellini's first films, which were considered new or 'realist', that there is always also a scene with some incredible grotesque. Just a moment in the film. Later, that person, that moment, grew to become almost the entire film. Real, simple people were pushed right to the walls. Fellini is passionate about them all; it's just that the proportions have shifted. That's what I'd have to do, and I guess I'd have to do it consciously if I wanted to reach a wider audience that is not quite so sensitive.

You make a movie to find out what it is that made you want to make the movie. That's how it works for me. I very often don't know. I just know that on the journey to the end of the movie I will discover it. In retrospect, I could say *The Dead Zone* has got some differences: these are very small-town rural characters, as opposed to urban; they're simple and archetypally nice; they're called Johnny Smith; it's New England countryside; it does involve some politics. All stuff that I'm generally not interested in. Sexuality doesn't surface in *The Dead Zone* in the same way it does in my other films, but it's certainly there. It's a very repressed, restrained and frustrated thing. Personally the movie's just like me, but filmically I suppose not.

But you have a man who thinks he knows what's going on and where he is, and then suddenly an accident happens to him. Something physical; a disaster. Suddenly he realizes that he's not who he thought he was, that his life cannot be what he thought it could be. He is an alien. An outsider. He has the seeds of being a visionary, the same as a Scanner. At a certain point that comes out and destroys his life as he had known it. He tries to find another life that will accommodate his abilities as a prophet. He is an outsider. He looks like a normal guy, but he knows he's not.

He's cut off from the life he thought he had as his birthright as a normal human being by virtue of an increased sensitivity of some kind that is unbearable. It's not a gift, but a kind of curse. His girlfriend, his mother, his father, the town he was living in, the school that he taught at, are all gone suddenly. The loneliness and the melancholy and the impossibility of dealing with things. And yet the necessity to do it. That's what it was. It's Chris Walken's face. That's the subject of the movie; that's what the movie was about. All the things that are in his face. That's difficult to write about.

The folks in *The Dead Zone* tend to be God-fearing characters, whereas in my other films they are not. Because many of the scientists in

38 Christopher Walken in *The Dead Zone* (1983).

my early films are absent from the films themselves, although their influence remains, I think you could make a good case for saying that in *The Dead Zone*, God is the scientist whose experiments are not always working out and that the Johnny Smith character is one of his failed experiments.

Significantly for Cronenberg, and his supporters, The Dead Zone *was neither an original idea he had generated nor a script he would write.* Fast Company *had proved the only exception to a rule which had been a significant factor in establishing and maintaining his strong auteurist position. At a later stage, when the film was all but complete and the advance word was that it was very good indeed, Cronenberg was to remark, 'What'll bug me is if people think it's my best work because I didn't write an original script.'*

Because I had done *Fast Company* before, and because I hadn't written the two tape shows I did for the CBC either, *The Dead Zone* was different but familiar different. I didn't try to impose myself on the subject-matter. I had to assume that through the accumulation of the thousands and thousands of details that go into making a film, I would be there. And obviously I chose to do the project. I'd been offered a lot of things in the previous ten years, and this was the first one I'd accepted.

Stephen King's own script was terrible. It was not only bad as a script, it was the kind of script that his fans would have torn me apart for doing; they would have seen me as the one who destroyed his work. It was basically a really ugly, unpleasant slasher script. The Castle Rock killer in the middle of the movie becomes the lead, and it was 'Let's show lots of his victims.' It began with Greg Stillson torturing some kid in a back room, and it never went into Johnny's past. I didn't want to open the film with a kid being tortured, especially since, at that point, you don't know who Stillson is, what he's doing and why.

Each of the five scripts I was handed had stuff like that. I still didn't want to write it myself, but of all the scripts, the guy whose writing I liked the most, whose tone most approached what I'd seen in the book, was Jeffrey Boam.

Ironically, Boam had completed his first draft of The Dead Zone *for Lorimar the day Ronald Reagan was elected President. When De Laurentiis picked up the property, after Lorimar dropped its feature-film commitments, he had rejected Boam's draft and commissioned the*

Stephen King version. When this was rejected by the producer, De Laurentiis commissioned a further script from Polish director Andrej Zulawski. Cronenberg was never to see this version: 'I didn't read it. His script was apparently in Polish, then translated into English, and then into Italian for Dino to read. I don't know how that could have worked out.' When Debra Hill was taken on as the film's producer, these problems were solved: she put Boam and Cronenberg together to work on a final version.

As Boam observed: 'The basic difference between Stanley Donen's and David Cronenberg's approach to the material was that David ultimately wanted to see the story through Johnny's eyes. Stanley wanted it from an objective or outside point of view. This is when David first introduced the notion of visual representation of Johnny's visions. Stanley perceived it as a drama in which nothing weird was shown happening on screen. We would see Johnny experiencing the vision, but never the vision itself. Once we began the revision of my script, David never once looked back at the novel.'

Cronenberg was intent on 'personalizing' The Dead Zone into Johnny's story, as he had planned to do with Mary Shelley's monster a few years before (Walken even moves a little like Karloff in the final version), as he had done with Videodrome (in which Renn's 'visions' are inseparable from 'reality'), and as he would do in the future with his version of The Fly and Naked Lunch. For once Cronenberg also dropped a brain tumour (the cause of Johnny's 'dead zones' in the book) in favour of his increasingly explicit engagement with another 'disease': each of Johnny's visions ages him and brings him closer to death.

It's different when it's not your own script, but gradually it becomes your own and suddenly you can't tell the difference. I was involved in structuring the script and the characters from the beginning, so I felt very involved. I was the one who said, 'I want this scene and that scene; I'm not interested in this or that; I hate the boy in the movie: he's eighteen and has a Corvette and a swimming pool and he's blond. I hate him. Let's make him a little kid, the kid Johnnie knows he'll never have.' Stuff like that. But Jeffrey wrote it. He went home and did it. There is a certain last little distance you can't go because it's not yours.

Because its imagery is rather innocuous, it's more palatable. It's certainly the least offensive film I've made; the only one where grannies come out crying about the tragic love affair at the end. It's more gentle. Possibly that's one of the reasons I wanted to make it. For the emotional release; to deal with that. The unrequitedness of life in general, made specific through a love story. I completely understood my characters and what was going on. I was not condescending; it would be hideous to do a movie that you felt superior to. I enjoyed coming to grips with those archetypes and the simplicity of it. I felt a need of it. Having my own children and having gone through most things that one goes through, emotionally I was completely at one with it.

*Over the years Cronenberg had been responsible for creating a host of characters with names as unusual as their points of view: Adrian Tripod (*Crimes of the Future*), Dr Dan Keloid (*Rabid*), Nola Carveth (*The Brood*), Darryl Revok (*Scanners*), Barry Convex and Professor Brian O'Blivion (*Videodrome*) to name but a few. Johnny Smith of* The Dead Zone *was not a departure in name alone; like the characters around him, he was the kind of guy a mainstream audience could begin to approach, come to understand or sympathize with.*

There are many characters in *The Dead Zone* that people think are 'real'. That's ironic. I think in America in particular there's a feeling that anything that's sophisticated, articulate or complex is not really real. Take Martin Scorsese, who is incredibly articulate and verbal. His screen character, the projection of himself on screen – as say de Niro in *Raging Bull* – is totally inarticulate. Somehow the simple good people who live in the country and live simple lives are real.

But what I love about guys like Max Renn (*Videodrome*) and Seth Brundle (*The Fly*) is that they cannot turn the mind off; and the mind undercuts, interprets, puts into context. To allow themselves to go totally into the emotional reality of what's happening to them is to be destroyed completely. They're still trying to salvage something out of the situation: 'Maybe this isn't a disease at all. Maybe it's a transformation.' So I have my reasons for having my characters articulate a lot. It seems real to me. Characters who will not allow themselves to get bathetic. Seth Brundle has built his whole career, life and understanding of the world on cerebration and the thought process. He cannot totally let go of it. He has to get drunk to get jealous, to talk to the ape.

Stephen King has said that he is the Big Mac of literature, and I think it's right. He taps into a mass pulse, and that's his strength. He takes people along a path which they would not normally go. A lot of people. That restricts what he can do, as well. But in his case that's not a restriction; that is the ideal. He's doing exactly what he wants to do, and is an absolutely pure and integrated artist. I think it's as much a surprise to him as anyone else that it works for an enormous number of people.

The essence of *The Dead Zone* is a lost love story. There isn't that element in *Videodrome*. When I say I wanted to come to grips with that, maybe it's difficult for me to allow myself to be that melodramatic. But here was somebody else (Jeffrey Boam) who was doing it. Certainly Stephen King is never afraid to do that. It's a tear-jerker. And it's possible that I needed someone else to have done it and then build on that because I just can't bring myself to do it.

I did feel a great kinship with New England, and Melville's writing. I still look at the pictures of Norman Rockwell;[3] we used Rockwell as a model for the Stillson posters. The whole picture was lit like that. I was really into New England puritanism, that sort of cold and snow and loneliness. It was pleasing that a lot of critics said it was the first Stephen King movie that faithfully translated the novel. Amusing, because we threw a lot out. There was no attempt to slavishly reproduce it. But somehow the tone ... There was a tone to the book that did strike me and I distilled it out.

I was offered *Witness* after *The Dead Zone*. I didn't take it because I could never be a fan of the Amish, and the film required a certain glorification of their life: close to the earth; more godly; better. What I saw was a repressive, enclosed society. My least favourite kind. I knew I couldn't do that film well. I wouldn't have been doing the producers a favour by accepting that film.

The Dead Zone was a more successful release than *Videodrome* in terms of numbers, and some reviews. It certainly did a lot for people's awareness of my stature *vis-à-vis* working with actors. Here were not just two foreign actors and a bunch of unknown Canadians, but Chris Walken, Martin Sheen and Brooke Adams. And for some people the fact that I was doing a Stephen King was a step up somehow. Certainly a dipping of the toe into the mainstream.

The fact that The Dead Zone *emerged the most artistically successful adaptation for the cinema of a Stephen King novel or short story did not save it at the box office. Although a reasonable success in Europe, the film failed to attract the attention and audiences it deserved world-wide. And again there were marketing, distribution and exhibition problems. In Toronto, where no theatres were playing the Dolby stereo version, Cronenberg four-walled a cinema himself and ran a Dolby print for a month, breaking even without the help of the popcorn concession.*

39 Norman Rockwell revisited: Cronenberg in front of the Greg Stillson
campaign billboard in *The Dead Zone*.
40 The family Johnny missed: Brooke Adams in *The Dead Zone*.

Most importantly, however, the movie represented a major develop-
ment for the director. Although some loyal audiences were initially
dismayed at the conspicuous lack of flesh-tearing transformations, weird
science and creative cancers, the emotional charge of The Dead Zone
came as a welcome surprise to others. Staunch critic Robin Wood found
this the first Cronenberg picture he could admire, describing it as a
'healthy development'. No doubt assisted by not writing the original
story or the screen adaptation, Cronenberg had finally mined – with the
help of Christopher Walken – the emotional dimension of the Cronen-
berg Project. What had remained stillborn – most obviously and urgently
in the character of Max Renn – at last found release.

The Dead Zone also touched on politics, a subject Cronenberg hadn't
dealt with before in the strict sense of the word. Some critics, freed of the
'disgust' factor and trawling for other problems, were uneasy with The
Dead Zone's *(subordinate) political implications – the justification of*
assassination by 'visionaries' who can see the future.

I'm very balanced. I'm cursed with balance, which is to say I immediately
see all sides to the story. And they are all equal. That can be a curse,
maybe it's very Canadian too. This has been noted by some critics like
Carrie Rickey, who humorously said that my political stance, since it
seems to come down on all sides at once or none at all, seems to be very
Canadian. And that's true. There is a certain point when that can be
paralysing: it stops you from action. You don't move. If you shove one
way, even if it's the wrong way, at least what you get is motion. It's
certainly true that Americans, if nothing else, have moved, even
wrongheadedly, but they'd rather move than stand still. In Canada we'd
rather stand still.

Martin Scorsese thinks I don't know what my films are about. He said
once, 'I read your interviews, but it's obvious you don't know what
they're about, but that's OK, they're still great.' I hope I don't understand them. Scorsese deals with good and evil in very proto-Catholic
terms. But my curse is that I can't believe in the devil because I would
have to believe in a purely evil being, and I don't feel that I've met
anybody I could consider evil. I'm sure if I'd been raised a Catholic I
would have no trouble. My demon is that all sides appeal.

People are fascinated by the Nazi period. It's because suddenly there
was a society that set itself up to completely reorganize the moral order,
using people as objects, experimenting on people, killing people. That's
one of the reasons it's fascinating – because it's terrifying – but it was

invented by people. It's something people are capable of. Most people have considered murdering someone, whether or not they were kidding or serious. In a way, killing someone is the ultimate human experience. Especially in the twentieth century. One of the first things people want to know when they hear that somebody was in Vietnam is 'Did you kill anybody? Did you kill women and children? Were you involved in one of those horrible bloodbaths?' I do, and I don't think I'm alone in that.

If you begin with a political stance, and your film is an illustration of Marxist propositions or Fascist propositions or whatever political theory you happen to hold, then I think you're making a propaganda film, and to me that automatically means it cannot be art. Art and propaganda are poles apart. When I start to make a film I try to completely clear my head of all the intellectual and cerebral considerations of the times I live in. I try to get in touch with something that's more basic, intuitive and instinctive and then work outwards to details of time and culture. To me, any valid expression of that is legitimate art. Ferdinand Céline was a Fascist collaborator. That doesn't mean his works are not great. It doesn't mean that you thought his works were great until you realized he was a Fascist collaborator and then decided that his politics were wrong and therefore his books are trash.

After Videodrome, *Cronenberg had a deal with Universal Pictures to write another original script. This now emerged as 'Six Legs', both his first 'insect' picture and his first feature-length comedy. Although the film was never made, it was finally to be subsumed by Cronenberg's version of* The Fly. *Tiny aspects of 'Six Legs' also found their way into his solution to the problems of filming William Burroughs's* Naked Lunch.

After *The Dead Zone* Pierre David called me up and said, 'Universal are interested in an original project from you. Do you have something?' Despite the fact that people might roll their eyes, *Videodrome* wasn't like *Heaven's Gate*. The general attitude at Universal – the same as at Cinepix – was 'We know you've got some talent that's quite unique. If only we could channel it into the mainstream it could be fantastic, but you keep going off into this little side trickle.' I still get that.

'Six Legs' was about entomologists discovering an insect on a Caribbean island that is addictive when you eat it: the adventures of the main guy and his two strange friends. Weirdly enough it was a little bit like *Ghostbusters*, in that there were three eccentric guys running around in a van with a symbol on it – in this case a bug symbol – and it was a comedy. The idea that I might write my own comedy made sense. I wasn't going to do someone else's, so maybe I could do my own. I rushed the end to finish the first draft; the first third was pretty good, the second third so-so, and the end was probably pretty bad. They didn't want to continue with it.

Dino De Laurentiis also approached me for many things. Many Stephen King things, because he had a deal with him; he was Stephen King-infatuated. But one of the things he threw at me was Ron Shusset and *Total Recall*.[4] I'm getting a terrible headache just saying that; it's pulsing through my eye, like a big hatpin. I should have seen it coming and didn't. Or I wanted it to work out so badly that I pretended it could. It came very close.

I read the draft script that was around, by Ron and Dan O'Bannon. It was one of the famous unmade scripts that had been around ten years; the thing that would not die. The reason this one wouldn't quite die was because it had a terrific premise. Although it had some very soft, if not juvenile, silly stuff in it, it had this stunning premise. It's about memory and identity and madness. All kinds of neat stuff. But, as far as Ron Shusset was concerned, it was really 'Raiders of the Lost Ark Go to Mars'. Apart from the first third of the script, it was all action and shoot-up. So this was our struggle. Me trying to unravel everything I thought was implicit in the first third, and Ron thinking it could be a big hit.

Along the way I met Fred Schepsi, who had written several of his own versions. Richard Rush had been involved at one time, and Bruce Beresford after me was going to do it in Australia. If you read the Phillip K. Dick short story 'We Can Remember It for You Wholesale', it's unfilmable and it doesn't have an ending. But it does have this brilliant concept at the centre . I thought the movie could be much better. So it was a year, and over a dozen drafts I wrote myself, and trying to deal with Dino – who was trying to get an accord between me and Ron, but of course had his own very strong input. He didn't want it to be another $40 million movie like *Dune*. Of course now it's a $60 million movie with Schwarzenegger instead of a very mousy little clerk.

I didn't want it to be high-tech, because I wasn't excited by the gimmicks, the vehicles and the glass city. It was the human element that excited me. I did invent some stuff that I was very happy with, but I was never totally happy even with the last draft script because I felt even there I was making too much of a compromise *vis-à-vis* the action. There was more of it than I felt I needed, or felt. I tried very hard to make it significant in terms of its themes, rather than 'Now turn off your mind, and we'll have a car chase.'

I went to Rome several times, and worked in what is playfully called Dinocittà – Dino's studios – which had lain dormant since the 1960s and were reopened just for us. There was moss on the walls of the office. And lizards. They had artefacts left over from *Waterloo*, the last movie Dino had shot there. *The Agony and the Ecstasy* had been filmed there too, so it was thrilling for me. And I loved the Italian crews and the energy. It would have been my first foreign film: we were going to shoot Tunisia for the planet Mars. We went there to look for locations. You go out into the desert, wend your way in total isolation, finally crawl along and find the place where you have an angle on everything. Then your Moroccan guide says, 'Yes, in *Star Wars* they put the camera over there,' and points five feet away. It was neat.

It was a lot of work and effort on many people's part, and a lot of money was spent. A year after the first phone call I said to Dino, 'OK, here's draft twelve of the script. This is it. This is the one I want to make.' He read it and said, 'I think we should go back to draft nine.' I said, 'It's really hard to go back to the golden calf after you've seen God.' I couldn't do that, because I'd seen draft twelve. So he said, 'Well, what do we do? We don't do the movie?' And I said, 'If you won't bend and I won't bend, I guess we don't do the movie.' There was one time when he phoned me back and said, 'OK, we're ready to do it your way,' but by that time it was too late. I couldn't go back to it. I couldn't deal with Ron Shusset any more. One of the nice things that came out of it was that I made real advances in my Italian.

Apart from the Total Recall *débâcle, which took a valuable year out of his time with no resulting movie, Cronenberg was offered many other scripts, all of which he turned down or which came to nothing. Many were not obviously Cronenbergesque.*

When I say I was offered things, sometimes it was sent to me by my agent. I didn't know whether he would have to fight for it or whether he could get it for me. But Dawn Steele very much wanted me to do *Flashdance*. The offer to do *Witness*, which was called 'Called Home' at the time, was a definite offer. I was also sent *Top Gun*; it was called 'Top Guns' then. A lot of things came my way. At this point I think I'd taken it for granted that I would be offered stuff, and I was always flattered and felt happy that people did. *Beverly Hills Cop* came my way, when Sly Stallone was supposed to play the part.

I could have been tremendously rich if I'd directed all these movies (which would have been impossible because a lot of them were happening at the same time). But they were mainstream. Now, 'mainstream' is a subjective term; it doesn't necessarily have to do with the budget of a film or how much money it makes at the box office. I realize what mainstream means when I read a script, and by page three I know everything: there are these two LA cops and one is a drug dealer and they get into their Porsche ... A mainstream movie is one that isn't going to rattle too many cages, is not going to shake people up, push them too far or muscle them around. It's not going to depress them. That's why I don't think that *The Fly* is mainstream. No horror film is truly mainstream. When people say, 'Great, another Cronenberg movie! Let's take everybody and have popcorn' – then I'll know I'm mainstream.

If one day I don't have it any more – what I consider 'it' to be – that could be worse than directing some nice, big-budget, mainstream movie that does well at the box office. That's not the worse fate you could suffer. As long as it's my choice to do that, and I'm not forced to do it by circumstances. If I suddenly don't have anything to say, but am not ready to go to bed for the rest of my life, maybe that's not so bad. It's nice to think of the theory of survival being the essence of Canadian-ness.

During one trip to Los Angeles, Total Recall *finally fell through. Unlike the frantic rush-to-production years of Canadian tax-shelter finance, Cronenberg found himself without the next project – either an original, or one that he could happily accept as an assignment.*

I was totally back to square one. I phoned my wife and said, 'Dino and I are not making *Total Recall*. I've got to stay in LA for another two weeks, or as long as it takes, because I can't come back until I've got a movie.' I was in dire straits financially. I was just hoping that somehow something would happen that would be honourable, a movie that I could really be happy doing. I'd never been in that position before. I was desperate to do a picture.

Then my agent called and said that Mel Brooks[5] was interested in me doing *The Fly*. A friend of mine, Mark Boyman – who ended up co-producing *Dead Ringers* with me – had shown me this script sometime earlier. He was hustling and running around with a trunk full of scripts, and he thought that it would be great for me. I read it, but was doing *Total Recall* and therefore couldn't really try that one on for size; I wasn't interested mentally. Now I was approached directly by Mel Brooks's people and looked at it again. I remembered that I had really been struck by those elements – still in the movie – which felt so much like me it was unbelievable. I had not had that experience before. That was strange.

I figured out exactly what I wanted to do, and said to Mel and producer Stuart Cornfeld, 'The script starts on page nineteen. Throw away the first eighteen pages.' They said, 'Great.' I told them in detail what I wanted to do with it, and said, 'I've just been through this experience with Dino. It took us a year to realize that we were talking about two separate movies. I'm not going to do that again. This is what I want to do. You have to say yes, and that you're leaving it in my hands. Otherwise, I can't do it.' They really wanted me, and Mel made me a fantastic offer, so I came back to Toronto having agreed to do *The Fly*.

Mel is very bright, and he's very well-read. He knows the literary connections. Once he's decided that this is the right thing to do, he goes with it. He prided himself on being a producer who would do stuff that was not expected of him, that was not him at all as a film-maker or an actor. He was very excited. So then it was just a question of making all our intentions clear so that there was no mistake.

The Fly was to be produced by Brooksfilms, for release by Twentieth Century-Fox, on a budget of approximately US$10 million. Stuart Cornfeld had previously been responsible for introducing Mel Brooks to the delights of David Lynch's Eraserhead. *This had resulted in Lynch directing* Elephant Man *for them, a dramatic mainstream development for a film-maker also not suited in any obvious way to the assumed tastes of a large cinema-going public.*

Despite The Fly *technically being Cronenberg's first major Hollywood studio picture, it was again shot entirely in Canada, with sets constructed in the old Kleinburg Studios north of Toronto. Cronenberg assembled his usual crew for the project. This was to be his sixth feature film with John Board as first assistant director, Mark Irwin on camera, Bryan Day on sound, Carol Spier designing and Ron Sanders editing. Along with other regulars, this group had long been known not only as the 'Cronenberg crew', but also as some of the finest technicians and creators in their respective disciplines. Stuart Cornfeld found himself in the unenviable position of Hollywood producer in residence: 'He'd never known what windscreen washers were for, because he'd never been out of California. He was certainly fairly paranoid and felt rather isolated up here in the winter with a bunch of Canadians. I think he realized for the first time that Canadians really are different from Americans. I had to deal with that.'*

As with The Dead Zone *before it,* The Fly *was Cronenberg's second adaptation, this time preceded not only by an original short story but also by a film version. However, unlike his approach to Jeffrey Boam's script of the King novel – and perhaps because Charles Edward Pogue's script for* The Fly *had touched and twisted some familiar Cronenberg-esque nerves – he set about rewriting it.*

Most approaches to remaking a film are very uninteresting to me. It wasn't until I read this script that I thought, 'My God, the writer has really rethought and reunderstood it.' The basic premise of the movie was always good. The short story that it's based on is not good at all. The screenplay of the original movie by James Clavell – his first – was very good. But it was the rethinking of the basic premise which opened up huge vistas to me. It was very body-orientated, very body-conscious.

But I thought the characters were awful, the dialogue trite and the ending bad. But the details of stuff – like the fingernails coming off, like the idea that he gets super-strong – that was terrific. Also, the scientist becomes incapable of speech far from the end of the movie. To me that was an insurmountable problem. What fascinated me about the whole project was, how does this man deal with his disease: rationalize it, articulate it? If he's silent or – as in the original movie – if he uses a typewriter, it's not enough. I couldn't work it that way. He had to be made articulate to the end. I insisted on that. Otherwise, it took away too many of my weapons as a dramatist.

That's why I haven't dealt much with serious mental problems, because if your mind goes, then you are somebody else immediately; you have been transformed, more than in the body sense. That's part of the mystery; we're used to our bodies changing. First we grow up, then we grow down. There's only a moment where there are a few years of the illusion of stability. It doesn't last long. I read a nice article that talked about the older mind being a different kind of mind, with different strengths and weaknesses from the younger mind. Not a deficient version, just another kind, making connections in a different way. Having greater powers of comprehension and synthesis, but lesser powers of instant access to trivial data.

Stuart was very involved in the script development, being a story editor, as I rewrote the script. He was very sharp and good at that. There's one line of dialogue from Chuck's script that remains, but not one character. There was a scientist, and there had been before, but he's not the same character at all. I never talked to Chuck. I never met him until after the movie was released. He told me how much he liked the movie, and felt that it was strong on the things that he had felt were good in his script.

I remember when the arbitration came up – because when a director wants a screenwriting credit you have to have a judgement from the Writers Guild. I sent them a letter saying, 'I believe I've written more than 60 per cent of this script'; a director has to do that, whereas if you're a writer, it's only 30 per cent. But I also said that there was no question that Chuck Pogue should get the first credit; there couldn't be a Cronenberg version if there hadn't been a Pogue version. The Writers Guild felt that was honourable. I wouldn't have done the movie if I had had to do Pogue's script. On the other hand, what got me excited was his script.

Pogue had used the structure of the original movie. The scientist had a wife, and they had been together for a long time. I think he even had a kid in there. So you didn't see them meet; you didn't see them fall in love; it wasn't a fresh affair that is tragically cut short. So I invented Seth Brundle, and made him eccentric. In Chuck's version, he was rather a dull, clever techno guy; just a boring, handsome guy who was a scientist. I didn't think there was much juice to be gotten out of that. Pogue's approach was to play them as a normal couple who are afflicted by this disaster. That's all right, except that the response of a normal couple to disease is something you can read in a newspaper. I wanted a guy who was eccentric enough to get a weird take on what was happening to them – to talk about it. That wasn't happening in the script, or in the original movie. I wanted everything in this movie to be edgy, revealing and incisive; not just the obvious parts to be extraordinary.

To me the film is a metaphor for ageing, a compression of any love affair that goes to the end of one of the lover's lives. I can be a sucker for a romantic story, believe it or not. I'm not totally cynical. Nor do I think I'm pessimistic. But the reality is undeniable, especially if you don't believe in the afterlife – where you walk hand in hand through the clouds together. Every love story must end tragically. One of the lovers dies, or both of them die together. That's tragic. It's the end. That was only really in Chuck's script by necessity. It was never a conscious theme or an understanding. But it did trigger this off in me.

41 Al Hedison and Patricia Owens: *The Fly* (1958).
42 Jeff Goldblum and Geena Davis: *The Fly* (1986).

In the Cronenberg/Pogue version of The Fly, *scientist Brundle becomes fused with the insect – during a teleportation experiment – at the molecular/genetic level, as opposed to emerging from his telepod with the head and claw of a fly. This results in his manifesting 'a form of cancer', apparently intent on transforming him into something else. Not a fly, but something that never existed before. Cronenberg had not made an obvious 'disease' movie since* The Brood (1979). *As* The Fly *became a widely distributed and popular horror film in the late 1980s, introducing new audiences to Cronenberg's work, some critics and cinema-goers were tempted to see the movie's subtext as dealing with AIDS. Cronenberg is resistant to such a reading, because he does not want his own strain of horror films to be subjected to specific societal and political interpretations.*

However, it was inevitable that the timing of The Fly's *release should trigger such a response, and that the film should in part function as a discussion of that disease, in societies attempting to come to terms with a very real virus. Despite the director's own philosophical imperatives, part of* The Fly's *meaning and cathartic effect was divined from this inescapable context. Cronenberg's intention and desire to produce art was here perhaps matched by audience desire to seek and find some consolation, some answers and some way of appropriating a specific threat, as Cronenberg himself continues to do with his own particular demons.*

If you think of *The Fly* as an AIDS movie, then you have to think that Geena Davis gave it to him, because he's a guy who's never been fucked before. Then, is she going to die? That's why I don't want it to be AIDS, truly. If you go all the way with that, and you look at it that way, you have to answer some fairly gloomy questions which don't work with the movie. That's why I resist it.

People forget what syphilis was at the turn of the century; how terrifying it was, what a scourge and a plague on people who went to prostitutes it was. How many well-known people had their noses and ears fall off. It wasn't as deadly as AIDS, but it often took thirty years to manifest itself. If AIDS hadn't been around, I would still have made *The Fly*, and I did make *Shivers* and *Rabid*. In retrospect, people say 'My God, this is prophecy,' but I think it's just being aware of what we are. There was the Black Death and there was Corman's *Masque of the Red Death*. Was that prophetic? No. It's an examination of what is universal about human existence, and that hasn't changed.

Reviewers are very plugged in to what's happening *now*. The connections they tend to make are of the moment. But these perceptions about disease have always been very immediate and accessible to me. Because of AIDS – the concept, publicity and fear of it – suddenly these things are common perceptions and awarenesses. There's a sign on the doctor's wall in *Shivers* that says 'Sex is the invention of a clever venereal disease.' Well . . . AIDS: a brilliant publicity coup for a venereal disease. But ten years ago my movies were potent and thirty years from now – when hopefully AIDS doesn't exist – they should still be as potent. Then they will be about ageing and any kind of disease you can still get. They will be about cancer, death, a compression of mortality. All lovers are young lovers, even when they're sixty. Old people don't think they're old. There's no such thing as an old person. There's a person who has been broken on the rack of pain and infirmity, but there's really no old person. When someone dies at eighty, it's the death of a young person. I see that.

When you have a dream that has terrified you, and you can't shake the fear, you tell somebody the dream. As it comes out of your mouth you know it's flat, it's not working. You're saying exactly what happened, but the terror isn't there. You can tell by the look on the person's face that it's not scary. You're saying, 'But you had to be there. The dream had a tone and a colour and an ambience that was terrifying. It wasn't the concept. It wasn't the action. It was the dream itself that was terrifying.' That's the thing. It's the tone. Intangible. And yet it's palpable, in the sense that you wake up and you're still living in it. You're not in the narrative any more, but the half-life is still there. I had a dream that I was watching a film and the film was causing me to grow old fast. The movie itself was infecting me, giving me a disease, the essence of which was that I was ageing. Then the screen became a mirror in which I was seeing myself age. I woke up terrified. That's really what I'm talking about, more than any puny virus.

So the AIDS connection is very superficial. I see it as talking about mortality, about our vulnerability, and the tragedy of human loss. The difficulty in accepting it, and the difficulty of coming to terms with it when you've got it. We've all got to do that. When children die, we feel it's more tragic because they're not supposed to die, they're supposed to live to be eighty. There's a potential that never happened. That's tragic. AIDS is tragic. But, beyond it all, I'm digging deeper. We've all got the disease – the disease of being finite. And consciousness is the original sin: consciousness of the inevitability of our death.

Part of my cinematic voyage has been to try and discover the connection between the physical and the spiritual: what we are physically; what is the essence of physical life and existence. It's still a conundrum that drives me mad: the old Bertrand Russell riddle. What's mind? No matter. What's matter? Never mind. Catholic imagery of the Middle Ages is very body-conscious and very obsessive, all for the same reason: the illumination of the mind, the spirit, the soul versus the body. For different reasons, but it's the same philosophical discussion. You could be a Catholic and be obsessed with torture, pain, decay and disintegration, as the entire medieval world was in all its forms.

Cronenberg cast his two leading roles in The Fly *with a real-life-romance acting couple, Jeff Goldblum and Geena Davis, previously seen together in* Transylvania 6500. *Stuart Cornfeld was initially resistant to Davis playing opposite her already cast boyfriend, but Cronenberg was determined.*

Jeff is a very particular and eccentric screen presence. I wanted a woman who could match him for that, and yet be attractive and sexy, as she is. Geena is funny and sexy, and to me that is just the most diabolical combination. You can't beat it. Stuart thought it was too obvious maybe, but I said, 'The obvious thing is that they're both tall. But it's hard to line up the shots if one is much taller.' Stuart was being a tough Hollywood producer, looking after his director. He made me look at other actresses, but they were all disasters. He admitted it.

It had its advantages and disadvantages. Jeff and Geena did have a real ease with each other in terms of nudity. Jeff in particular was willing to go beyond what I was asking. In fact, I shot some stuff that was steamier than ended up in the picture. Stuart Cornfeld turned out to be a little prudish about that, although in terms of his visual and sexual imagination he's not the slightest bit prudish. But when it comes to what's on the screen, he's slightly squeamish. But I didn't expect anything extra from them sexually, as I didn't with Jeremy Irons and Geneviève Bujold in *Dead Ringers*. It also never occurred to me that they wouldn't do stuff, because it was in the script.

Maybe it's naïve of me, but I figured that if Jeremy and Geneviève knew that these people were going to tie each other to the bed and fuck each other – because it says so in the script, and we've talked about it, and they know I want to do the scene – we're going to do it on camera. OK, I don't need to see pubic hair or breasts even. But I expect they will do it. If they're both attractive people, which is often the case, then at

43 Jeff Goldblum and Geena Davis.
44 David Cronenberg on the set of *The Fly*.

least between 'Action' and 'Cut' they can get it up for each other. I expect
them to be able to act sexually hungry with each other. Good actors on
location tend to be sexy together, unless they hate each other.

The other side of the Jeff and Geena coin was that they were much too
familiar with each other. Geena is a terrific mimic, and Jeff has a very
infectious style of speech and body language. Geena, when you met her
with Jeff, did Jeff. So I said, 'Look, Geena, you've just met this guy, you
can't talk like that; you can't be a mirror image of him.' So the bad part
was just making sure they were more separate, because in the movie they
never really get to be as close to each other as Jeff and Geena actually
were.

Again The Fly *was a major development for the director. The movie
achieves a difficult synthesis: the 'gloopy' side of Cronenberg's work –
the obvious trademark of all his features up to* Videodrome *– with a
newly found special effect: an emotional intensity and deep melancholia
realized (for the first time in* The Dead Zone) *through performance. The
successful fusion, of touching love story with Chris Walas Inc.'s Oscar-
winning make-up and special effects, transformed* The Fly *into the first
movie truly to integrate Cronenberg's evolving concerns and passions.*

Mel didn't say, 'I don't want you to get artsy,' but he may as well have.
He didn't mean in terms of the elegance of shooting, or the intelligence of
the film. He meant 'Don't get squeamish. Don't think this is Mel Brooks
doing *The Elephant Man*, therefore this has to be an art-horror film – as
opposed to a horror-horror film – and therefore I will hold back and be
circumspect about the horror aspects.' No. He said, 'I want you to go all
the way. Let yourself go, and don't hold back.' There were no restraints.
They were willing to lose that percentage of the audience that would have
liked the love-interest stuff, but couldn't take the horror.

The essence of *The Fly* was to say, 'We're going to do this and show it
to you. It's not going to be easy, but if you look at it, it's going to take
you someplace else.' It was never just gloop; it was always conceptual
gloop. Everything in it had a bizarre conceptual element. And anyway, in
terms of just audience squeamishness, who comes to see a version of *The
Fly* that I've directed?

John Donne's definition of metaphysical poetry was poetry in which
normally unharmonious elements are violently yoked together. That's a
paraphrase, but it's close. I was a big fan of the metaphysical poets. Take
'The Flea', a perfect example to base a wonderful sexy love poem on: the

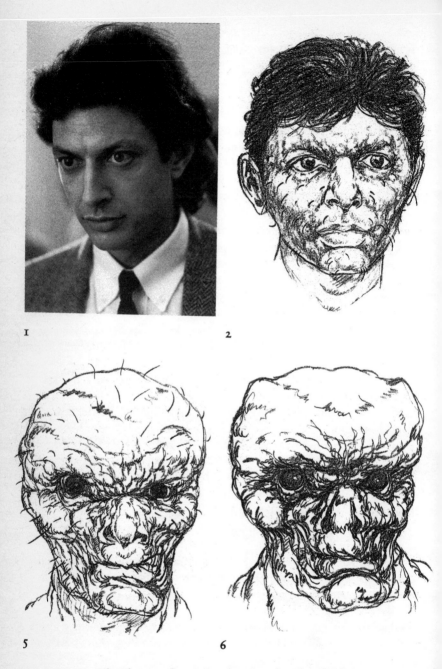

1

2

5

6

45 *The Fly*: transformation drawings by Chris Walas.

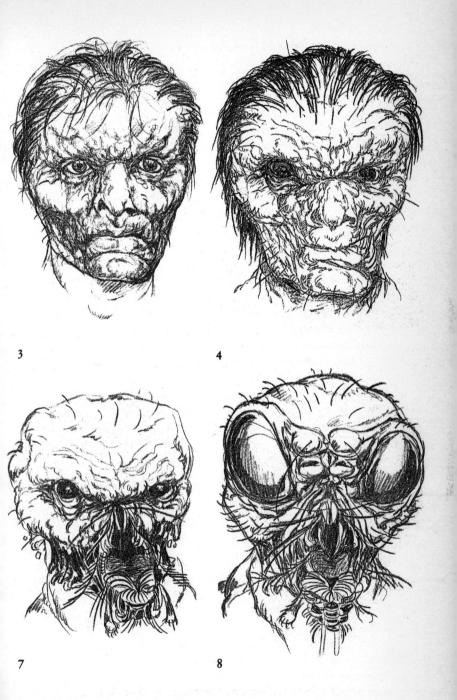

3

4

7

8

concept of fleas sucking the blood of both lovers and therefore mingling it together. Let's say that *The Fly* is metaphysical horror. It pleases me to do that, to show what the genre can do, especially at a time when for most people horror is *Halloween* or *Friday the Thirteenth*. That's too bad.

The Fly *had many alternative endings, including a scene in which Veronica (Davis) finally gives birth to a baby by the diseased Brundle. The audience, already alerted to expect the worst by the film's nightmare sequence of her delivering a giant maggot (at the hands of Cronenberg himself), is pleasantly surprised to see a butterfly child. As written, the scene contains an element of sceptical optimism, missing in the final version.*

We did a lot of work on that – the butterfly child. We tested the film with what we had of that ending. The fact was that when Brundlefly died it was so devastating that the audience could not recover for the coda; they couldn't switch gears. I had a version where she wakes up in bed at the end with Stathis Borans, because she's married him, and they're having a baby – or she dreams she's pregnant. Audiences hated that.

We were always taught that one of the strong distinguishing characteristics in Shakespearean tragedy was that at the end there was an undercutting of the tragedy with the suggestion that (say) the kingdom will go on in a much better way. Things will be stronger. It helps to ease the tragedy. That's what I was trying. I had tried that with *The Dead Zone* too. I shot something that suggested Brooke Adams had Johnny Smith's baby from that one time they made love together. The thing is, nobody wanted to know. Johnny Smith does save the world, but on a personal level it ends tragically.

The Fly got good reviews and made a lot of money. That's unusual for a fairly extreme horror film. It's my biggest financial success; it made more money than all the other films combined. It might well be my biggest success ever. It's conceivable that I'll never make another movie that is that successful.

Despite The Fly's *success, Cronenberg was to encounter even greater difficulties in raising interest in, and production finance for, what finally emerged as his next feature:* Dead Ringers. *This project had begun to take shape in the offices of Carol Baum of Lorimar in 1981. Cronenberg wanted to make a movie about twins; Baum cherished a remake of the*

Robert Siodmak/Olivia de Havilland twin sisters noir movie The Dark
Mirror. *The good-side/bad-side approach to twins held no interest for
Cronenberg, but both were familiar with the case of the Marcus
brothers.*

*Stewart and Cyril Marcus, identical-twin gynaecologists, were,
according to* New York *magazine, 'found gaunt and already partially
decayed in their East 63rd Street apartment amidst a litter of garbage
and pharmaceuticals. Stewart was found face down on the floor, nude
except for his socks; Cyril was found dressed in his shorts and face
down on a big double bed. Stewart had died several days before Cyril.'
The coroner announced cause of death as barbiturate withdrawal.
Baum pointed Cronenberg to a book loosely based on the case,* Twins
*by Bari Wood and Jack Geasland, and xeroxed copies of every article
ever written about the brothers.*

I'd first heard about the Marcus twins through a blurb in the paper:
'Twin docs found dead in posh pad'. I thought they were making it up.
It was too perfect – better than 'Two-toed man falls to death in bathtub', another of my favourites. Then every day I would read something
else about these twin gynaecologists, until it became a huge subject,
because it involved medical scandal and holding back evidence of mal-
practice. Eventually there was an article in *Esquire* called 'Dead
Ringers', a very good article. Then came more, in *Ms* magazine and
Harpers, because it had such resonance for the women's movement;
there were interviews with women who had been their patients and so
on. I remember thinking at the time, 'Somebody has got to make a
movie of this!' I thought it was a natural. As the years went by nobody
did. After taking ten years to try and do it myself, I realized why not!

*Baum introduced Cronenberg to Joe Roth, then an independent pro-
ducer. She and Roth were partners and, on leaving Lorimar, took Cronenberg to Sylvio Tabet – a rich Lebanese producer – with the intention
of financing a fictionalized film version of the Marcus twins' story.*
Twins, *the book, also disclaimed any connection with the actual case
history. When Tabet agreed to proceed, Cronenberg enlisted Norman
Snider as scriptwriter.*

Norman is in *Crimes of the Future*, and *Secret Weapons* – my suppressed film – which he actually wrote. We had met at university and
liked each other. We were very hot on literature and writing, and both

loved Burroughs. He is now a very successful journalist and has done some good screenwriting. I couldn't write the script because of what I was doing (I can't remember what), so it was natural that I should turn to him. We felt that because the book had been written we had better option it. The writers hadn't been sued by the survivors of the twins, and because the book existed and there were all these overlaps, we would just do it the straightforward way: get an option and say the movie was based on the book.

Norman did the first script, which had some terrific things in it, and a lot of bad things. Some of the bad things were due to his attempting to use some of the stuff in the book. Because we had the rights in it, we felt we should. But the script was not shootable as it was, in my opinion. I don't know why I felt I had to do a movie about these twins. It wasn't because it was grotesque; it wasn't because it had sensationalist aspects. I didn't know what it was. I just knew Norman's script didn't get it, although on a functional level it did do some things.

I approached Sylvio, Joe and Carol with it. Joe and Carol agreed with me, but Sylvio said, 'I love this script. Let's shoot it.' I didn't know whether he was serious, whether he just didn't get it, or whether he had some financial reason for wanting to get this movie under way. But I said I wasn't going to shoot it as it was; I wanted another draft. He said, 'I'm not going to pay for another. I want this.' I went to Norman and said, 'I'm not happy with this draft. As a first attempt, sure. But the first of many.' I told him what the situation was. He was mortified, but did another draft for nothing to try and rectify the situation. I then showed it to Sylvio and said, 'This is getting there'; there was still awful stuff in it that was clinging to the novel. Sylvio said, 'I hate this script. I still want to do the first draft.' Then I don't know what happened. Maybe he got petulant or mad. Anyway, he wouldn't pay me; he owed me $7,500 as director overseeing the writing. He still hasn't paid me. So it died at that point in 1982. It would have been up to Carol and Joe to find someone else to put money into it, and then pay Sylvio back the money he had invested. He would have been agreeable to that.

Some two years later Mark Boyman, a Toronto producer, approached Cronenberg to direct The Incubus, *on which he passed: 'The script was undo-able, I thought.' However, this led to Boyman acting as a co-producer for Cronenberg on* The Fly, *and then running with the 'Twins' project. Then dividing his time between Canada and Los Angeles, Boyman energetically set up punishing schedules of meetings about the project in Hollywood. Cronenberg's name got them through the door, but Boyman's energy secured the appointments. In commando-raid fashion, both would attack these scheduled meetings in spurts, get depressed at the lack of interest, only to return to Los Angeles six months later (to meet a whole new set of executives in the same positions within the same companies) to do it all again. It was the basic material of 'Twins' that met with consistent corporate Hollywood opposition.*

'Do these guys have to be gynaecologists? Can't they be lawyers?' The number of times I heard that. 'Do they both have to die?' 'Why do you want to make this movie?' Stuff like that. Most of these people had heard of the Marcus twins; they remembered that they couldn't get the story out of their minds – the tone of it. Like a dream. Gynaecologists are weird enough, and then also being identical twins who worked together . . . And then to die together. They knew there was a hook, because it was already hooked into their subconscious. But when it came to trying to make it work as a real movie, they couldn't accept it.

Of course, they were all male. You get hot reactions from women about *Dead Ringers*, but one thing they aren't is squeamish about it. It's their bodies; they do it all the time. The men were squeamish, also about the drug thing, but that depended. This project went over many eras, and there was a time when it was thought that a good, hard drug movie could be hot – especially one that was moralistic. And of course these guys don't survive; it's tragic. So there wasn't always a resistance to the drugs, but there was always a resistance to the gynaecology, to the darkness. That was the phrase, always: 'It's too dark!'

'Pitch' meetings were odd, and this was the most practice I've ever got at pitching a project or a story. It's like performance. You had a matinée and an evening performance; a morning performance and a lunchtime performance. Sometimes you're depressed and tired and not that sharp. Other times you get a good response, so it encourages you and you have a great meeting. This was all new to me at that time. One thing about the tax-shelter era was that it was like a blotter hungry for ink; people would soak up every word you said. You never had to pitch twice.

At one time, the project did find sympathy with Bob Bookman at ABC Motion Pictures. In order not to complicate matters, Norman Snider had to be dropped as scriptwriter, as did the book as source material and, therefore, Carol Baum and Joe Roth. Cronenberg auditioned other writers, and decided on Andy Lewis – screenwriter of Klute.

The idea was that the woman who gets involved with the twins should survive, and that the story should be told a little more from her point of view, so that it wouldn't be so dark at the end; she has learned things about herself, and so on. That's what we basically agreed with Bookman on how to get the movie made. It could then be palatable to ABC. But later I got the impression that Andy didn't want the twins to be special; he didn't want to impose any kind of mythology on twins. He wanted to demystify them, and not let them be amazing or strange. He wanted all twins to be normal people who just happened to be twins. That's very humanistic of him, but that wasn't the movie.

One of the things that was very common when Mark and I were pitching the project was 'We've got another twin script. We're not crazy about yours, but we'd love to work with you on ours.' And they were always *The Dark Mirror* or the original *Dead Ringer* with Bette Davis: the killer twin and the naïve twin. Identical, except that one killed people. Those movies are very unrevealing about the nature of twins; they're just gimmick. In *The Parent Trap* there's confusion about there being two Hayley Mills, but nothing about how they're different people. Twins are desperate to share everything, which is why I wrote the line in *Dead Ringers*, 'You haven't fucked her until I've fucked her. You haven't done anything until I've done it too.' It's like lovers wanting to share everything.

Lewis delivered a script that was of no interest conceptually to Cronenberg, strong as it was on dialogue and structure. Now the director had yet another script that he didn't want to shoot. Bob Bookman left ABC Motion Pictures, to be replaced by a less than enthusiastic Stu Samuels. The company folded shortly after that. 'So we had two aborted foetuses, but no movie and no script.'

Despite Cronenberg's Total Recall trauma, the project was finally taken up by Dino De Laurentiis, who happened to have an identical-twin dentist. It was De Laurentiis's idea that the more experienced, sexually aggressive twin should 'pass down' the woman to his more timid and inexperienced brother, based on his own dentist's behaviour. 'Twins' would be produced by De Laurentiis's DEG company, with the involvement of his daughter Raffaella, then head of production. Cronenberg finally wrote his own draft script, based on Norman Snider's two drafts from 1981/2.

I really didn't know after all that time if I could do it. Maybe that's why I'd been avoiding hitting the keys myself. I was afraid that I'd try and wouldn't be able to find it. For me, it started with stuff that was maybe not crucial to the movie, but things that I needed: the instruments; the dream sequences; the opening with the kids; the Mantle Retractor. None of these were in Norman's drafts, but they were touchstones, to get me around and through. I eventually got a draft that I was happy with, which was about 60 per cent me and 40 per cent Norman. Dino finally said, 'If you can make it for under $10 million, we'll do it.'

With some difficulty, Cronenberg succeeded in casting the main roles in the film. Many film actors did not regard portraying two bodies with one soul – Elliot and Beverly Mantle – as a challenge from heaven. No 'marquee name' North American actor was willing to rise to the occasion, despite the opportunity offered by the movie to showcase acting ability and provide constant exposure (few scenes do not feature at least one brother). In addition, the female lead role of Claire Niveau was unlikely – due to scenes of gynaecological examination, if nothing else – to attract conservative or image-conscious actors. To their credit, both Jeremy Irons and Geneviève Bujold (after meetings and discussions of specifics with Cronenberg) finally agreed to be cast. 'Twins' was up and running. However, along with the many other movies on DEG's impressive production slate, it was not to be.

I visited Raffaella De Laurentiis. She had her hair up and back, so I knew I was in trouble. The lights in her office were out. Something was up. It was very early in the morning – for me an unusual occurrence. She said, 'You're going to kill me when I tell you this, but we can't do the movie. We're in trouble.' Apparently they were on the verge of bankruptcy, having extended themselves too far. *Dead Ringers* was now not a movie they could do. They couldn't do another *Blue Velvet* kind of film. They didn't lose money on that movie, but they did only break even. DEG was set up to accommodate that; it could have been great, doing movies to make money and movies for prestige that would just break even. What people don't realize, because they hear about *Batman* costing $52 million and making $300 million, is that for normal movies $2/3 million in or out of the budget is the difference between a successful movie and a flop. On that level, a movie you can make for $5 million will not get off the ground at $8 million, because that's where the profit is. DEG had come out with a string of movies that just hadn't appealed, like *Million Dollar Mystery*. Total disaster. The worst opening of a film in the history of the world. And *Dune* didn't do it either.

46 Hayley Mills: *The Parent Trap*.

47 Olivia de Havilland: *The Dark Mirror*.
48 Jeremy Irons as Elliot and Beverly Mantle: *Dead Ringers* (1988).

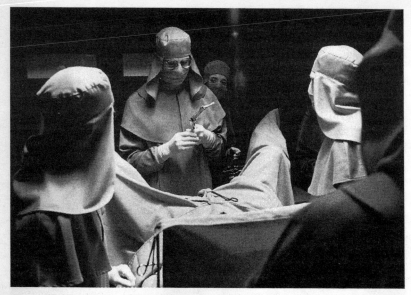

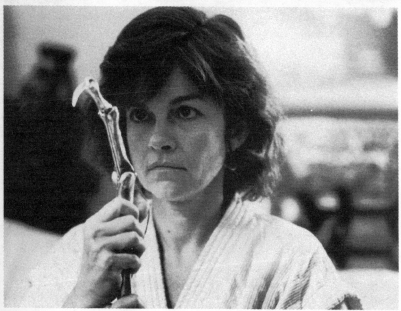

49 Beverly Mantle reveals new instruments in *Dead Ringers*.
50 Geneviève Bujold as Claire Niveau, with a 'gynaecological instrument for operating on mutant women' in *Dead Ringers*.

I couldn't believe it. But I didn't go crazy, throw things around, or scream and yell. I didn't talk betrayal, because I liked them. I am Canadian; my curse is that I can see everybody else's point of view. That's hard, when you need to push. I just thought, 'OK, they're in trouble and can't do it. What can I do now?' But it was disastrous; we had already built sets worth $300,000 in a building we were leasing, and had Jeremy Irons's agreement to do the movie. That was the beginning of ten months of agony like I've never experienced. I knew that if the sets came down – which would have cost another $30,000 just to get rid of them – that would all have to be added to the price tag for the next financiers.

Cronenberg needed to maintain the set construction already completed. To achieve a convincing 'twinning' effect – and to accommodate other special effects – the sets for 'Twins' were built to certain specifications. Firstly, they had to be very solid, to allow computerized motion-control camerawork for the twinning shots. Secondly, they were built on high platforms, to allow the special-effects team to operate from below. The solution arrived at was to rent non-set space in the leased building to anyone wanting to film commercials/rock videos, etc., until replacement finance was found.

Suddenly, David Cronenberg Productions became landlords overnight and Cronenberg himself, in collaboration with Mark Boyman, became a producer. His regular crew remained on standby – all, that is, apart from cameraman Mark Irwin. Irwin took a job in the States, a break in the family chain Cronenberg remains somewhat bitter about and disappointed by. When the time came, British cinematographer Peter Suschitzky joined the 'Cronenberg crew'.

In the meantime, Joe Roth was on the verge of forming Morgan Creek Productions, in partnership with Jim Robinson. After some six years, Roth became involved again with 'Twins'. Eventually, at the end of tangled negotiations comprising pre-sales, Morgan Creek and Rank Films, finance was finally secured to make the movie ($9 million approximately). Old friend Ivan Reitman, poised to make his latest Hollywood picture, Twins, *with Arnold Schwarzenegger and Danny De Vito, managed to talk a co-founder of the Canadian Film Co-op into changing his title. Cronenberg's most mature and profoundly disturbing cinematic experiment to date was now to be christened* Dead Ringers. *Inevitably, Cronenberg's story of Elliot and Beverly Mantle concentrated on the twins' biology and therefore – within a feminist context – on the unacceptable notion that Biology is Destiny.*

Not just for women. Everybody has heard of the phenomenal research coming out of Minneapolis showing that twins separated too early to remember later prove to marry women with the same name, for example, or smoke the same cigarettes or dress uncomfortably alike. You have to ask yourself if our chromosomes and genes are so detailed that they will programme us to respond to the sound of a name of a woman in twin fashion. It's very mysterious, but the implication of all this is that a huge amount of what we are is biologically predestined.

The whole concept of free will resists the idea of anything determining destiny. Freedom of choice rests on the premise of freedom from physical and material restrictions. But the twins research suggests a fair amount of biological predestination. Twins just provide a basis to investigate that, not as an aberration but as cases in point of genetic power. There are religious and philosophical questions attached to this that make it even more disturbing in a society like ours. Do I like it? Like everybody else, I'm attached to the notion that I am free and that my will determines my own life, and maybe I'm wrong.

In one way, *Dead Ringers* is conceptual science-fiction, the concept being 'What if there could be identical twins?' Some might say, 'But there are.' But I'm suggesting that it's impossible, and let's look at them really closely. I can imagine a world in which identical twins are only a concept, like mermaids. The fact that Elliot and Beverly are identical twins is their evolution into something monstrous. They are creatures, as exotic as *The Fly*. So there's a double game there; the mind/body split is still very much on my mind (and possibly my body too), but here the body is separated into two parts. Twins tend to love *Dead Ringers* because it talks about stuff that no one else talks about. It's like seeing your home town on screen.

For some people the movie is a lot harder to take than *The Fly*, which has the shield of fantasy in front of it. *Dead Ringers* is too close to home. The feeling is like an aquarium, as though these are strange exotic fish creatures. That's why I wanted their apartment to be purply and blue and sub-marine. It's very cool. People find it extremely disturbing. The fact that they can't exactly say why – there isn't much blood, etc. – makes it more so. With *The Fly* you can say, 'Yes, it was yucky. I had to turn my head. Other than that, it was neat.'

I think the movie is disturbing because it's all existential fear and terror: the evanescence of our lives and the fragility of our own mental states, and therefore the fragility of reality. I was playing with that in *Videodrome*. This is where *Naked Lunch* connects with all these things.

One of our touchstones for reality is our bodies. And yet they too are by definition ephemeral. So to whatever degree we centre our reality – and our understanding of reality – in our bodies, we are surrendering that sense of reality to our bodies' ephemerality. That's maybe a connection between *Naked Lunch, Dead Ringers* and *Videodrome*. By affecting the body – whether it's with TV, drugs (invented or otherwise) – you alter your reality. Maybe that's an advance. I don't know if I'm evolving at all in terms of the struggle.

Gynaecology is such a beautiful metaphor for the mind/body split. Here it is: the mind of men – or women – trying to understand sexual organs. I make my twins as kids extremely cerebral and analytical. They want to understand femaleness in a clinical way by dissection and analysis, not by experience, emotion or intuition. 'Can we dissect out the essence of femaleness? We're afraid of the emotional immediacy of womanness, but we're drawn to it. How can we come to terms with it? Let's dissect it.'

People who find gynaecology icky say, 'I don't find sex icky.' They've never gone into why. Men who put their fingers up their girlfriends can turn around and say the concept of gynaecology is disgusting. What are they talking about? That's one of the things I wanted to look at. What makes gynaecology icky for people is the formality of it. The clinical sterility, the fact that it's a stranger. The woman is paying the gynaecologist – let's say it's a man – and allowing him to have intimate knowledge of her sexual organs, which are normally reserved for lovers and husbands. Everyone agrees to suppress any element of eroticism, emotion, passion, intimacy. There's not a gynaecologist in the world who would tell you he's been intimate with eight hundred thousand women.

The other reason gynaecology weirds men out is that they are jealous. Their wife is known better, not just physically because, yes, you could look up there yourself with a flashlight. The gynaecologist's understanding of what it all does and how it works is greater than yours. And he does it all the time. He can compare your wife with other women: structure – does it look pre-cancerous? – all this stuff. It's his knowing stuff that you can never know. I don't want to discuss whether I've looked up my wife with a flashlight or not, but absolutely I wouldn't be afraid if I needed to. Neither would she. But it's something else. It's a very potent metaphor, such a perfect core to discuss all this stuff.

Strikingly, Dead Ringers' *own twin movies are Cronenberg's early featurettes* Stereo *and* Crimes of the Future. *In the aquamarine design of the Mantle twins' apartment, and their strange 'otherness', is the fish-tank approach Cronenberg applied to his characters in those early avant-garde experiments. This is explicitly signalled in the opening sequence, in which the young Mantles discuss the fact that humans are compelled to have sex only because they don't live in water. There even seems to be an equivalent of Ron Mlodzik's gay sensibility at work again, albeit at a more subtextual level. As Jeremy Irons observed about the twins: 'I find their attraction fundamentally homosexual, but Platonic. It allows them the freedom to relate to other bodies – women's in their professional life, their lovers, or each other's – on an unfettered physical level rather blind to emotional implications.'*

Dead Ringers, Cronenberg's ninth feature, also reopened the can of worms labelled 'pornography' – not the first movie he had made to be attacked with such ill-defined and easily mobilized adjectives as 'pornographic'.

I don't think we should debase the language, in the sense that if anything we say is to mean anything we have to at least agree on what our terminology means. Pornography is art or non-art that is specifically designed to arouse sexual desire. That's not eroticism. For political reasons people want to make a distinction between pornography and eroticism. Pornography technically is writing about prostitutes. Porno is whores, graffiti is writing. That's what pornography originally was: writing with prostitutes as characters. It was meant to be stuff that would arouse people. I suppose if someone was a very elegant writer, and an artist, he could do pornography that would be erotic.

The standard joke is that what I like is erotic, and what you like is pornographic. Many feminist factions support eroticism, and they try to discuss it in terms of equal power between the male and female parties – if they're talking about male/female – with no dominance of one over the other. That leads you into ridiculous conundrums. You have to have equal time with the woman on top and then the man. It just gets ridiculous.

The assertion is that eroticism is tender and gentle, and pornography is nasty and violent. But I could create for you a version of each that would fall into those categories which would not be acceptable to either side. It's extremely difficult to accept the concept of eroticism in art but say, at the same time, that pornography must be banned. It's so subjective. It's culturally subjective too. What is erotic in one society is completely disgusting and pornographic and anti-religious in another.

The use of the word pornography as a metaphor has become very popular: the pornography of war; the pornography of hunger. To talk about a pornographic idea or a pornographic concept really creates total confusion. *Peeping Tom*[6] is an interesting film because it deals with the creation of pornography: one man's version of pornography on film. I think that anyone now who pushes against what are considered very safe standards of behaviour and imagery is open to being accused of being a pornographer of some kind. It's almost a compliment now.

When was the last time a gynaecologist was in a movie, even as a figure of fun? There's something taboo there, something strange and difficult. A lot of people say, 'I suppose women find this movie much harder to take.' The answer is, 'Not really.' For a lot of women, the opening scene of gynaecological examination is no big deal. Later on, when it gets weird, of course it's uncomfortable. But, for a lot of men, that very first scene is the worst. They've never been there; they've never seen it; they don't want to think about it.

I felt, when I was working on the movie, that I made it primarily out of the female part of myself. Maybe that's why it was so successful in terms of its revulsion factor: I was doing these twins from a woman's point of view. They are so horrific, and yet still charismatic and exotic. In a crude sense, it's certainly the least macho movie I've done: there are no guns, no cars. *Scanners* was very masculine by comparison. Even *The Fly* was machinery-dominated. In *Dead Ringers* the machinery is the gynaecological instruments. They're very menacing on screen, but actually rather effete. *The Dead Zone* had a lot of femaleness in it, and not just because it's more emotional. But it's too simplistic to say that when a movie's emotionally right out there it's female and when its repressed it's male.

In *Dead Ringers* the truth, anticipated by Beverly's parents – or whoever named him – was that he was the female part of the yin/yang whole. Elliot and Beverly are a couple, not complete in themselves. Both the characters have a femaleness in them. The idea that Beverly is the wife of the couple is unacceptable to him. He can't accept that they are a couple. Elliot has fucked more women, has a greater facility with the superficialities of everything, with the superficialities of sex. But in terms of ever establishing an emotional rapport with women, Elliot is totally unsuccessful. Beverly is successful, but he doesn't see this success as a positive thing. He sees that as another part of his weakness. He's a part of his brother's view of society and has great difficulty accepting

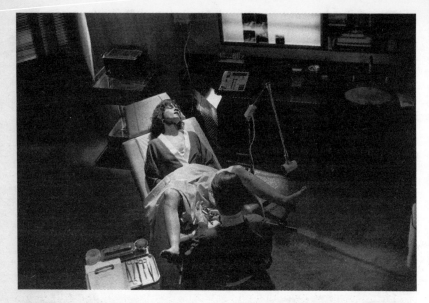

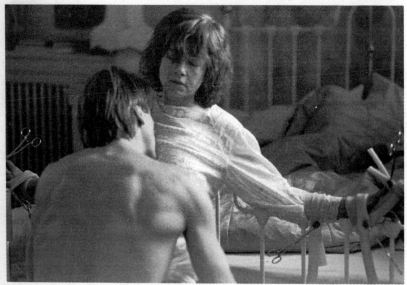

51 One of the Mantle twins is intimate with Geneviève Bujold in
    Dead Ringers.
52 One of the Mantle twins is intimate with Geneviève Bujold in
    Dead Ringers.

his own version. He's been colonized; he's bought the imperialist's line about what is beautiful, proper and correct. He has a lot of trouble hearing his own voice.

I've had a response to the movie that I've never gotten from any of the other films. I went to one of the first public screenings in Toronto and one guy, a doctor, said, 'Can you tell me why I feel so fucking sad having seen this film?' I said, 'It's a sad movie.' Then I heard from someone else that a friend of his saw it and cried for three hours afterwards. So I thought, 'That's what it is. That's what I wanted to get at.' I can't articulate it. It's not really connected with gynaecology or twinness. It has to do with that element of being human. It has to do with this ineffable sadness that is an element of human existence. It's a distillation of that; the way poetry and really good art often distil an essence which is not the whole story, but is perhaps so potent, one drop would kill you. It had come through a story about twins and gynaecology, because it has to do with women, birth, frustration and unrequited life. Not just love. But the sadness wasn't in the script.

The wonderful thing is when you get a guy like Howard Shore. As soon as I heard the music he wrote for the movie, I knew he'd got it too, and he couldn't articulate it either. When I talk to Howard we get very specific about where the music should come into the scene, where it should leave, and between which two phrases the musical sting will appear and disappear. We get down to the frame. But the tone of it, like the tone of those dreams, is ineffable. You cannot speak it. If Howard didn't get it, his music wouldn't get it, and you'd lose something. Because of the stupidity of a bunch of legal and other things, that music isn't available on disc or tape. That kills me, because it's gorgeous, sensuous, sad. Really moving.

I love the music in *The Dead Zone*. It's heartbreaking music, sumptuous. That was Michael Kamen. But I think *Dead Ringers* was much harder to get a handle on. It was more challenging. You really know what *The Dead Zone* is. You know what it needs. *Dead Ringers* was more slippery.

Having first been subjected to audience preview screenings with Universal Pictures on Videodrome, *Cronenberg was by now familiar and at ease with 'testing' a movie.* Dead Ringers *originally contained two dream sequences, the most visceral and extreme of which featured Jeremy Irons imagining an aged version of his other brother growing out of his abdomen. Although the sequence was costly, and involved weeks*

of preparation for the special-effects team, it was cut by the director
himself from the final film.

I used to think that, to be pure, all art should be like poetry; you write
it in your garret and it's there. It's taken for what it is. Then I realized
that poets regularly had readings. Certainly in the oral tradition, they
would modify their work depending on whether they got a laugh in the
right place or not. All those great poems were usually honed against
audience reaction. So even from the purist point of view, given that
you're making a film for an audience, eventually you have to let them
see it. Why not know in advance? The wonderful thing is you can never
totally gauge every response. You don't have to pay attention to it.
Politics within the studio system is another matter. The way I do my
own test screenings is that I control them; I'm not really answering to
anybody. *Dead Ringers* was perfect that way because I was also the
producer. I was free to ignore everyone's response. But I wanted to
know. It's painful, but it's worth going through. You have to do it
sooner or later.

This led to some hard decisions. The most obvious was the two
dream sequences. I knew there would be critics who'd say I'd almost
made a naturalistic movie (whatever that is), but couldn't resist falling
back on special effects and having to do some schlocky stuff. On the
other hand, I felt they were crucial to the movie; they would get into
Beverly's inner life in a way you can't do with dialogue. This was the
best way dramatically to get at what was going on inside him – the
shape of his anxiety about his brother, his dependence on him and his
fear that they will be separated by this woman.

I screened several versions: one without the dreams; one with a single
dream; one with both dreams. I asked on the card: 'Do you think these
dream sequences belong in this movie?' The only reason I found for
taking one out – in terms of the audience response, as opposed to
critical examination – was that people were squeamish. In terms of the
movie, it made me feel confident that I should leave one in. Not two.
The second did go too far. It broke that pact with the audience.

After the two adaptations of The Dead Zone *and* The Fly, *Cronenberg*
had returned – despite the 'stranger than fiction' real-life basis of Dead
Ringers *and of the book* Twins *– to his own original and essential*
impulses and materials, the quintessential 'stuff' of the Cronenberg uni-
verse. Not surprisingly, therefore, Dead Ringers *opened some old critical*

wounds. Accusations of sexual disgust and misogyny stalked the discourse of some responses to the movie like the walking dead – the issues that would not die, certainly in the face of such confrontational material. Cronenberg continues to console and defend himself with ease whenever such criticism fatally confuses or collapses his (unknown) personal day-to-day relationships with those of his characters. In short, movies do not deliver the self in any obvious way.

I don't experience revulsion in sex. That's why I know from the inside that the reality of a person as he or she lives their life, intimately, day by day, from the pores outward, is not what's delivered directly in their art. I am being this clinician, this surgeon, and trying to examine the nature of sexuality. I'm doing it by creating characters I then dissect with my cinematic scalpels. Why does that make them me, their sexuality my sexuality? I'm driven to look at it and want to see what it means because it keeps provoking me.

Venereal disease is very pro-sex, because no sex, no venereal disease. I know that some people think this is disgusting stuff, but in *Shivers* I was saying 'I love sex, but I love sex as a venereal disease. I am syphilis. I am enthusiastic about it in a very different way from you, and I'm going to make a movie about it.' It's trying to turn things upside down. Critics often think I'm disapproving of every possible kind of sex. Not at all. With *Shivers* I'm a venereal disease having the greatest time of my life, and encouraging everybody to get into it. To take a venereal disease's point of view might be considered demonic, depending on who you are. In a way, Robert Fulford's attack on me at the time is more understandable; he was a good bourgeois, responding with horror to everything I did. He would not take the disease's point of view, not even for ninety minutes.

Even someone who ought to know better, like Martin Scorsese, was terrified to meet me. He said afterwards he expected me to be a maniac. It's so compelling, the identification of the person with the art, even he couldn't separate them. And he's been on the wrong end of that particular stick himself.

When I'm having someone take a shower in a script, what's that based on? It's based on how I do it, how I see other people do it, how I've read people do it and how I've seen it done in other movies: a synthesis of all these. Then, my decision on how it works best for the character in the film. That's imagination, and it isn't. It's part of my nervous system up there. People say, 'What are you trying to do with your movies?' I say, 'Imagine you've drilled a hole in your forehead and that what you dream is projected directly on to a screen.' Then they say, 'Gee, but you're weird. How come you do that strange stuff?' I can then say, 'You would do the same if you had access, if you allowed yourself access.' Everybody would have weird stuff up there that an audience might think antisocial, perverse, whatever. It might even look that way to the person who created it.

That's not just your imagination up there; it's a huge synthesis of things. 'He's got a weird imagination' trivializes it and says it's just a little arabesque. Nothing serious. Not the real person. Not the essence. But I think it is the essence of the person. Maybe the exercise is to deliver an essential part of you that cannot be delivered in any other way. Most people have too exalted an idea of what art must be to connect their own impulses to create with delivering themselves.

I don't know how many movies it would take to equal the complexity and variety of a movie-maker's life, his or her actual inner and outer life. How many fictional novels would it take to deliver the author? Thousands. For some reason, the medium does tease out and induce particular states of creative mind. Something that might obsess you in the everyday might be absolutely not inspiring as a film subject. To make a film that's going to take two years and involve a lot of people, you have to find the big socket – the big juice, not the little juice. It's delivery of your sensibility, your aesthetics. You're not giving your audience something they can jump into bed with. Because of the *People* magazine cult, audiences might think that consumption of human beings – of their personalities, their essences – is what art is all about. I think it's possible to be a great artist and not be very self-revealing at all.

If you do a Woody Allen and put yourself physically in your movies, that's getting closer. The only reason I played the gynaecologist in *The Fly* was because Geena Davis begged me to. She didn't want a stranger between her legs, and felt more comfortable with me there. And it was a very convenient place to direct the scene from. Also to see how the effects were working. Because I was wearing a mask I thought, 'I can always ask Bobby de Niro to dub me if I hate my performance.'

My films spring from the traditions of wonder and phantasm, the fantastic. If you go back to the two founders of film tradition – Lumière and Mèliés – then I come from the Mèliés side: *Rocket to the Moon*.[7] As for specific influences I often point to Vladimir Nabokov and William Burroughs. But I just don't feel I can point to any particular film-maker. This has nothing to do with arrogance; I'm not saying that I'm unique among film-makers and have no predecessors, because obviously I do. This was one of the reasons why film was very liberating. Despite the fact that I had seen everybody who is normally considered a huge influence – Fellini, Bergman and Antonioni – I suppose I was just consuming them, rather than studying them.

I was very affected by Nicolas Roeg's *Don't Look Now*. As a film, as a story – just totally affected. But that film features a lot of tricks you just don't think of using. There are a lot of directors I admire, that I'm interested in. But I'm merely interested, as opposed to all those people who are obsessed with Hawks and Hitchcock. There's quite a difference between how I got into the film business and how the guys who went to UCLA to study movies got into it. They had the weight of film history on their backs. First, because they're American, and second, because they were scholars before they were artists. That's always a very difficult way to do it.

I'm anti-Hitchcockian when it comes to filming. I can't think of anything more hideous than planning everything on paper before you shoot, and then enduring the process. Hitchcock himself liked to say it was just 'grinding it through the machine'. He did that in an attempt to exalt himself – I mean that affectionately – and to de-emphasize the creative input of others. To say he only had to shout 'Action' and 'Cut' on set, and nothing else, meant he had total control – the complete puppet-master. What a hell. By the time we get to 'take two' I usually know just what it is I want. My eye for composition is very specific. I feel physically ill when I look through a lens and things aren't properly composed.

In *Dead Ringers*, the operating-room scenes as written are very realistic. I had to confront the dreariness of the average operating room and all that bankrupt imagery at the very point I needed very potent imagery, a metaphor. So I had to come up with the idea of the 'college of cardinals' approach and develop my own operating room completely. It's a total fabrication (although I like to tell people we really do it that way in Canada!). I love the fact that every day brings the possibility for some complete novelty, some emergent evolution, that will clarify everything and snap it into focus. By the end of the film you have something you could not have anticipated from the script, and yet can truthfully say, 'That is the script.'

It's joyous fun to make a movie on some levels. We lose sight of that. It's back to Orson Welles saying, 'This is the greatest train set any boy could have.' Despite all the heavy talk, I'm making myself like a child when I make a movie. It's make-believe, dress-up; creating things that didn't exist before. I'm not talking Steven Spielberg or George Lucas. That's substantially different. But if you don't have that sense of being a child, you can't make movies as an adult. There comes a point when you're asking this guy to stick on a funny moustache, put on clothes he doesn't normally wear and say things he doesn't normally say. You're asking people to believe it. When you shoot you have to believe it. You can't do that as an adult. It's not an adult thing to do. Underneath the patina of professionalism and the veneer of artistic and philosophical endeavour comes the childlike. Which is why even the most pessimistic film-making has some optimism behind it. Just making a film is a positive act, some act of faith.

Notes

1 Cronenberg was a friend of John Landis (1951–   ) and subsequently played a cameo role in Landis's *Into the Night* (1985), on which he met Jeff Goldblum, later to star in *The Fly*. Landis's other film credits include *The Blues Brothers* (1980), *Trading Places* (1983), *Coming to America* (1988) and *Oscar* (1990).

2 Dino De Laurentiis (1919–   ), the Italian producer, launched the career of Italian actress Silvana Mangano (later to become his wife) with *Bitter Rice* in 1948. Joined forces with Carlo Ponti in the early 1950s, producing Oscar-winning films such as Federico Fellini's *La Strada*. After this partnership dissolved in 1957, De Laurentiis went on to produce international blockbusters, building the giant studio complex 'Dinocittà' in Rome in the early 1960s. With the crisis in Italian cinema, due primarily to deregulated television and an increasing dominance of American product, De Laurentiis sold his studios and moved his operation to the States. His new company produced many box-office successes in the 1970s (*Serpico, Death Wish, Three Days of the Condor*) as well as some impressive failures in the 1980s (*Dune*). Production was wound down at the point DEG boasted an impressive slate of forthcoming, adventurous products from a number of interesting directors (Cronenberg, David Lynch, Peter Bogdanovich, etc.).

3 Norman Rockwell (1894–1978) became popular as the cover illustrator for the weekly American tabloid paper the *Saturday Evening Post* from 1916 to 1963. His work often depicted a charming, rosy-cheeked, vignette-style middle America, as opposed to the harder, more stylized 'American gothic' images of Grant Wood. Rockwell also illustrated such classic American texts as Tom Sawyer and Huckleberry Finn.

4 *Total Recall*: the film was finally produced by the major Hollywood independent company Carolco in 1990. Setting new standards for techno-style special effects and production cost (rumoured to be anywhere between $53 million and $75 million), the movie was directed by Dutch film-maker Paul Verhoeven (*Robocop*), with his customary flair for sadistic violence and action setpieces. The result couldn't have been more removed from Cronenberg's 'vision' of the piece if it had tried. Arnold Schwarzenegger was starring.

5 Mel Brooks (1926–   ), best known for his 'tasteless' comedy movies such as *The Producers*

(1968), *Blazing Saddles* and *Young Frankenstein* (1974), *High Anxiety* (1978), etc., writes, directs, produces and performs. He made his name as an irreverent nightclub stand-up comedian, and as creator of several successful American TV shows (including *Get Smart*). Of late, Brooks's films as director have deteriorated, reaching their nadir with his Star Wars pastiche *Spaceballs* (1987).

6 Written by one of Britain's top code and cypher experts, Leo Marks, and directed by Britain's greatest director, Michael Powell, *Peeping Tom* tells the story of sympathetic psychotic Mark Lewis, and his attempt to film fear. Although it is in all respects a remarkable and dark meditation on the very creation and viewing of cinema, hysterically adverse critical response to the film when released in 1960 all but destroyed the 'career' of Michael Powell in Britain. Significantly, the film was released in the same year as Hitchcock's 'classier' *Psycho*. Both films marked the beginning of a daring new approach to psychological horror, setting many precedents which were to be exploited later (they were both perhaps models for the 'stalk-and-slash' subgenre, as well as the first pre-video 'video nasties').

7 With brother Auguste, Louis Lumière (1864–1948) projected the first moving images, on 22 March 1895, in Paris: a short entitled *La Sortie des usines Lumière*, showing workers leaving their factory. Thereafter, Lumière's films tended to record real life and current events, predecessors of newsreel and documentary traditions. Dubbed the father of cinema, the Lumière tradition ran contrary and quite distinctively to that of Georges Mèliés (1861–1938) in the development of the art of film. A conjurer and illusionist, Mèliés was inspired by the Lumière invention but quickly developed his own practice: one of fantasy, imagination and the inventive use of the camera. His most famous film remains the influential *Le Voyage dans la lune* (*A Trip to the Moon*), made in 1902.

53 David Cronenberg and William S. Burroughs on the set of
Naked Lunch (1991).
54 Peter Weller as Bill Lee in *Naked Lunch*.

CHAPTER 7

Bugs, Spies and Butterflies:
Naked Lunch and *M. Butterfly*

In 1981, on the occasion of Scanner's *release in the States, Cronenberg had said in an interview for* Omni *magazine, 'Some part of me would love to make a movie of William S. Burroughs's* Naked Lunch.' *As was observed by critic Mitch Tuchman some five years later, a part of him already had. Not only had Burroughs (along with Nabokov) possessed Cronenberg's early writing to such an extent that he found it difficult to locate his own 'voice', but his first commercial feature –* Shivers *– was already infected with Burroughsian imagery. In* Naked Lunch *Burroughs's lecherous candiru are described thus: 'small eel-like fish or worm ... long patronizing certain rivers of ill repute'. These little creatures bear a remarkable likeness to the venereal/faecal parasites of* Shivers. *Both gain access to their victims through their genitalia.*

As Tuchman points out, in Rabid *the 'morphologically neutral' skin graft that transforms Rose's armpit into a blood-sucking phallic syringe is Burroughs's 'undifferentiated tissue, that can grow into any kind of flesh ... sex organs sprout everywhere'.* Scanners *also shares Burroughs's obsessions with telepathy, Senders and control. Tuchman concluded that Cronenberg's homage to Burroughs was 'largely iconographic. Their principle difference [was] Burroughs's impassioned moralism and Cronenberg's bloodless agnosticism ... Without Burroughs, Cronenberg may be without imagery.'*

Whatever the influence Burroughs exerts on Cronenberg, for the director to approach a film version of Naked Lunch *was a fitting form of cinematic destiny. Their nervous systems had been connected for years; both men shared the same nightmares and visions; both evinced a puritan disgust of the flesh (though at least one of them would deny this); both had been criticized and censored for their extreme imaginings.*

On its original publication, many reviewers of Naked Lunch *were repulsed, horrified and depressed by the novel. Some were made hysterical by it (again, a more serious parallel to the critical response awaiting* Shivers). *One such review states: 'Privacy of speech and nightmare – the fact that we keep some of our blackness and bed-smell inside – is one of the conditions of political and moral freedom.' Such a response begs certain questions about issues of the social responsibility of artists and creators, something Cronenberg feels particularly strongly about.*

As an artist, one is not a citizen of society. An artist is bound to explore every aspect of human experience, the darkest corners – not necessarily – but if that is where one is led, that's where one must go. You cannot worry about what the structure of your own particular segment of society considers bad behaviour, good behaviour; good exploration, bad exploration. So, at the time you're being an artist, you're not a citizen. You don't have the social responsibility of a citizen. You have, in fact, no social responsibility whatsoever.

If someone says, 'Now you must be the citizen and step back to see what happens, examine why you have an impulse to create and show these things,' that puts me in a different position. I'm no longer being an artist; I'm being an analyst of the act itself. There are many artists who don't feel the need to examine the process, or who fear that if they do, it will go away or change.

Nabokov said that and nobody threw rocks at him. I could say in the same breath that I am a citizen and I do have social responsibilities, and I do take that seriously. But as an artist the responsibility is to allow yourself complete freedom. That's your function, what you're there for. Society and art exist uneasily together; that's always been the case. If art is anti-repression, then art and civilization were not meant for each other. You don't have to be a Freudian to see that. The pressure in the unconscious, the voltage, is to be heard, to express. It's irrepressible. It will come out some way.

When I write, I must not censor my own imagery or connections. I must not worry about what critics will say, what leftists will say, what environmentalists will say. I must ignore all that. If I listen to all those voices I will be paralysed, because none of this can be resolved. I have to go back to the voice that spoke before all these structures were imposed on it, and let it speak these terrible truths. By being irresponsible I will be responsible.

Once you go deeper into what social responsibility consists of, you inevitably end up examining personal responsibility. You don't have one without the other. If you're trying to consider something pure and innate, as opposed to just culturally relative, you have to dive deep inside yourself, and that can be very perilous.

People ask me, 'Don't you feel you have a huge responsibility because of the films you make? How can you bear the weight of that responsibility?' To them I say, 'I'm carrying the weight of that responsibility very well. I think these films are good for people. They're not bad for people.'

Some people say that movies tend to support or encourage a certain philosophy. But the movie doesn't do anything. It just sits in the can. So, are we talking about the writer, the director or the producer? Who possesses the will behind this hypothetical movie that is saying – for example, in *Dead Ringers* – that misogyny is good, that I approve of it, partake in it? Where does that come from?

If it's to be a true art form, it's conceivable that the author himself, and the people making the film themselves, do not, in the process of making the film, know exactly what the film is saying. They don't know what the film is supporting or expressing. It's in the process of making that you start to come to some understanding of that. Therefore, you cannot have a group of people searching amongst the entrails of a movie at mere script stage for its meaning, social significance, political correctness, etc. Ultimately that's bullshit. In perspective you might be able to say something truthful about it. But who has the balance, the magisterial cosmic perspective that he or she can look at a script and say, 'This is irresponsible and must be suppressed'? What you get are little committees of scared, timid people who are fumbling around. If there was this Godlike person we agreed could arbitrate, OK. If someone would say to me, 'David, I know you don't think *Dead Ringers* is going to enhance misogyny in society but I, God, tell you that in the light of the next 2,000 years it will,' then maybe I could submit to that arbitration. But basically, I refuse to be suppressed.

The director who had said years earlier, 'I want to show the unshowable, speak the unspeakable' was finally about to film the unfilmable. Since 1984, when British producer Jeremy Thomas had attended Toronto's Festival of Festivals, he and Cronenberg had been talking about making a film version of Naked Lunch. *In 1985 Thomas, Cronenberg, Burroughs, James Grauerholz (Burroughs's secretary for eighteen years) and Hercules Bellville (head of development with Thomas's production entity, Recorded Picture Company) had all gone to Tangiers to retrace the footsteps of* Naked Lunch. *This was to be Burroughs's first trip to the 'Interzone' that had given birth to the novel, since he had been there in 1973.*

However, it was not clear how the film might be adapted for the

55 Producer Jeremy Thomas and Cronenberg on the set of
Naked Lunch.

*screen. Other film-makers had been interested in trying: among them
Stanley Kubrick and Antony Balch (who proposed a quite different,
low-budget attempt in the early 1960s, from a script written by Brion
Gysin). In the event, Cronenberg made* The Fly *the next year and,
although there was still talk of the project going ahead after this was
complete, then went on to make* Dead Ringers.

*Finally, in 1989, the project went ahead with Recorded Picture
Development. Cronenberg began the unenviable task of an adaptation
while starring in Clive Barker's film* Nightbreed,[1] *and living in London.
His approach, appropriately, was to fuse himself with Burroughs, one
schism he has been very successful in healing, for what was always a
marriage made in heaven. Or hell.*

James Grauerholz had shown Burroughs my films on tape, and earlier
took him to see some movies. He'd seen *The Fly*, and *The Dead Zone*. I
think he's seen *Videodrome*. He says he likes them to the extent that
when he was in Toronto he said he felt that I was the only person who
could do *Naked Lunch*. I don't think he would have said that if there had
been no belief in it whatsoever.

Of course, it's my version of *Naked Lunch*. I've seen other screenplays,
and attempts to do it. If you literally translate *Naked Lunch* to the
screen, you get a very nasty kind of soft, satirical, social satire of the
Britannia Hospital variety, with no emotional content and without the
beauty, grace and potency of Burroughs's literary style. So, as with *The
Dead Zone* – but in a much more subtle way – I had to abandon the
project of a direct translation, knowing it to be impossible, in order to be
faithful to it. I had to fuse myself with Burroughs in order to bring
something of *Naked Lunch* to the screen. I can hear some crude
producer/director saying that, but really meaning that he wanted to
dominate it and impose his own will on the material because he was too
insecure to be faithful. But you can't.

There are two main problems. One is the scope of it. It really is quite
epic. It's the mother of all epics. It would cost $400–500 million if you
were to film it literally, and of course it would be banned in every country
in the world. There would be no culture that could withstand that film.
That is what I was faced with: the difficulty any audience would have
plugging into it. As a book, you dip into it, you don't read it from start to
finish. It's like the Bible; it's a little bit here, a little bit there; cross-
references. You find your favourite parts, like the *i ching*. You look in it
when you need it, and you find something there.

Those are the main problems, but they excited me. It meant I was forced to do something else: to fuse my own sensibility with Burroughs and create a third thing that neither he nor I would have done on his own. It's like the Rubaiyat of Omar Khayyam. Borges has written a wonderful critical essay on that poem, saying that the English translator, Edward Fitzgerald, was no good as a translator because his work on the Rubaiyat is very faulty; that Khayyam was actually not a very good poet. But somehow, over the span of nine centuries, they combined to make this little gem of a poem that would never have happened otherwise. I feel that's what's happening with *Naked Lunch*. It's like Burroughs and myself fusing in the telepod of *The Fly*.

What I do is very different from Burroughs. There are influences and there are connections. One of the reasons you find a writer so compelling is that they crystallize for you stuff that's in you already. Images of addiction and body-consciousness, say. I think everybody has a literary imagination. People walk around with metaphors bursting out of them all the time. They usually come out as clichés, but everyone speaks in metaphors; they talk about their heads exploding and things like that. It's not restricted to academics.

Mine? Well, there it was in Burroughs. Not all of it. Not all of it in Burroughs, and not all of it in me. But so much of it, right there, stuff I could have written, except Burroughs had been doing it so much better and for so much longer.

I wasn't intimidated by the prospect, because behind this façade I am actually very arrogant. I felt I could do it. I didn't know how, but I knew I was going to be absolutely ruthless when it came to using Burroughs's material. I did go to him, and we talked several times. One of the things I said to him was 'You know, I'm not gay and so my sensibility, when it comes to the sexuality of this film, is going to be something else. I'm not afraid of the homosexuality, but it's not innate in me and I probably want women in the film.' So, I got my blessing from the Pope and he said that was fine; he's the last person to try and censor you.

It was, however, very cathartic for me to write the script of *Naked Lunch*, because I started to write Burroughsian stuff, and almost felt for a moment, 'Well, if Burroughs dies, I'll write his next book.' Really not possible or true. But for that heady moment, when I transcribed word for word a sentence of description of the giant centipede, and then continued on with the next sentence to describe the scene in what I felt was a sentence Burroughs himself could have written, that was a fusion.

Burroughs had nothing to do with the writing of the script once it was under way. When the first draft was completed in December 1989, he simply gave his blessing to what had emerged. The resulting script combined imagery and small pieces from the book with Burroughs's own life. It also opened with a scene adapted from the Burroughs short story 'Exterminator' (the writer had at one time been a bug killer in New York). As Cronenberg had also mentioned to Burroughs before attacking the problem of an adaptation, the homosexuality had been played down – as in his telling of the Marcus twins' story. The book Twins portrays one of the gynaecologists as gay, and at one point they have sex with each other, thereby making it a story about gayness and incest as well.

To me that just felt wrong. If one of them is gay and one of them is not, then already they are different in a very essential way, when the point of the whole story should be how similar they are. One of Norman Snider's comments about the first draft script of *Naked Lunch* was 'It's not as aggressive and predatory in its homosexuality.' But this is a fusion of several things together: me and Burroughs for one thing. Also, Burroughs the writer and Burroughs the work. Once again we're dealing with separation. If you read his letters, prefaces and other things he was writing, you realize that Burroughs had not at that point come to terms with being homosexual. You expect something else from someone as extreme as Burroughs, but he was capable of saying and writing in a letter exactly this: he felt that maybe writing *Naked Lunch* had cured him of his homosexuality, and that he was really looking for cunt. That's not very subtle, is it?

Earlier, he also accused Ginsberg, I think, of being a wimp in terms of his homosexuality, saying, 'Allen, you're a faggot, for God's sake. Why don't you just admit it?' Ginsberg was also in therapy to cure his homosexuality, thinking of it as maybe an aberration, because his mother was so dominating. And so on. Both of them were afraid, basically, of the social vulnerability of being homosexual. Not wanting to deal with that.

I'm giving you the doubt that was there in the life at the time. I think Burroughs himself saw the aggressive predatoriness as maybe so cathartic and so extreme that maybe he wouldn't have to live out of it any more. I was trying to see beyond, to the reality of the situation, which is much more ambivalent and ambiguous in terms of sexuality. In the script, the Burroughs character Bill Lee creates this insect controller. It tells him he must be a homosexual, that he's got to play the role because it's a good cover for him as an agent. But he has created this; he's making it his excuse. He's demanding of himself that he must do it. But it's for 'other reasons', not because he's homosexual. He has to do this as a noble, social act. And I like that. That portrays some of the complexity of Burroughs at that time. Now he's reached another point entirely, where he would happily not have anything to do with women at all – not see them, talk to them or know they exist.

Sexuality is not the only element of difference between Burroughs and Cronenberg. Their nervous systems may have been linked from an earlier time, but the two men couldn't be more different. Burroughs had been a drug addict; he had shot his wife; he had been in prison, and had lived in exile. Indeed, part of the defence of Naked Lunch *during its prosecution in America for pornography had been that the writer had experienced much of what was described in the book. Cronenberg, on the other hand, has always stressed that he is a middle-class Canadian, for whom anti-social or dangerous behaviour (beyond the making of his films, of course) is an anathema. Their 'vision' was similar, but Burroughs had lived his nightmares in a more concrete sense.*

Burroughs and I are not alike personally; in terms of our backgrounds and our upbringing we're extremely different. In fact we couldn't be more different, given that we were both raised as middle-class children in North America. I had nothing like the drug experience Burroughs did, until the 1960s, like everybody else. I used to think that drugs were for jazz musicians. And yet, as a metaphor for control and addiction, it was very understandable to me. He could have made up all his drug talk. He could have been the only person on the planet who ever did drugs and it wouldn't have mattered, because I understood the metaphorical side. That's what I responded to.

I started to think about what I didn't want to do with *Naked Lunch*. I didn't want it to be a movie about drugs, because I think Burroughs is more about addiction and manipulation and control. I didn't want people to think of Nancy Reagan when they saw the movie. So I knew it couldn't be about the cocaine problem, or the angel-dust problem or the crack problem. I knew the drug had to be invented. By inventing my own drugs they would have internal, metaphorical connections attached to them, rather than external, social ones. I could stay away from the social problems of what it's like to live with a junkie or whatever.

I also knew that I wanted it to be about writing: the act of writing and creating something that is dangerous to you. That's not an obvious discussion in *Naked Lunch*; it's buried in there. In other Burroughs writings it's a more obvious surface discussion. When you see the list of movies about writers, it's quite extensive – everybody from F. Scott Fitzgerald to Dashiell Hammett to Kafka. But the problem is always the same: the act of writing is not very interesting cinematically. It's a guy, sitting. Maybe he's interesting, maybe he wears a hat, maybe he drinks and smokes. But basically he sits and types. It's an interior act. In order to really convey the experience of writing to someone who hasn't written, you have to be outrageous. You have to turn it inside out and make it physical and exterior. That's what I've done with *Naked Lunch*. I've seen a lot of movies about writers and I don't think one of them has gotten to the insides of the process. You can't do it in a realistic, naturalistic way.

One of the things I asked Burroughs about was the afterlife. I said, 'Do you believe in the afterlife? Because I can feel that from your writings. And does that mean you are not afraid of death?' He said, 'No, no. Death is very frightening, because if you do it wrong you might end up in the wrong company. You might be setting yourself up because of what you write; because of what you reveal; because of what you create.' So in the film I've made things created by my writer Bill Lee physically present. They do influence him and tell him what to do. On one level it's like telling himself what to do and, on another, it's not. It's him creating something that will then take him through his life. If he's created the wrong thing, it's going to take him to meet the wrong company.

I also knew that I wanted the movie to have characters; I knew that I wanted a woman to be an important character. I knew that I wanted it to have narrative cohesiveness. All these things weren't because it was a movie that was going to cost X million dollars and would therefore have to have those things. I did deliberately stall and delay. Jeremy Thomas and Burroughs and I had been to Tangiers in 1985, and I still didn't write it. It was after Jeremy had had his hit with *The Last Emperor* and I had mine with *The Fly* that we thought it was time – if we were ever going to do a very difficult project.

Now I think, 'Thank God, it didn't happen earlier,' because I don't think I was good enough to do it properly. You hope that you are constantly maturing and getting better. Eventually, you have to admit to yourself that you're getting worse. As long as you are on the upward curve, it's good as long as your pet projects are just near your peak. I can just feel myself being stronger. I know stuff now that I didn't know before. *Naked Lunch* will probably be the most complex movie I've done in terms of the number of levels that things are working on. I must have known that, because I didn't even try to write the script until two years ago.

I really didn't know what was finally waiting for me in my little laptop computer. I said to Jeremy Thomas, 'There's a lot of hi-sci-fi and horror imagery in Burroughs, particularly in *Naked Lunch*; there are Mugwumps, and all kinds of creatures. But I don't think I want to make an effects movie. I don't want you to expect that and be disappointed.' I could tell by his reaction that he *was* disappointed. He thought, and I think rightly so, that that would be one of its main strengths and selling points: an effects movie for adults. The book itself was a sort of sci-fi horror novel for adults.

When I started to write, of course, I didn't get three scenes into it when the creatures started to appear. There was nothing I could do about it. Once you're writing, it's got to be what it's got to be. I was as surprised as anyone else that suddenly *Naked Lunch* was a heavy-duty effects movie, with effects that also talk a lot. That worried me, because if the effects don't work, all the dialogue goes as well. It's like casting an actor who turns out to be bad.

The script required some fifty Mugwumps, Sex Blobs, typewriters that mutate into giant bugs with talking sphincters, giant centipedes and some transformation set pieces. Chris Walas Inc. were hired to realize all this for a film the budget of which could not be excessive. Six months before shooting began, they went to work on a large number of creature puppets at CWI's base in San Rafael, Marin County.

Predictably, Naked Lunch *proved difficult to finance, its original Japanese backers dropping out at a late stage. However, Jeremy Thomas replaced his usual investors with other Japanese interests, adding top-up monies from Telefilm Canada and the Ontario Film Development Corporation to what became a UK/Canada co-production. With a budget of approximately US $17 million, the film commenced principal photography on 21 January 1991 in Toronto, starring Peter Weller as Bill Lee and Judy Davis in the dual roles of Joan Lee and Joan Frost.*

The production was scheduled to shoot all interiors and special-effects work in Toronto, moving to Tangiers in April for all exterior work. However, due to the Gulf crisis, it became impossible to secure insurance for the film to go to North Africa. Once again, location shooting outside Canada was to elude Cronenberg. Tangiers would have to be brought to

56 Peter Weller as Bill Lee: *Naked Lunch*.
57 Judy Davis as Joan Lee/Joan Frost: *Naked Lunch*.

Toronto, with the aid of production designer Carol Spier and her expert team, as part of a massive and last-minute rethinking of the film and its look.

I did a three-day instant rewrite of the script a few days before we started shooting. It was like 'Oh my God, what are we going to do? Maybe the picture can't go ahead,' and so on. I had one day of being depressed, because we had found all these wonderful locations. But it was really only one day. Then I got very excited, sat down and wrote the new script. I knew it was better, and so did everybody else, from the actors, to the crew, to my producers. It brought out things which had been latent, waiting in the script for me to find. I realized that we had been seduced by the biographical element: Burroughs was in Tangiers when he wrote most of *Naked Lunch*. In 1985 we saw the places where it all happened and gradually the assumption was made by all of us – a mass hypnosis – that we must go there.

   In fact, Interzone is, of course, a state of mind. That concept would have been damaged by splitting it between a real place that Bill Lee flees to and his strange state of mind. So it was now more pure, and everything started to fall into place. Connections were made. Everything was clarified. Once again, if the vibes are right, if the karma is right, the right actors will say 'No' when you approach them to play difficult roles, and the right countries will say 'No' to you when you want to go shoot there.

Naked Lunch was to see Cronenberg working through his long-standing conceptual and visual association not only with Burroughs's work, but with his beliefs that writing is a dangerous business. Cronenberg himself had often linked imagination with the idea of a disease: something that is catching and can cause harm.

To make a metaphor in which you compare imagination to disease is to illuminate some aspect of human imagination that perhaps has not been seen or perceived that way before. I think that imagination and creativity are completely natural and also, under certain circumstances, quite dangerous. The fact that they're dangerous doesn't mean they are not necessary and should be repressed.

   This is something that's very straightforwardly perceived by tyrants of every kind. The very existence of imagination means that you can posit an existence different from the one you're living. If you are trying to create a repressive society in which people will submit to whatever you give them, then the very fact of them being able to imagine something else – not necessarily better, just different – is a threat. So even on that very simple level, imagination is dangerous. If you accept, at least to some extent, the Freudian dictum that civilization is repression, then imagination – and an unrepressed creativity – is dangerous to civilization. But it's a complex formula; imagination is also an innate part of civilization. If you destroy it, you might also destroy civilization.

We've become very blasé in the West about the freedom, the invulnerability of writers. We take it for granted, particularly on the level of physical safety. But look what happened to Salman Rushdie. And now we find that under their dictatorship, Romanians had to register their typewriters as dangerous weapons! They couldn't own photocopiers. Every year you had to supply two pages of typing using all the keys, so that anything typed on your machine could be traced back to you. That is true fear of the power of the written word.

But even in the West, writing can be perilous. Taking his cue from Jean Genet, Burroughs says that you must allow yourself to create characters and situations that could be a danger to you in every way. Even physically. He in fact *insists* that writing be recognized and accepted as a dangerous act. A writer must not be tempted to avoid writing the truth just because he knows that what he creates might come back to haunt him. That's the nature of the bargain you make with your writing machine.

The bargain David Cronenberg had struck with his own first laptop in attempting to adapt Naked Lunch *proved a critically successful one. The film not only laid claim to eight Genie Awards (Canada's equivalent of the Oscar), but went on to win the National Society of Film Critics award for Best Director and Best Screenplay. The New York Critics' Circle also awarded* Naked Lunch *Best Screenplay, and Judy Davis Best Supporting Actress (also for her role in* Barton Fink*). Yet another award for Best Screenplay came from the Boston Society of Film Critics.*

Naked Lunch *also triggered a rash of Cronenberg retrospectives worldwide, the most complete and prestigious being in New York in January 1992 and Tokyo in March 1993. The Japanese tribute was accompanied by an exhibition 'The Strange Objects of David Cronenberg's Desire', comprising some 200 objects, drawings and props. The combination of Cronenberg, Burroughs, Peter Weller and* Naked Lunch *had produced the desired effect. Purists, however, were quick to complain. As Cronenberg was later to observe: 'The commonest negative*

58 Bill Lee with typewriter in *Naked Lunch*.

criticism came from the "hipper than thou" journalist. They said "This isn't as hip as Naked Lunch," *as though these guys were on the cutting edge when the book came out and of course immediately recognized it as a masterpiece. We all know that trick.'*

Some of this response was no doubt prompted by the fact that the emergent film was clearly more Cronenberg than Burroughs. In what Cronenberg had described as a fusion process, the fly – inevitably – had won. And in focussing to a large extent on actual events in Burroughs's life as a way of attacking the material, the film had become as much an adaptation of Ted Morgan's biography of Burroughs, Literary Outlaw *(the most visible book on set), as it was* Naked Lunch.*

After the demands of Videodrome, *Cronenberg had felt it necessary to find a less personal project. The result was* The Dead Zone, *a movie adaptation of pre-existing, successful material, and the only Cronenberg film for which the director took no writing credit. A similar condition began to manifest itself as* Naked Lunch *came to a close. By the time the film had opened in the States, Cronenberg's next project was beginning to emerge. If* The Dead Zone *had caused ripples of concern amongst his auteur-driven admirers, this one might be expected to produce a schism. It was a successful Broadway play . . .*

I love *The Dead Zone.* I mixed my blood with it well and I still have a great affection for it and thought that I did things that I really am very happy with and proud of. It isn't the same kind of film-making as *Naked Lunch* or *Dead Ringers* or *Videodrome*, but it's valid film-making for me and satisfying. It's probably been a mistake for me to avoid this kind of film-making exclusively just because it's not perfectly auteurist.

I said to my agents, 'I really don't want it to be another three years before I do another movie. If I do it the way I've been doing it – independent production, very difficult subject, writing the script myself – I know it's going to take three years. Financially and creatively I just can't do that.' On the other hand, I didn't want to get caught doing something I hated because then, six months into the movie, you just want to commit suicide. So I said to my agents, 'I know there usually isn't anything around that's unusual and interesting, but I'd like to find something like that. But it has to be with a major studio; with serious people, so I don't have to worry about raising the money.' One I'd heard about and that they mentioned to me was *M. Butterfly*. I'd seen the logo, I knew basically what the plot was, but I hadn't seen the play. It was with David Geffen and Warner Brothers and had the right feel. The problem was that it was out to (I think) Peter Weir, who had just turned it down. My agent Mike Marcus said, 'I think you're not in David Geffen's top five list. He's going to approach Stephen Frears next.' I said, 'Fine, let me read it anyway. Why should he think of me for it? That doesn't mean anything to me.'

So they sent me the script that the playwright David Hwang had written on his own – in the sense of not with a director, but with a producer or an executive at Geffen who had been overseeing it. I thought there was tons that didn't work, but I thought there was stuff that really did work very well and it was very intriguing. Then I read the play. I'm not good with theatre. I really have trouble with that suspension of disbelief and, anyway, I thought there were other things about the play that I wasn't crazy about. I was very glad that I'd read the screenplay first because there were many things in it that weren't in the play. They weren't necessarily the best things, mind you. But it was obvious that David Hwang was interested in experimenting and trying to create something new and that he wasn't going to be upset by transferring the play to the screen.

The play M. Butterfly, *written by David Henry Hwang, had opened on Broadway in March 1988, winning the Tony Award for Best Play of that season, subsequently playing in over 30 countries. Its proven stage success predictably led to dozens of companies bidding for the film rights, but David Geffen – who produced the Broadway version and whose independent company Geffen Pictures had a deal with Warner Bros – retained them. Inspired by real events,* M. Butterfly *tells the extraordinary story of French diplomat René Gallimard, who is so obsessed with Song Liling – a diva from the Beijing Opera – he is unaware that the object of his desire is really a man. And a spy for the Chinese government. It is only when both are arrested for espionage that Gallimard is forced to face the reality of Song Liling's sex.*

Perhaps understandably surprised by Cronenberg's interest, Geffen was happy that he direct the movie version provided it could be budgeted at the right price. Geffen was also keen that Hwang write the script. Only if Cronenberg wasn't completely happy with Hwang's solution could the director do his own draft. 'I said "Fine" because I'm lazy and it is his play. What the hell.' With the expertise of Cronenberg's regular production crew, the budget was pegged at a very acceptable $17/18 million, which left the issue of the script.

When I started to talk with David Hwang I told him what I was interested in and what I wasn't interested in. There was a whole sub-plot in his first draft that had to do with Americans in Vietnam, and there were scenes of bombs falling on Vietnam. I said, 'I'm not interested in that; it's about these two people and what goes on with them.' Apparently the Geffen executive felt the script needed that stuff to make it cinematic. So we threw it out and started from scratch. Also, its sexual politics were very easy, very standard; you read them every day in the paper. A particular brand of feminism and sexism. I thought we could be a lot more subtle, more complex and probably more emotional. I didn't get any emotional buzz from the play at all. I finally saw it performed in LA where it was played very broadly, so that emphasized the cartoon nature of it. You were watching schematic struggles between forces rather than individuals.

I said, 'First of all I don't buy your basic premise which is that everybody in Western culture is caught up with this mythology of the East. That's really too pat. You've really stacked the deck against Gallimard; he's obsessed with the opera *Madame Butterfly*, he's a total nerd and he's sexually inept. That suggests to me that you're not so confident of your premise because technically you could take any man off the street in Western culture and he would believe all of these things. He doesn't have to ever have seen *Madame Butterfly*.' In fact, the first draft of the screenplay began with a young René Gallimard at his mother's knee watching *Madame Butterfly* and crying and being totally emotional and sexually aroused and all of that stuff. I said, 'That's really making it such a special case and yet you're trying to suggest that this is a cultural truism. Why not test it. Let's take away the crutch of *Madame Butterfly*, let's say he's never seen it before.'

I can see that some people might accuse me of de-politicizing the piece. I think all of the politics *vis-à-vis* sexuality and cultural mythology is definitely there but it's more subtle, in keeping with my understanding of what film can do. It's a more subtle medium in the areas that matter to me – particularly dialogue, knowing that I was going to have to see René and Song, face to face, saying these things. On stage they're declaiming, and of course the structure of the play exacerbated that because it was René walking you through his life from the vantage point of the future and commenting on himself. That was another thing in the screenplay that I thought was bad and have since changed. There's a little too much self-awareness on the part of Gallimard and it comes from that old structure of the play.

It's clear from the playwright's own Afterword to his published play that David Hwang, the son of first-generation Chinese Americans, is overtly –

perhaps primarily – interested in M. Butterfly's *cultural, sexual, political dimensions. On reading a two-paragraph story in the* New York Times *about the real-life Gallimard (diplomat Bernard Boursicot) and Song Liling (Shi Pei Pu), he was gripped by the idea of doing 'a deconstructivist Madame Butterfly'. The play's resulting didacticism about racist and sexist stereotyping, politics and polemics is at odds with Cronenberg's own views on politics and – more importantly – its possible function within artistic practice. He had to make the story his own – mix some more blood with another foreign body – at the same time developing what he found so intrinsically of interest at the heart of the Hwang/ Boursicot/Gallimard story: the desire and capacity for physical and mental transformation.*

I remember distinctly when I got David's second draft I got little goose bumps, and I got it in many places. I didn't really try to analyse why because really that just puts me in the position of playing critic, which I can do. But the idea of transformation is there everywhere. The scene with the dragonfly is mine and it wasn't in any of David's writing and wasn't in the play. I put it into the movie because it seemed so perfect, subtle and obscure to me: the idea that these dragonflies have come out as a result of a transformation. I feel that René is responding to that unconsciously; he is transforming himself, into what we don't know. It's the idea that reality is created by human beings, that there is really no other kind of reality for us. René is creating a reality for himself and, for her own reasons, Song is helping him. I find that a very interesting version of stuff that I've done before but probably would not have done this way.

At one point my cinematographer Peter Suschitzky said, 'I really miss your dialogue,' and I knew what he meant, but that's part of what's exciting. You can't deliver the dialogue in this movie the way you can do it in *Naked Lunch* or *Dead Ringers*. I didn't want to spurn the theatrical basis of *M. Butterfly*, I wanted to go with the operatic and the theatrical. I felt it would be a mistake to try and turn this into to, say, street language, because Gallimard is in the process (unknown to him) of creating his own opera. He is creating the opera of his life, preparing to become the diva of it. I therefore thought of semi-theatrical dialogue where you could say, 'No one talks that way,' and you'd say, 'Of course not, but they do in this movie.' Let Song say those proverbs, especially once you realize what her goal is and how she is going to help Gallimard create their romance, their fantasy. It should be operatic, not realistic.

59 Diplomat to diva. Jeremy Irons transforms in *M. Butterfly*
60 Only a man knows how a woman should act. John Lone as
Song in *M. Butterfly*

There's a scene where Song's sitting on the bed and she says, 'I despise this costume and all the bourgeois perversions, but for the sake of the great helmsman I want to do it.' Being forced to be a homosexual and loving it, of course, and needing and wanting it and at the same time being humiliated by all those things. It's an interesting mix of stuff and of course it's in the play, I didn't invent it. It does have that resonance — being forced to do things that you really want to do anyway. You want to desperately, but it's no good unless you're forced. But, like the play, we don't get into Song's psychology, what does she do alone in a room, we don't see much of that.

I think that's part of the transformation theme. People want to be forced to come out. I don't only mean sexually, because that's only one kind of covert life you can live. Their secret life suggested this possibility of transformation; allowing yourself to become something else and let go of what you are, your past, your culture, your emotional life, everything. It's a scary thing and an incredibly seductive thing too.

Cronenberg cast Jeremy Irons as Gallimard. For the first time we see a Cronenberg Man making a re-appearance in another story. The effect is unfamiliar, chilling and strangely resonant. Surely the Cronenberg Man lives only in the hermetic hell of a specific narrative? He has no life, and no future, beyond either an (unseen) awkward destiny or his apparent self-immolation. The very sight of Irons on location in China – made more concrete by virtue of his uncanny performance(s) as Elliot and Beverly of Mantle Clinic fame – produces a sense of unease and imminent danger. A Cronenberg Man has stumbled into the real world. We can expect the worst.

Jeremy's a combination of Beverly and Elliot in this movie. He's Beverly aspiring more to be Elliot. We joked about it. It was interesting to have a past to refer to when discussing scenes and how to play them. It works the way it works with your cameraman and your production people. You don't get bored with each other, you challenge each other. It's not an ego thing, it's the challenge of the work. And then you're very efficient. That's one of the reasons we came in under budget; we didn't have all the ego stuff that takes a lot of time and money to deal with. So we felt very much like a guerilla operation – really tight and efficient. That has a lot to do with all the people I work with, and also my brutality with the script. Despite the fact that this is my biggest budget, it still felt tight. I'd hate to lose that feeling. I think it's important.

On one level of course it's a totally different movie, but I thought, 'Will Jeremy and I be bored with each other and know each other's tricks and not get the best out of each other?' And yet we're both edgy enough I think, comfortable but edgy, that we didn't take anything for granted. It was dangerous enough, and of course John Lone was a very strong presence on set. There was a lot of interesting stuff going on between John and Jeremy, so that immediately alters everything, because with *Dead Ringers* it was just Jeremy and Jeremy. There was really no one else. In a way John Lone was a version of the Geneviève Bujold character in *Dead Ringers*. He was so scrupulous about being a woman on set. He wanted Jeremy to not ever see him as a man. He really was the girl on the set and that was great. If you needed femaleness, he was it.

M. Butterfly is the first Cronenberg movie actually to make it to a location beyond Canada. It was filmed in four countries – China, Hungary, France and Canada – from August to early December 1992. One unforseen shock result was the film's first trailer, prepared prior to its completion by Warners to generate theatre bookings in the U.S. Maximizing the film's location shots and crowd scenes, Cronenberg appears to have made a movie of epic proportions and vision.

However, what actually emerges from the film itself, what is Cronenberg's most remarkable achievement for his first foreign location movie, is his determination and ability to subordinate landscape. The breath-taking beauty of the Great Wall of China is appropriately framed to contain intimate, delicate emotion, in an almost anti-David Lean gesture. René and Song seem to project this landscape themselves, rather than rattle around in its spectacle in search of any meaning beyond their unwitting participation in an elaborate and expensive tourist trigger for the big screen.

When David Geffen saw the trailer he said, 'Is this stuff in the movie? Are we selling something we don't have?' I said, 'No, those are all shots that are in the movie, but it is not like a David Lean picture.' I'm joking when I say it's my first David Lean picture, because that's what the trailer makes it look like; an epic like *Doctor Zhivago*. But of course it's not. Warners were stunned. They said, 'You've made this movie for what we've been going over on all our other movies! God, for 17 million dollars we got a fucking 50 million dollar epic!' So they were very excited. I was excited because I had done this for not much money, but it was all stuff that I felt had an absolutely right metaphorical place in the film.

I didn't want it to be like *The Russia House*, for example, which I thought was a very strange lesson to watch. I didn't think it was very successful artistically because there was this obsession with showing you the real streets of Leningrad and so on. The camera was drifting to show you what was outside the window when really you just wanted to see the actors' faces. I couldn't believe how often the camera would just steadicam its way over to see the nice onion domes and stuff. I thought, 'God, I don't want to make that mistake.' In *M. Butterfly* the stuff is there when it's there. Some of the stuff I really wanted to capture most was the feel in the backstreets of Beijing because I'd never seen that before. You always see Tiananman Square or the Forbidden City. I didn't want to be a tourist, and yet the structure of the piece is so perfectly set up for that because Gallimard is really falling in love with China.

The audience gives a little gasp when you first cut to the shot of René and Song by the Great Wall of China. But it ends with a big close-up of Song and that's what it is. There's no 360-degree pan showing you that landscape. The wall isn't window dressing. Gallimard is being seduced by the combination of the Wall and being there with Song, but he feels it more than the audience. It's for him to be overwhelmed more than the audience.

Scanners and *Rabid* were very much out on the streets; incredibly low budget, guns, tanks, explosions, car crashes, stuff like that, all subject to the vagaries of location (for me Montreal is a location, I'm not home there). So it was just once again: how do you make it work for the movie? It wasn't a problem, and of course ultimately this movie is two people in a room.

Dead Ringers was to be called Twins *until Ivan Reitman's movie came on the scene.* Naked Lunch *had to contend with a small avalanche of films about writers (including Stephen Soderbergh's* Kafka *and the Coen Brothers'* Barton Fink*). 'I laughed and I cried' is how Cronenberg describes his reaction to the appearance of Neil Jordan's* The Crying Game *during* M. Butterfly's *production. Jordan's story of an IRA affiliate (Stephen Rea) falling in love with the girlfriend of a black British soldier he first helps to kidnap then allows to die, only to discover that the girlfriend (Jaye Davidson) is really a man, was like a small bomb exploding behind* M. Butterfly's *transsexual lines. Not only that, the movie became an unlikely smash hit in America (for a low-budget British feature) before his very eyes.*

61 David Lean à la David Cronenberg: *M. Butterfly*
62 'Why is she dressed like that?' Song testifies in *M. Butterfly*

As soon as you start to make a movie it seems that it crystallizes that particular force in the universe and they start popping up all over quite independently. Now there's nothing but transvestite movies. I expect that by the time we come out, there'll be at least ten other ones. It would be wonderful to make a movie that was so 'out there' that no one came close with anything remotely resembling it.

We'll never know what the history of this movie would have been without *The Crying Game* because I think they're linked, unfortunately. I say unfortunately because you can't see it clear of that movie now. *The Crying Game* made that thing of two men having a love affair – where one didn't know that the other one was a man – kind of sweet and innocent and pure and, in a weird way, not threatening. An amazing number of straight heterosexual middle-class men loved *The Crying Game*, to my total surprise. This is me being the Devil of course, but I think it's because she (Jaye Davidson) really *is* a woman, even though she's got a cock. There's that scene where her hair gets cut. You were supposed to go, 'Oh my God, she really looks like a guy.' But it didn't happen because she was even more female with short hair. That's why I wanted John Lone, not the equivalent of Jaye Davidson. I didn't want an unknown who was incredibly female, who was like a wonderful drag queen and almost undetectable. I wanted a man. When Gallimard and Song are kissing I wanted it to be two men. I wanted the audience to feel that. I think for all of those reasons this is a much more public act than *The Crying Game*, which came from nowhere with a complete unknown who didn't want to do publicity.

I did audition some transsexuals who were so female that you'd have to see them naked to believe that they were men. They were so perfect. I was watching one of them, an English/Chinese 'woman' on tape and I'm saying, 'She isn't a man, she's a woman. She is totally a woman.' I realized at that moment that that was not what I wanted because you'd have to strip this woman and zoom into her crotch to make sure that everybody knew you hadn't made a switch. That's the wrong trick – especially when I had some candidates who were convincing as women, but had no power in the court room scene, no power in the paddy wagon scene. They were either boys or they were still women and that was no good. *M. Butterfly* for me is about a transformation; that's what attracted me to it. There must be this transformation into a man, and you can't get that if you get someone that is such a perfect woman that you can't transform them.

It must be convincing only in that Jeremy has to have enough to work with – that René Gallimard has enough femaleness to work with so that he can create a fantasy of femaleness. I don't want him to be a total fool. I want the audience to understand why he doesn't twig to it. By the end of the movie you should realize that there's a will involved in this; he's determined not to accept that Song is a man and he has his own reasons for that. Several of them. So it's complex.

There are even more parallels between *M. Butterfly* and *The Crying Game*; not only is it transsexual, but it's transracial and transcultural as well. Both take place under very hot political circumstances. So there are many, many comparisons to be made and yet it's so different. In a way, my attempt to do the prologue was probably induced by the reaction to *The Crying Game*. To give them credit, the guys at Warner Bros saw that. They said, 'We think you're overreacting. You should just forget it; it's another movie. Just make this movie. It's going to have its own life.'

'The prologue' refers to Cronenberg's attempt, at one test screening, to short-circuit the potential problem of an audience accepting John Lone as a woman and, as in The Crying Game, *therefore being able to surprise them with something of the same revelation. The test prologue gave the game away in advance, telling the audience that Song turned out to be a man. However, the screening revealed that granting the audience this certainty didn't give them the real comfort they perhaps needed. They remained disturbed by the scenes of tenderness and physical love (the latter being absent from* The Crying Game) *between the two men. The prologue, designed to second-guess a post-*Crying Game *audience's expectation of shock revelation or not, was therefore dropped. M. Butterfly's more subtle purpose was retained. This purpose is perhaps most eloquently expressed in Jeremy Irons's face at his first ever sight of Song as a man in the courtroom during their trial for espionage.*

We were playing several things with that reaction shot. One of them was, 'Why is she dressed that way? Why is she pretending to be a man?' A little laugh and then a little confusion and then a little feeling of, 'I knew anyway but I didn't want to know.' It's very complex. That's why *M. Butterfly* is less mainstream in a bizarre way than *The Crying Game*, which you might think would be the fringe movie of the two.

We'll find out later if *M. Butterfly* is more disturbing sexually to a middle-class audience. Artistically, that would make me happy. Commercially, it might make us all sad. Naturally, I want it to make a huge amount of money because I want people to see it. On the other hand, I didn't back off some of those difficult things in the same way that *The Crying Game* really copped out. For example, the Stephen Rea character should have killed the black soldier. He should have shot him and that would have made the movie so much more powerful because his guilt would have been so much greater. To have him chase the guy who then gets killed by a tank is almost a Hollywood solution to the problem: 'We don't want the audience to not like our main character.' I didn't want Gallimard to be too sympathetic.

It's the 'going native' theme really. Gallimard is about being dissatisfied with your own culture and then throwing yourself bodily into another culture to abandon your own culture. It's a kind of self-hatred to do that; people who learn another language and marry a woman or a man of that other language and become completely consumed by that other culture and abandon their own culture and their own friends and their parents and their own paths and themselves. It's an illusion, because the culture that you're taking on is not your culture, you're always an outsider, especially in a culture like that of the Chinese or Japanese. There's no melting-pot mentality; they don't want you to be Chinese.

There's some of that in the movie, that dissatisfaction with the self and with the culture that goes together, but as we're not examining Gallimard's lone past, it's more the process that we're seeing rather than the psychology. The desire to transform, to become something totally 'other'. One way to do it is culturally. Another way of doing it is sexually.

It would be simplistic to say that this is a story of repressed homosexuality, and if it were that, then it wouldn't have the suicide at the end, not the way it's done, not with Gallimard accepting that he is the woman. That's complex and strange. But I think there is an element of that – coming to terms with his own sexuality. I don't know that, if I'd approached the material to write a screenplay without the play existing, I might not have stuck closer to the real story in this respect. The real Gallimard met his Song as a man, was introduced to him as a man who played female roles in Peking Opera, a very female man but a man who wears suits. He doesn't wear dresses. They became very close friends. After a year of them being really close friends there was a moment when his Song said, 'I'm really in love with you, you can fuck me, we can be lovers, we don't have to just be two guys. My mother wanted a boy because in China only boys are valued and after she had a bunch of girls she just said I was a boy and raised me as a boy but I'm really a woman.' It was as though his Song sensed that the real Gallimard was in love with him but couldn't allow himself to come out and be a homosexual and that they be homosexual lovers. He had to create a woman for his Gallimard to love and that's real interesting. Without Hwang's play I might have been tempted to do that version of it. But then that would only be a story of repressed homosexuality.

M. Butterfly *ultimately pivots on one scene. After their trial, René and Song ride the paddy wagon together through Paris; René on the way to prison, Song on the way to the airport to be extradited. It provides the only chance for reconciliation and understanding for the characters and for the audience. René must face Song's physical sex. In* The Crying Game *the sight of Jaye Davidson's cock prompted Stephen Rea's charac-ter to vomit, and the audience (if fooled) to marvel at the deception.*

The idea of doing the final scene between René and Song in a paddy wagon was mine because I just knew that it wouldn't play in prison the way it was in the play. It wouldn't be believable that Song be allowed to stand outside Gallimard's cell and take his clothes off and rant and rave and nobody come around. On stage, when it's in limbo, a sort of memory of something, it worked fine. To me that is the essential scene in the movie and I was a little worried about putting it in a paddy wagon. But where else can you put it? It's between court and prison. It was a gamble because we didn't shoot it in a real paddy wagon. That's the scene most people put down as favourite. Thank God it worked, and again it's two people in a fucking room.

I didn't want to show Lone's cock because suddenly it becomes a scene about a cock. I think it's important that Jeremy sees it for an instant, that's all. I don't think we need to see it. It's quite different from *The Crying Game* because you need to see it there or you'll never believe that Jaye Davidson is a man! Nakedness, not the cock, is important in our scene because Song says, 'Feel this skin, it's still the same skin.' In a way, it's his purpose not to show how different he is from the Song that was imagined, i.e. the woman, but to show how much the same he is.

Song is this creature: male, female, east, west, invented. Song is no longer this thing they created, and yet has the nerve to come whimpering to Gallimard in the paddy wagon scene saying that he should love it when, in fact, it doesn't compare to what they created together. It's really very applicable to a lot of normal relationships. A lot of marriages fall apart when that willed suspension of disbelief collapses and suddenly the thing that you've created together is not there any more. You see each other plain and you don't like what you see because it's not enough. Then you go off to create some other thing with somebody else.

'Only a man knows how a woman is supposed to act.' That was the line in the script and the play that made me want to do it; the idea that female sexuality is invented by men. The idea that the sexuality of each of us is an agreed-upon fantasy that we both create for each other. It's kind of sweet in some ways and kind of scary in others, because it means in a way there's no reality of sexuality; there's no such thing as absolute maleness or absolute femaleness. The premise of *Crimes of the Future* was that, in the absence of women, men have to discover the maleness and the femaleness in themselves to keep a balance. You should be able to have a story about two men or two women and still have all the maleness and femaleness play out. I think you can.

In Naked Lunch *Cronenberg had toyed with certain connections between homosexuality and spying. Bill Lee was 'forced' to adopt a homosexual cover for his covert operations in Interzone by his own hallucinatory bug controller. Whereas this provided an ingenious solution to specific questions in Cronenberg's mind about Burroughs's own sexuality, and to some of the problems of adapting* Naked Lunch, M. Butterfly *explicitly continues the theme. This time, Bill Lee's imagined bug controller becomes the very real Butterfly Song, manipulating René who – like his Burroughsian counterpart – is unsure of his sexual identity. But in* M. Butterfly, *the context is politically very specific compared to the shifting imaginary regimes of Interzone.*

Revolutions are used by people. This is a perfect example: a man saying, 'I'm desperately trying to become something else,' and then later, 'I cannot have the body of somebody else, I cannot give you the body of somebody else,' but at the same time willing it to happen, wanting it to happen and doing it internally instead. That's why I wanted to play down the politics; what you see in the movie is politics in the service of unstated individual will and desire. The whole Red Guard thing is exactly what René is trying to do – sweeping out the past; viciously, violently, cruelly, completely. It's a political manifestation of a very personal impulse. We create politics. There is no politics without human desire and madness, so to me it makes perfect sense that the two go together.

It would've been interesting to do more of that. I tried to keep them as parallel as I could. That was one of the things that wasn't clear in the play. I tried to add a little stuff to position Song a little better. Was she a spy before René met her? Unlikely. That's a pretty specialized sort of spy – only transvestite Peking Opera singers! So the way I talked to John Lone about it was that Song meets Gallimard, does her routine almost tongue in cheek, sees that he's actually falling for it, gets him isolated from his embassy staff in case somebody tells him that she's not a woman and sees how far she can go. She's flattered, excited and aroused to have him start to fall in love with her and be seduced by her. And then she is caught with him. That's why I added a shot – Song's housemaid Shu Fang peeking through the window at them – on the day of shooting. I wanted to suggest that she blows the whistle on Song, who is then forced to spy, or it's a serious labour camp for being a homosexual. So she can play the political game, play for time. She's forced to do what she wants to do anyway, but now there are strings attached.

Finally, the Red Guard come on the scene and they're a whole other force. This wasn't too clear to the American eye, so I added the line 'All artists are now considered criminals' and the voice-over loudspeakers in the labour camp. I also added the drunk's off-camera line about leftist students in the bar in Paris. People were very confused about what the Chinese were doing in Paris. They didn't get it, and of course I realized, why should they? They live in Santa Monica, they might be 20 and what the fuck do they care? I didn't mind. The changes clarified that this new political force comes along that will not indulge Song. The old regime was decadent and allowed such terrible things to happen. The new politics will not, despite the fact that it's expedient to use her. She's too perverse to be allowed to do this and therefore she goes to a labour camp.

M. Butterfly's success with audiences may ultimately depend on their ability to accept the notion that Gallimard is – at least on one level – shocked and surprised to learn that Song is a man. Easier to accept in theatrical form, its cinematic equivalent inherits the inevitable problem of making places, characters and actions more concrete, more real. And yet, historical events seem to show that Boursicot had relations with Shi Pie Pu for some 20 years. During his trial in 1986, Boursicot maintained that he had passed on secrets for love, not money, and told the court: 'We were forced to keep our romance secret and often met in the dark. That could explain why I made this mistake. I never saw his sex completely. He was very modest. I thought it was a Chinese custom.'

Cronenberg's characteristic determination, not only to face this head-on, but to make Irons's Gallimard a sexually experienced married man (unlike Boursicot, who was 20 when he first met Shi Pie Pu) makes the premise even more confrontational. Their scene of love-making in a back room, glimpsed by a tracking camera, is – in this context – doubly challenging.

When you get to the paddy wagon scene I think you have to accept that there's something more going on. When I was young, it was a stunning thought that you might go off with a hooker and she turns out to be a guy. Well now, it's like forget it. It's everywhere! It's hard to find a hooker who looks like a woman and actually *is* one. It would be bad only if the audience didn't buy Gallimard's apparent stupidity; that they felt it to be a mechanical device that doesn't work. Then you're in big trouble. But if they can find a way to make it work in their head as part of his character, that's fine. In a way, I removed that safety net deliberately, I hope not foolishly, when I took away the whole element of Gallimard being just a total sexual nerd and inept so that you could believe he might be fooled. But then I might not have cast Jeremy, because of his presence on screen; it's hard to buy that with him. I wanted Jeremy precisely because you'd feel that it was a willed suspension of disbelief. He's not fooled. He *wants* to be fooled.

I'm always surprised when people's version of why they can't believe Gallimard's ignorance of Song's real sex is that naturally he would have wanted to stick his cock up her cunt. Only that satisfies a real guy, so how come he didn't? They don't want to even think about him sticking it up her ass. I think the real Gallimard still claims that he didn't do that, that it was between Shi Pie Pu's thighs. I'm thinking, 'Yeah, between his thighs, with hands with mouths.' I emphasized that a little bit more. Song is inventing a fake Chinese culture, she is inventing a fake ancient Chinese sexuality and making it very wonderful and very attractive.

The little scene in the back room where they're having some kind of – I don't know what it is – sex. Is it her hand doing it? Is it between her legs? Is it up her ass? Where is it? I think people have got to accept how weird people really are. In the Victorian era men certainly went 20 years without ever seeing their wife's cunt. It's not so amazing. Human sexuality is an incredibly potent force; it has become detached from the physiology of reproduction and so it now is almost an abstract force. There's a lot more that could be done with it, perceived as an artistic form all by itself.

Notes

1 Clive Barker is the successful British horror writer, who is much admired by Stephen King. Barker began film-directing in 1987 with a version of his own short story *Hellraiser*. Barker co-produced *Hellraiser 2: Hellbound* in 1988 and directed *Nightbreed* (starring David Cronenberg as Dr Decker) in 1990.

CHAPTER 8

Wounds, Scars and Twisted Cars:
Crash

If Cronenberg's 1992 adaptation of William Burroughs' The Naked Lunch *seemed overdue, his filming of J. G. Ballard's 1973 novel* Crash *looks and feels as if it was made long, long ago in a parallel universe. For one is forcibly struck by the overwhelming impression that this is early Cronenberg. Unblinking, undiluted, unrepentant and downright provocative.*

For those unfamiliar with Ballard's novel, it tells the story of James Ballard (James Spader) and his wife Catherine (Deborah Unger). Locked in a practice of compulsive sex with strangers, they compare notes, seeking any physical experience that makes sense in a bleak, passionless world of multi-lane freeways. Ballard becomes involved with Helen Remington (Holly Hunter) after he accidentally ploughs into her car, killing her husband. Their mutual crash-victim status brings them together, ultimately delivering them into the sump-oil-soaked world of the pathological Vaughan (Elias Koteas).

Renegade scientist and leader of a strange subterranean group, Vaughan is only able to achieve sexual release by crashing into people on the motorways surrounding Heathrow airport. His tattered leathers smell of stale semen. His cock only responds to twisted metal, beautifully formed chrome, shards of windscreen glass and blood on instrument panels. He photographs crash-sites and victims, and dreams of the ultimate orgasm: ramming into a Rolls Royce carrying Elizabeth Taylor.

In the film, his band of scarred and semi-mutilated crash victims (including Rosanna Arquette) spend their time looking at videos of simulated accidents, fucking in cars, or attending Vaughan's own 'illegal' performances – such as his restaging of James Dean's 'Death by Porsche'. Ballard, his wife and Helen Remington are all drawn into Vaughan's crazed orbit, and his dream of a new conceptualized relationship of flesh and metal: man and machine.

The book was (and is) shocking, by any standards. Naming the novel's first-person hero after himself seemed calculated to shock the reader into confronting the book's hardcore fantasy reality. The author was being totally honest about his own imaginative life.

Given the novel's scenario, in which humans realign their minds, bodies and sexuality to dominant technology, it was always perfect Cronenberg material. And it had echoes that might satisfy the director's personal interest in cars (he's an amateur racing driver).

Although the book is set in London, the cars are often American (Vaughan drives a '63 Lincoln, the car in which Kennedy was assassinated). It feels like the future, but is steeped in the present. The novel's dystopic vision seems as contemporary in the 90s as it did in the 70s.

The movie relocates the story to Cronenberg's home town of Toronto, that most archetypal of North American cities. The perfect quasi-sci-fi backdrop. Nowhere. No time. A brilliant solution to the novel's sense of America, and that country's very particular relationship to the car and its development.

Its spare, no-holds-barred script is structured around a number of sometimes perverse, sometimes joyless, sometimes verbally excoriating sex scenes. Characters pair off in various permutations. Not since actor Udo Kier fucked his own monster in Andy Warhol's Flesh for Franken- stein *have audiences witnessed the erotic opportunities offered by an open wound: to Cronenberg, a neo-sex organ.*

Like the earliest Cronenberg experiments, Crash *evinces no waste, no mercy, no way out. Despite the overheated nature of the raw material, it is handled with the precision and formal restraint of an expert surgeon with years of experience behind the scalpel. The film's power to disturb lies in its apparent coolness, its refusal to get too excited. When so much of contemporary cinema is in a permanent state of premature ejaculation over nothing,* Crash *gives us every reason to boil over, but continually chills the blood. Unable to seek refuge in the delirium of a fever, the viewer is therefore consigned to an unsettling state of total awareness in the face of delirious behaviour. And, as in the very best of Cronenberg, when a hard-won emotion eventually surfaces, a single frame of that scene could put twenty mainstream American movies on permanent life support.*

When Cronenberg embarked on Crash, *perhaps he glimpsed his original creations in the rear-view mirror and saw them fast retreating, like a landscape he didn't want to leave behind. Maybe he saw the Starliner Apartments of* Shivers, *disappearing like a concrete-and-glass sun below the horizon. The sight obviously triggered a longing in him. He slammed the car into reverse gear and crashed into his own arms. Now we're back where he started when he declared 'I want to show the unshowable. Speak the unspeakable'. Twenty years on, his wants are undiminished.*

Great books often make very bad films. J. G. Ballard's Crash *is so original and so complete a vision in itself that it must have seemed a daunting challenge.*

It's also hermetically sealed. But there was something about it that I thought really *did* lend itself to being distilled and transformed into a film. You can only go on your instinct. When I finally started to write it, I was surprised just *how* directly it distilled. I thought I would be doing a lot more funny stuff, like inventing other characters, changing things structurally. But it distilled in a very *pure* way. And what was left was not only the essence of the book, but a living thing in its own right.

With The Naked Lunch, *you said it was a matter of choosing exactly when to do a film adaptation. That you had to let it alone until you felt you could assert yourself over the material. Was that the case with* Crash?

I might have put the book away before I finished it, because I was afraid that I *was* going to want to make it into a movie. That was probably the gestation period: between when I didn't finish it and when I did. But then I didn't think about it for a couple of years. I think it needed that time to settle.

Have you managed to make Crash *the novel into a Cronenberg film?*

Every day you're making a thousand decisions about what a film should be. It's hard to feel that it's *not* you. I think this is a lovely fusion of me and Ballard. We're so amazingly in sync. We completely understand what we're both doing. Right down to why he called the main character 'James Ballard'. There was never a question in my mind that I wouldn't call that character James Ballard. I knew why he did it. For some people it might seem strange. It *is* quite unusual. It might be unprecedented for an author to write a book like *Crash* and name the main character after himself. All of these things just seem so right to me.

You and Burroughs are very different as people, in that Burroughs lived his books. Are you closer to Ballard? He has always distinguished between his imaginative life and his 'ordinary' daily existence.

I think that's true. Although I don't know if I could live in Shepperton! But even when you talk to Burroughs he'll say, 'Look, I spend 70 per cent of my life sitting at a desk, so how adventurous is that?' And now he lives in Lawrence, Kansas. That makes Toronto seem adventuresome! But I do know what you mean. The Ballard character in *Crash* could just as easily have been called David Cronenberg, and it would have the same relationship to me as Ballard the character does to Ballard the writer.

The shooting script of Crash *is only 77 pages. Very short. Was that intentional?*

Yes. I've been doing that for some time. It's part of what I think is my strength as a producer/director. It's a question of control. I shoot slow, with a lot of attention to detail. I'd rather focus microscopically on 77 pages. I like to have the script really pared down.

It's also an issue of budget. If I'd had a 120-page version of *Crash*, I couldn't have afforded the movie. My shooting schedule wouldn't have been any longer in terms of days, but it would have been almost half the time that I needed to do it right. I remember George Bernard Shaw saying that the length of a play is dictated by the capacity of the human bladder. You've got to get up and pee!

I like things to be taut and intense. To make a two-hour movie of *Crash* would be so draining people would hate me for it! If you're going to do *different* material on low budgets, that's a critical thing. Also, with a 77-page script I'm building a protection for myself and my actors. I can guarantee them that I have control, that I have final cut. That's part of directing actors.

It's a very hardcore script. When it was completed, were there any 'worried' reactions initially?

My then agent at CAA, who I still like very much, said, 'Do not do this movie. It will end your career.' When I said, 'I really want to do this,' he said, 'OK, then forget I said this. As a friend and business associate I felt I had to tell you.' I changed agents ultimately, and certainly that moment had something to do with it, because he really wanted me to do films like *The Juror* with Demi Moore. So I figured that we weren't talking about the same stuff. We'll see if *Crash* ends my career. I don't think so. I've never been in competition at Cannes before. That's definitely a good career thing!

To get this script made, did it have to be low-budget?

It was *always* going to be a low budget. There was no question. It was obvious from the word go that under $10 million was really what we were talking about. The question then became how far under 10 million.

After the big-budget location extravaganza of M. Butterfly, *was* Crash *intended as a back-to-basics Cronenberg movie?*

Absolutely. That was very conscious. But it wasn't just the budget. It was also subject matter. My last three pictures have basically been studio pictures. Even *M. Butterfly*, despite the location shooting. Here we were shooting in Toronto locations with available light. There was no way we could afford to light three miles of road. It was very much like shooting *Scanners*. This means you have to absorb and incorporate what's there. It's much more like found art, and that's very exhilarating.

What's interesting is that this extended to the music as well. Since *Dead Ringers* my composer, Howard Shore, had gotten into the habit of going to London and recording with an 84-piece orchestra! We didn't have the budget, so he came to Toronto. He hasn't recorded in Toronto since *Videodrome*. So it would be: first day, do the whole movie with three harps; second day, do the whole movie with six electric guitars; third day, do the whole movie with two percussionists. Very much like we did on *Scanners* and *Videodrome*. We had many discussions about returning to the old style, except we felt we were a lot better at it! But the techniques and the parameters were like the old days.

Seeing Crash, *I was immediately reminded of very early Cronenberg.* Shivers *and* Rabid *mainly. Like those two, it is uncompromising, very stark and very bleak.*

I don't disagree. I was also thinking of the Darryl Revok character in *Scanners*. Vaughan in *Crash* does seem very much like my own creatures, who were emerging at the same time Ballard was writing his creatures.

There also seems to be a sci-fi link. Ballard's version of science fiction isn't dissimilar to the worlds of Videodrome, Scanners *or* Shivers. *Is it or isn't it the future?*

Yeah. The conceit that underlies some of what is maybe difficult or

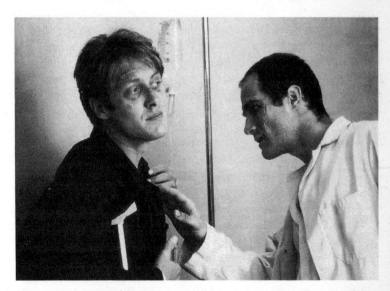

63 One of Cronenberg's visceral versions of Vaughan: Darryl Revok
(Michael Ironside) in *Scanners*.
64 Vaughan (Elias Koteas) admires Ballard's (James Spader) bruises.

baffling about *Crash*, the sci-fi-ness, comes from Ballard anticipating a future pathological psychology. It's developing now, but he anticipates it being even more developed in the future. He then brings it back to the past – now – and applies it as though it exists completely formed. So I have these characters who are exhibiting a psychology of the future.

I think that'll be tricky for some people. If they try to apply the normal movie psychology to these characters, they're doomed to be confused, baffled and perhaps frustrated by *Crash* Where are the sympathetic characters? Where is this recognizable domesticity that is then destroyed by Vaughan?

Some potential distributors said, 'You should make them more normal at the beginning so that we can see where they go wrong.' In other words, it would be like a *Fatal Attraction* thing. Blissful couple, maybe a dog and a rabbit, maybe a kid. And then a car accident introduces them to these horrible people and they go wrong. I said 'That isn't right, because there's something wrong with them right *now*. That's why they're vulnerable to going even further.' The novel is uncompromising in that way. Why shouldn't the movie be?

Ballard loves the film and says it is even more extreme than the book. Do you agree?

In the book you're in the head of the character James Ballard. There's that interior monologue thing that fiction does so beautifully, and which movies cannot do at all. Maybe that would give people more of a feeling of empathy for the character. But not much. When Ballard says that I go even further than the book, that delights me. I don't know how accurate it is though. I think it might just be a difference in the media. The immediacy of movie reality might do that on its own.

Hearing that Holly Hunter was to play Helen Remington, it sounded like radical casting. How did you decide on her?

I've had some people saying angrily. 'I don't know what Holly Hunter was doing in this movie!' Outraged. But that's Holly. She wants to outrage those people. She was the first in! I hadn't even sent the script out. Her agent phoned me and said, 'Holly wants to play Helen Remington.' Holly is tough in ways her fans don't realize. She's not afraid. She had let me know as far back as *Dead Ringers* that she liked my movies and wanted to work with me. So you see an actor saying, 'OK, so

65 Consenting sex between crash victims: Ballard and Remington
(Holly Hunter).
66 Back-seat love – while Ballard gazes.

67 Rosanna Arquette's caged, neo-sex organs.

I've got some power now. I've got some fame and clout and what I want to do is work with these people who always seem to do things that I wish I was in.'

We did have some discussions, but always with the understanding that she was already in. This was a character she wanted to explore. You can imagine the kind of things that Holly must get offered. None of them would be like Helen Remington! So we talked about the function of the character in the script.

What about James Spader?

Well, I was really surprised that right away he wanted to do it, because he's done so many different kinds of movies it's hard to know. It was obvious he wasn't afraid to play unromantic or strange characters. But I didn't realize the depths to which he was willing to go in terms of exploring the *dark*. He really was an incredible collaborator and buddy once we started. He said that he was afraid of the script, as well as being intrigued, terrified and mystified by it. But he absolutely wanted to do it. So I thought, 'He's my kind of guy.' He *did* want to know who else was going to be in *Crash*, because he said, 'After all I *do* fuck everybody in the movie.' So I thought, 'He's going to be fine.' And by God he was more than fine.

How did he cope with doing certain scenes? He has to fuck a wound in Rosanna Arquette's crash-damaged leg!

In the character that Rosanna Arquette played, there's a definite humour involved. But people are pretty grossed out by that scene, I must say. But for me and for James it was just, 'Well, it's in the book, and it's in the script.' It made perfect sense and was integral to what's happening with those characters at that time: being involved in a strange sexuality that is a mutation – not genetically but physically – through scars, car crashes, and self-mutilation. It was just a question of how to do the scene *effectively*. The way you would do a dialogue scene.

I did a little rehearsing with this movie because the actors requested it. As Holly put it, it's really a matter of comfort. Getting to know each other, given what everybody had to do. So we sat and talked and told stories, read scenes, discussed what were the nuances of the dialogue and how could we best make them work.

There's another very confrontational scene of anal sex between Deborah Unger and Spader. They're in bed, and Unger talks throughout their fucking about Vaughan and his car. How it must smell of stale semen et cetera.

She's very verbal there because what's happening is that they're incorporating Vaughan into their sex life. So the way she talks – getting her husband aroused by talking about him having homosexual sex with Vaughan – means there are really *three* people in that scene. That is very close to how the scene is in the book.

That *was* a difficult scene to do, but in bizarre ways. You can't get hair to look the same when it's messy! You can't get pillows to scrunch up the same way! I had those agonies, as well as getting the scene to work. For the movements to be sexy, elegant but awkward. And finding the right tone. It's difficult for actors physically when you're doing a lot of takes.

You did a lot of takes on that!?

Oh yeah. Several masters, and several of each close-up. We had to take breaks and stuff. One of the ways that I worked in this movie was to let the actors look at tapes of what they'd done. I've known directors who won't tape what they're shooting, or who deliberately use horrible black-and-white monitors so the actors won't look good. I had the *best* colour monitor I could possibly find, and I showed my actors whatever they wanted to see. It was a measure of trust. They could see exactly how they looked naked, how they looked talking, or where their ass was when their skirt was pulled up. If they were going to freak out and be upset then fuck it, they were going to freak out and be upset and we'd discuss it. I found it was well worth the time on the set in terms of just finessing what they were doing.

The sex in the movie is rarely face to face. It's usually rear-entry or anal. Why is that?

It's the choice I made. I liked the way it looked. It felt right, getting both the actors looking towards the camera and not at each other. It helped that sort of 'disconnected' thing. It's been suggested that I'm obsessed with asses, but I like everything, you know. I don't think I'm too overly obsessed with asses. It's more, 'How do you have sex when you're not quite having sex with each other?' That kind of thing.

The movie begins with three sex scenes in a row. Again, this seems very confrontational.

It is. There are moments when audiences burst out laughing, either in disbelief or exasperation. They can't believe that they're going to have to look at *another* sex scene. To me that was replicating the tone of the book, which was absolutely unrelenting and confrontational. I thought that was one way I could replicate that.

In fact, rarely does a sex scene appear in isolation. They usually come in pairs!

And they all mean different things too. Each one leads to the other one. The first scene is of Deborah Unger with this anonymous guy in a airplane hangar. Then James Spader with an anonymous camera girl. They're parallel of course. And then James and Deborah come together, fuck, and compare notes. That's how they develop their sexuality. In one of my little test screenings someone said, 'A series of sex scenes is not a plot.' And I said, 'Why not? Who says? It worked for Arthur Schnitzler.' And the answer is that it *can* be, but not when the sex scenes are the normal kind of sex scenes: lyrical little interludes and then on with the real movie. Those can usually be cut out and not change the plot or characters one iota. In *Crash*, very often the sex scenes are *absolutely* the plot and the character development. You can't take them out. These are not twentieth-century sexual relationships or love relationships. These are something else. We're saying that a normal, upper-middle-class couple might have this as their norm in the not-so-distant future.

I was struck by the desire in the film to merge with metal and technology. It reminded me of ideas like the handgun in Videodrome.

A car is not the highest of high tech. But it *has* affected us and changed us more than anything else in the last hundred years. We *have* incorporated it. The weird privacy in public that it gives us. The sexual freedom – which in the 50s wasn't even subtle! I mean, the first guy who had a convertible in high school was the guy who had the sex. He could take girls out to the country and do things to them. You'd have to take the fucking bus, and that's not the same. He had a mobile bedroom. That's exactly what it was, and that element hasn't changed. Maybe that's why people still refuse to take public transport! If they had little isolated sleepers in the subways, maybe it would work better.

So we have already incorporated the car into our understanding of time, space, distance and sexuality. To want to merge with it literally in a more physical way seems a good metaphor. There is a desire to fuse with techno-ness.

And yet in Crash *doing this seems to lead inevitably to death. The body is destroyed in this process of merging.*

That's just an acknowledgement of the way it works with humans, which is more disguised than – let's say – with a salmon. After salmon spawn, they're so exhausted they die. Their sexuality and desire lead them to death. But there's a sense in which *Crash* – the book and the movie – are totally above death. They are about how much human control, and human will, are going to be involved in that.

When Ballard claims the dead Vaughan's car at the end, it's as if he's claiming his body. The movie does seem to imply that after a fatal crash, a merging has taken place.

Yes. I still remember when Marilyn Monroe's body wasn't immediately claimed. As a kid I thought, 'Well fuck, *I'll* claim her body. OK, she's dead, but she's still Marilyn Monroe.' I thought, 'Boy, that's very strange. This body that was the most desired body in the history of humankind, and no one will claim it.' Taking the car in that scene is exactly like claiming Marilyn Monroe's body.

Is the movie tapping into current obsessions with body-piercing and scarification?

Oh yeah. I've seen some very middle-class people with eyebrow rings and stuff like that. I think they would be mortified if you said it was self-mutilation, or very primitive, or related to scarification but without the ritual tribal structures that justify it. It's a huge, not-so-far underground culture. And tattooing. That's why I had a Lincoln steering-wheel shape tattooed on Vaughan's chest towards the end. That was my invention. But I'm sure someone somewhere has that – anticipating having a steering wheel buried in their chest in a crash.

Can you discuss your view on the characters' desire to explore the sexual excitement of the car crash?

It's making very conscious what is already out there. It's not so far-fetched. Apparently at one of the early LA screenings of *Crash* they were doing some focus-group thing and a guy came down waving his arm – which was in a cast – saying, 'I've just been through the hell of a motorcycle accident and I broke my arm and there was nothing sexy about it. It was just hell and I think Cronenberg's gone psycho.' I don't think too many people will take the movie on that level and maybe go out and do it. But one of the reasons this movie puts pressure on the unconscious is because this is something that has flitted through every-one's mind on one level or another at some time.

Ballard really touched on those aspects of writing about cars that can really arouse you. Surprise you. You find things arousing that you never thought could be: his descriptions of semen on steering wheels and instrument panels, and of how it got there. It was techno-sex.

Vaughan and his motley group reminded me very much of the low-life souls at the Cathode Ray Mission in Videodrome. *Or the scanners, who were derelicts.*

In most sci-fi movies it's usually the elite who are on the cutting edge of whatever's going on, but I think it's quite the contrary. It's going to be a grassroots-type movement. Those are the ones who are not fighting it, not analysing it, not organizing it. They're just experiencing it.

The characters want to embrace the car crash, a potentially life-threatening event, rather as characters approach disease in your earlier films. In the script, Vaughan actually says that we must see the crash as a 'fertilizing' event. Not a destructive one.

Yeah. That is a line right out of Ballard. And yet it is so much my line about parasites being a good thing rather than a bad thing. Or viruses being a creative force rather than a destructive force, if seen from their perspective. Absolutely.

But it's also about the tension between reality and that whole idea of an idealized life. It's strange to me that we can conceive of a life that possibly no one has ever lived and say that that life is ideal: what we should aspire to and strive to attain. That's always seemed quite odd to me, even though fantasy often precedes reality. You need the fantasy to give shape to the reality you're trying to move towards.

In *Crash* I'm saying that if some harsh reality envelops you, rather than be crushed, destroyed or diminished by it, embrace it fully. Develop it and take it even further than it wanted to go itself. See if that's not a creative endeavour. If that is not positive.

And the more strange and grotesque the circumstances, the more interesting it becomes. It's also me picking up on some of the philosophical tone of Ballard; trying to figure out once again my own little philosophy of life.

About the look of the movie. It's very stark. Simple. Very European in sense.

It feels that way to me, too. I like things to be deceptive in their simplicity. But sometimes the simplest things are the most difficult to do. The way I put the camera on the cars, for instance. The framing is not quite normal. I was thinking, 'I'm not going to do the usual tricky stuff. I'm not going to use wide-angle lenses from above and underneath, because it's so distracting.' And yet I *do* want to suggest people wrapped up in their cars: their relationship to their cars. So the framing is unusual, but in a very simple way.

It's really a matter of exactly where you put the camera. Not that simple. Each day, after choreographing the first scene to be shot, that would be the first thing I would do. I put it more *outboard* of the car body so that the windshield pillar was halfway through the frame, and the other half is looking right down the car body. That meant building rigs. You don't see that much because it takes a lot of time and it's hard to do. Shooting on a platform means you can dolly while the cars are moving. We had six Lincolns; one of them cut in half, one of them made into a pick-up truck so that I could dolly and put lights on from behind.

We got the roads department in Toronto excited about the movie. They closed a lot of things for us that they swore they would never close. Much to the dismay of some politician. We were going to get the Gardner Freeway because they were working on it, but they finished it early. Politicians came out and said, 'Due to the wonderful efficiency of your politicians, we now can open the road *this* weekend.' So we said, 'Sorry. You promised that *we* would have it that weekend.' So they had to *keep* it closed. Embarrassing.

The car crashes are unusual for 90s cinema in that they're very unspectacular. Why was that?

I wanted them to be fast, brutal and over before you knew it. There's not one foot of slow motion. No repeated shots. I wanted to make them realistic in a cinematic way, because it's the *aftermath* that is delicious: that can be savoured and apprehended by the senses. What happens during a crash itself is too fast to feel without slow-motion replay. Most of us don't get replays on our car crashes.

Ballard says that Crash *is a cautionary tale from the eye of the hurricane. Do you think it's timely in that we're approaching the millennium, and this century has definitely been the century of the car?*

Well, the place of the car in the world economy can't be overestimated. Although people don't think of cars as being very high tech, every high-tech development is represented somewhere in a car. Whether it's fibre-optic electronics, or in the metallurgy. All of these incredible industries serve the car.

So if suddenly we said, 'There can't be any more cars, we're stopping today,' it would be the end of the world: economies diving, people not knowing what to do with themselves. Our attachment to it, as discussed in the movie, is very primitive indeed. It has become the quintessential human appendage. I think it won't go away easily. It's got a lot of shape-shifting to do before it disappears.

What surprised you most about making Crash?

It has become a very *emotional* movie. In the beginning it wasn't, and certainly I would never have said that about the book. I find that people come away having been really shaken, feeling very emotional but not knowing why or how. It doesn't push any of the usual buttons. And that's really good. There's going to be a lot of different reactions. I do think we might get a lot of people throwing things. I'm prepared for that. But I don't really like being rejected. You know that. I really do want to make movies that everyone loves!

For your last movie you went to the Great Wall of China. Was there a sense with Crash *that you were – in more senses than one – coming home?*

Definitely. And I took considerable strength from that. We literally shot the whole movie within half a mile of my house. I like that very much. I'd drive by all the locations every day on my way to the editing room. There's a wonderful sense of this movie being physically and tangibly a part of my life, a part of my daily, mundane life as well as my artistic life. That's very satisfying. Something that I haven't experienced quite that way for some time. It's good.

68 On the verge of a breakthrough, the Ballards (James Spader and Deborah Unger) consummate survival.

Filmography

1966

Transfer

'*Transfer*, my first film, was a surreal sketch for two people – a psychiatrist and his patient – at a table set for dinner in the middle of a field covered in snow. The psychiatrist has been followed by his obsessive former patient. The only relationship the patient has had which has meant anything to him has been with the psychiatrist. The patient complains that he has invented things to amuse and occasionally worry the psychiatrist but that he has remained unappreciative of his efforts' (David Cronenberg).

Director: David Cronenberg
Screenplay: David Cronenberg
Cinematography (colour): David Cronenberg
Sound: Margaret Hindson, Stephen Nosko
Editor: David Cronenberg
Cast: Mort Ritts, Rafe Macpherson
7 mins, 16mm

1967

From the Drain

'*From the Drain* is a surrealist sketch in which two men, fully clothed, sit and talk in a bath at a veterans' home in the distant future. They discuss changes that have taken place in human and plant biology. A plant comes up from the drain and kills one of the men and the other man disposes of the shoes which have been left behind in a closet full of shoes. It becomes evident that a plot is underfoot to murder the veterans of the war so that they will not talk publicly about it' (David Cronenberg).

Director: David Cronenberg
Screenplay: David Cronenberg
Cinematography (colour): David Cronenberg
Editor: David Cronenberg
Cast: Mort Ritts, Stephen Nosko
14 mins, 16mm

1969

Stereo

The future. The Canadian Academy for Erotic Inquiry is investigating the theories of parapsychologist Luther Stringfellow. Seven young adults submit to a form of brain surgery which removes their power of speech and increases their potential for telepathic communication. An unseen group of students observes the results. As the experiment progresses, Stringfellow's theories are borne out. Later, aphrodisiacs and various drugs are introduced into the subjects' diet in order to expose an inherent 'polymorphous perversity'. Finally, they are isolated from each other, provoking antagonism and violence between them, and two suicides.

Production company: Emergent Films
Producer: David Cronenberg
Director: David Cronenberg
Screenplay: David Cronenberg
Cinematography (black and white): David Cronenberg
Editor: David Cronenberg
Production aides: Stephen Nosko, Pedro McCormick, Janet G. M. Good
Cast: Ronald Mlodzik, Iain Ewing, Jack Messinger, Clara Mayer, Paul Mulholland, Arlene Mlodzik, Glenn McCauley and others
65 mins, 35mm

1970

Crimes of the Future

The future. Millions of post-pubertal females have died from Rouge's Malady – a disease caused by cosmetics and discovered by mad dermatologist Antoine Rouge. Although Rouge has disappeared (possibly a victim of the disease), his clinic The House of Skin is managed by loyal disciple Adrian Tripod, lost without his master's guidance. He meets an old colleague at the Institute of Neo-Venereal Disease, whose body is producing mysterious, functionless new organs. With the remaining male population in psychic relapse, Tripod joins the Oceanic Podiatry Group's therapy programme, but is approached by Tiomkin, who heads a conspiracy of heterosexual paedophiles. Their sole purpose is to impregnate a little girl brought prematurely to puberty to avoid Rouge's Malady. The girl is kidnapped, but no one in the group will impregnate her. Tripod is chosen but hesitates in front of her, sensing the presence of Antoine Rouge . . .

Production company: Emergent Films, with the participation of the Canadian Film Development Corporation (CFDC)
Producer: David Cronenberg
Director: David Cronenberg
Screenplay: David Cronenberg
Cinematography (colour): David Cronenberg
Editor: David Cronenberg
Production assistant: Stephen Nosko
Titles: Jon Lidolt
Cast: Ronald Mlodzik (*Adrian Tripod*), John Lidolt, Tania Zolty, Jack Messinger, Iain Ewing, Rafe Macpherson, Willem Poolman, Donald Owen, Norman Snider, Stephen Czernecki and others
65 mins, 35mm

1971

While in France, Cronenberg scripted, photographed and directed the following 16mm fillers for Canadian television:

Jim Ritchie Sculptor
The work of Montreal sculptor Jim Ritchie, living in France at the time. No narration. Music track.

Letter from Michelangelo
Text: Michelangelo
Voice-over: Paul Mulholland

Tourettes
No narration. Music track

1972

On returning to Canada, Cronenberg scripted, photographed and directed the following 16mm fillers for Canadian television. All are 5/6 mins with music track only:

Don Valley
Fort York
Lakeshore
Winter Garden
Scarborough Bluffs
In the Dirt

Secret Weapons
1977. After five years of civil war, the gigantic drug company General Pharmaceuticals has taken over society, and seeks a monopoly in supplying troops with meta adrenalines. A former research scientist, now experimenting with aggression stimulants, is recalled for security vetting. Unwilling to surrender his findings, he is sent to a retreat run by the Holy Police. Using psychic judo he escapes and makes contact with a resistance group – a bike gang led by a woman who believes only in rebellion itself.

Production company: Emergent Films for the Canadian Broadcasting Corporation (*Programme X*)
Executive producer: Paddy Sampson
Associate producer: George Jonas
Director: David Cronenberg
Screenplay: Norman Snider
Cinematography (colour): David Cronenberg
Commentary: Lister Sinclair
Cast: Barbara O'Kelly (*motorcycle-gang leader*), Norman Snider (*the scientist*), Vernon Chapman (*the bureaucrat*), Ronald Mlodzik, Bruce Martin, Tom Skudra, Moses Smith, Michael D. Spencer, G. Chalmers Adams
27 mins, 16mm
Broadcast: 1 June 1972

1975

Shivers

(a.k.a. *They Came from Within*, *The Parasite Murders*)

Dr Emil Hobbes has supposedly been breeding a form of parasite that can take over the function of failing body organs, in order to save life. However, his true purpose is to cure man's over-rationality. The Hobbes parasite is actually a sexually transmitted bug which, having entered the body, acts as an aphrodisiac, thereby ensuring that it continues to spread to other bodies. Having implanted it in a sexually active young girl who resides in the luxurious Starliner Towers apartment complex, Hobbes realizes the imminent danger too late. Killing himself and the girl, the bug is already at work in Andrew Tudor, another of the girl's lovers in the Starliner. Despite efforts by resident physician Dr Roger St Luc and Hobbes's duped partner Rollo Linsky, the bug spreads throughout the luxurious apartments, transforming them into a high-rise orgy of chaos, death and destruction. At the end, the surviving infected inhabitants calmly leave their haven in convoy, setting off to infect the world.

Production company: DAL Productions Ltd, with the participation of the CFDC
Producers: Ivan Reitman, John Dunning, André Link
Director: David Cronenberg
Screenplay: David Cronenberg
Cinematography (colour): Robert Saad
Sound: Michael Higgs
Editor: Patrick Dodd
Music: Ivan Reitman
Special make-up and creatures created by: Joe Blasco
Cast: Paul Hampton (*Roger St Luc*), Joe Silver (*Rollo Linsky*), Lynn Lowry (*Forsythe*), Allan Migicovsky (*Nicholas Tudor*), Susan Petrie (*Janine Tudor*), Barbara Steele (*Betts*), Ronald Mlodzik (*Merrick*), Barrie Baldero (*Detective Heller*), Camille Ducharme (*Mr Guilbault*), Hanka Posnanka (*Mrs Guilbault*) and others
87 mins, 35mm

The Victim

Donald makes crank phone calls. His small apartment is littered with images of bondage, female underwear and a collection of news clippings about rape and violence. He continually pesters Lucy, a housewife, who refuses to be intimidated by his calls. Eventually she asks him over. When he enters her apartment, he finds himself in a custom-built cage, with Lucy now the dominant, sexy animal-tamer.

Production company: Canadian Broadcasting Corporation (*Peep Show*)
Executive producer: George Bloomfield
Producer: Deborah Peaker
Director: David Cronenberg
Screenplay: Ty Haller
Cameras (colour): Eamonn Beglan, Ron Manson, John Halenda, Dave Doherty, Peter Brimson
Sound: Brian Radford, Bill Dunn
VT editor: Garry Fisher
Art director: Nickolai Soliov

69 David Cronenberg and Ivan Reitman (kneeling) during the shooting of *Shivers*.

Cast: Janet Wright (*Lucy*), Jonathan Welsh (*Donald*), Cedric Smith (*man on park bench*)
27 mins, 2″ VTR
Broadcast: 22 January 1976

The Lie Chair

Neil and Carol are stranded in their car one stormy night. They take refuge in an isolated house where two old ladies, Mildred and Mrs Rogers, live. With the phone out of action, they are encouraged to stay the night. Gradually they are also persuaded to inhabit the identities of the ladies' long-departed grandchildren.

Production company: Canadian Broadcasting Corporation (*Peep Show*)
Executive producer: George Bloomfield
Producer: Eoin Sprott
Director: David Cronenberg
Screenplay: David Cole
Cameras (colour): Eamonn Beglan, George Clemens, Tom Farquharson, Peter Brimson
Sound: Roland Huebsche, Bill Dunn
Set designer: Rudi Dorn
Cast: Richard Monette (*Neil*), Susan Hogan (*Carol*), Amelia Hall (*Mildred*), Doris Petrie (*Mrs Rogers*)
27 mins, 2″ VTER
Broadcast: 12 February 1976

1976

The Italian Machine

Lionel, Fred and Bug, a trio of bike freaks, hear that a local dealer has come into possession of a Ducati Desmo Super Sport, an extremely rare and beautiful Italian motorbike. However, it has already been sold to Mouette, an art collector. Posing as journalists for *Techno Art World* magazine, they visit Mouette and find the bike on display as a sculpture in his living room, along with Ricardo, also kept by the dealer and his wife Lana as an art object. Lionel bribes Ricardo by offering drugs in exchange for his interesting Mouette in the metaphysical proposition of one 'artwork' purchasing another – an event surely worth documenting by the New York art magazines. Mouette agrees, Lana acquires a new 'living' sculpture, and the boys ride off on their machines.

Production company: Canadian Broadcasting Corporation (*Teleplay*)
Executive producer: Stephen Patrick
Director: David Cronenberg
Screenplay: David Cronenberg
Photography (colour): Nicholas Evdemon
Sound: Tom Bilenky
Editor: David Denovan
Music consultant: Patrick Russell
Art director: Peter Douet
Cast: Gary McKeehan (*Lionel*), Frank Moore (*Fred*), Hardee Linehan (*Bug*), Chuch Shamata (*Reinhardt*), Louis Negin (*Mouette*), Toby Tarnow (*Lana*), Geza Kovacs (*Ricardo*), Cedrick Smith (*Luke*)
28 mins, 16mm

Rabid

Montreal. Hart and his girlfriend Rose are involved in a bad motorcycle accident in the countryside, near the Keloid Clinic. Dr Dan Keloid has to perform emergency plastic surgery on Rose, in order to save her life. His relatively untried radical techniques backfire when neutralized tissue refuses to form the intestines she so desperately needs. When she comes round, Rose finds that the only food she can digest is blood, which she extracts from her victims through the penis-like organ she has developed in her armpit. Scared, and now a vampire, she escapes the hospital to seek the sustenance her new body requires. By extracting a little blood, Rose spreads a form of rabies which transforms her victims into violent crazies, all of whom eventually die. The city of Montreal becomes a major danger zone, and martial law is declared. Hart tracks her down, and confronts her with the truth. Disbelieving herself to be the cause of the epidemic, she locks herself in with one of her victims and is killed by him. Along with thousands of others, she ends up thrown in the back of a large rubbish truck.

Production company: Cinema Entertainment Enterprises (for DAL Productions Ltd) with the participation of the CFDC
Executive producers: André Link, Ivan Reitman
Producer: John Dunning
Director: David Cronenberg
Screenplay: David Cronenberg
Cinematography (colour): René Verzier
Sound: Richard Lightstone
Editor: Jean Lafleur
Music: Ivan Reitman
Art director: Claude Marchand
Special make-up design: Joe Blasco Makeup Associates
Cast: Marilyn Chambers (*Rose*), Frank Moore (*Hart Read*), Joe Silver (*Murray Cypher*), Howard Ryshpan (*Dr Dan Keloid*), Patricia Gage (*Dr Roxanne Keloid*), Susan Roman (*Mindy Kent*), J. Roger Periard (*Lloyd Walsh*), Lynne Deragon (*nurse Louise*), Terry Schonblum (*Judy Glasberg*), Victor Desy (*Claude LePointe*) and others
91 mins, 35mm

1979

Fast Company

Corrupt Fastco team manager Phil Adamson forces veteran drag racer Lonnie 'Lucky Man' Johnson to take his team mate Billy Brooker's car at a race meeting in order to beat independent driver Gary Black in the 'funny car' class. Let down, Lonnie later denigrates Fastco's products in a TV interview. Adamson attempts to persuade Billy's girlfriend to seduce the interviewer, and fires her when she refuses. After a fight with Lonnie, Adamson gets Black's mechanic Meatball to fix his car, resulting in a fireball. Adamson has their team car stolen, but it is discovered in a motorshow exhibition hall. Lonnie enters it in a grudge contest with Black at the Edmonton raceway but, unaware that Adamson and Meatball are again plotting, offers the ride to Billy. However, Black falls victim to Meatball's sabotage and dies. Attempting to escape by plane, Adamson is chased along the runway by Lonnie's dragster, and crashes. Lonnie and his crew rejoin the circuit.

Production company: Michael Lebowitz Inc. (for Quadrant Films Ltd) with the participation of the CFDC
Executive producer: David M. Perlmutter
Producer: Michael Lebowitz, Peter O'Brian, Courtney Smith
Director: David Cronenberg
Screenplay: Phil Savath, Courtney Smith, David Cronenberg, from an original story by Alan Treen
Cinematography (colour): Mark Irwin
Sound: Bryan Day
Editor: Ronald Sanders
Music: Fred Mollin
Art director: Carol Spier
Cast: William Smith (*Lonnie Johnson*), Claudia Jennings (*Sammy*), John Saxon (*Phil Adamson*), Nicholas Campbell (*Billy Brooker*), Cedrick Smith (*Gary Black*), Judy Foster (*Candy*), George Buza (*Meatball*), Robert Haley (*P.J.*), David Graham (*Stoner*), Don Francks ('*Elder*') and others
91 mins, 35mm

The Brood

Dr Hal Raglan has perfected the practice of Psychoplasmics: the treatment of serious mental disorder through its physical manifestation in the body. One of his patients is Nola Carveth, a woman full of rage for her parents and estranged husband Frank. She is kept under lock and key at Raglan's Somafree Institute in the country outside Toronto. When daughter Candice returns home from one of her visits to see her mother with bruises on her back, Frank decides to investigate further, and legally to prevent Nola having access to the child. Both of Nola's parents are mysteriously and brutally killed by strange midgets, who also attack and murder Candice's teacher, who has some affection for Frank. One of these creatures is found dead, and appears to have no navel. Frank breaks into Somafree, and to Nola's lair, where he discovers that her rage manifests itself in the form of self-made children – the brood – who act on her anger. With the help of a repentant Raglan, who is ultimately murdered by the brood, Frank strangles his wife and escapes with Candice. On the drive home, neither notices a small developing welt on her arm . . .

Production company: Les Productions Mutuelles and Elgin International Productions, with the participation of the CFDC
Executive producers: Victor Solnicki, Pierre David
Producer: Claude Héroux
Director: David Cronenberg
Screenplay: David Cronenberg
Cinematography (colour): Mark Irwin
Sound: Bryan Day
Editor: Alan Collins
Music: Howard Shore
Art director: Carol Spier
Special make-up: Jack Young, Dennis Pike
Cast: Oliver Reed (*Dr Hal Raglan*), Samantha Eggar (*Nola Carveth*), Art Hindle (*Frank Carveth*), Cindy Hinds (*Candice Carveth*), Henry Beckman (*Barton Kelly*), Nuala Fitz-Gerald (*Juliana Kelly*), Susan Hogan (*Ruth Mayer*), Michael Magee (*Inspector Mrazek*), Joseph Shaw (*Dr Desborough, coroner*), Gary McKeehan (*Mike Trellan*) and others
91 mins, 35mm

1980

Scanners

The near future. Social derelict Cameron Vale is taken to the mysterious Dr Paul Ruth, who understands his particular problem. Vale is a scanner – a telepathic misfit troubled by the unheard thoughts of others, and possessed of great powers of telekinesis. Ruth helps him with the drug ephemerol, which suppresses the voices, but he is also working for Consec, an organization specializing in international security, weaponry and private armies. Ruth is rounding up all known scanners to recruit them for intelligence purposes. Darryl Revok is the psychotic scanner leader of a rival group, attempting to do the same but to bring society to its knees. Vale is used by Ruth and Consec to penetrate this scanner underground, which he does with the help of Kim Obrist, a defector from Revok's group. Vale discovers that Revok is manufacturing vast quantities of ephemerol and supplying doctors nationwide, who are administering it to pregnant women to produce a new breed of scanner children. In a final confrontation Revok explains that he is Vale's brother, that Ruth was their father and inventor of ephemerol – originally a tranquillizer for pregnant women. He tested it on his own wife – their mother – and produced the first and strongest scanners: Vale and Revok. After a scanning battle between the brothers, Vale is physically destroyed but moves his mind into Revok's body.

Production company: Filmplan International Inc. with the participation of the CFDC
Executive producers: Pierre David, Victor Solnicki
Producer: Claude Héroux
Director: David Cronenberg
Screenplay: David Cronenberg
Cinematography (colour): Mark Irwin
Sound: Don Cohen
Editor: Ron Sanders
Music: Howard Shore
Art director: Carol Spier
Special make-up: Stephan Dupuis, Chris Walas, Tom Schwartz
Cast: Jennifer O'Neill (*Kim Obrist*), Stephen Lack (*Cameron Vale*), Patrick McGoohan (*Dr Paul Ruth*), Lawrence Z. Dane (*Braedon Keller*), Michael Ironside (*Darryl Revok*), Robert Silverman (*Benjamin Pierce*), Adam Ludwig (*Arno Crostic*), Mavor Moore (*Trevellyan*), Fred Doederlein (*Dieter Tautz*), Sony Forbes (*invader*) and others
103 mins, 35mm

1982

Videodrome

Max Renn, head of a Toronto cable station specializing in softcore violence and pornography, is looking for something that will 'break through'. Friend and ace satellite pirate Harlan 'accidentally' tracks down Videodrome – a snuff TV show comprising torture, murder and sadism – and is asked by Max to get a fix on it. A developing sadomasochistic relationship with radio personality Nicki Brand begins to escalate as Max becomes increasingly troubled by violent/sexual hallucinations. In attempting to locate the source of Videodrome, he discovers that it is encoded with a signal which induces a brain tumour, which eventually transforms the viewer's reality into video hallucination. Invented by media prophet Professor Brian O'Blivion as the next stage in man's evolution as a technological being, his partners – having killed him – intend to launch Videodrome as a mind-controlling device through Max's own morally bankrupt cable channel. Max, now suffering from extreme hallucinations of bodily mutation and murder, becomes the plaything of O'Blivion's daughter Bianca, the apparently treacherous Harlan and Barry Convex, the man determined to unleash Videodrome on a sick world. Max apparently kills his partners, Harlan and Convex, before going into hiding. On a television in a deserted barge, Nicki Brand appears and tells him to surrender the old flesh and embrace the new. He shoots himself.

Production company: Filmplan International II Inc., with the participation of the CFDC
Executive producers: Pierre David, Victor Solnicki
Producer: Claude Héroux
Director: David Cronenberg
Screenplay: David Cronenberg
Cinematography (colour): Mark Irwin
Sound: Bryan Day
Editor: Ron Sanders
Music: Howard Shore
Art director: Carol Spier
Special make-up design and creation: Rick Baker
Cast: James Woods (*Max Renn*), Sonja Smits (*Bianca O'Blivion*), Deborah Harry (*Nicki Brand*), Peter Dvorsky (*Harlan*), Les Carlson (*Barry Convex*), Jeck Creley (*Brian O'Blivion*), Lynne Gorman (*Masha*), Julie Khaner (*Bridey*), Reiner Shwarz (*Moses*), David Bolt (*Raphael*) and others
87 mins, 35mm

1983

The Dead Zone

Johnny Smith is to marry Sarah Bracknell, both teachers at their local school in New England. However, he is involved in a serious car accident, and awakes from a five-year coma to find that Sarah has since married someone else. Having to learn even to walk again, Johnny realizes that – even though his life has been dismantled – he now possesses the ability to see into people's lives: past, present and future. Now a local personality, he is asked by the police to help solve a serial-killer case with the aid of his 'gift'. He reluctantly agrees, having spent the only night he will ever have with Sarah. More and more reclusive, and cursed by his psychic ability, Johnny moves away and takes up private tuition, aware that every 'vision' takes him closer to death. Sarah reappears in his new life, campaigning for would-be Senator Greg Stillson. Johnny 'sees' that Stillson will, in the future, lead the world into nuclear conflict. The vision has a 'dead zone': a blank spot which indicates that he can intervene and change events. Johnny plans to assassinate Stillson but is shot in the attempt. While dying, he envisions Stillson committing suicide having been discredited by the event.

Production company: Dead Zone Productions in association with Lorimar Productions Inc.
Executive producer: Dino De Laurentiis
Producer: Debra Hill
Director: David Cronenberg
Screenplay: Jeffrey Boam, from a book by Stephen King

Cinematography (colour): Mark Irwin
Sound: Bryan Day
Editor: Ron Sanders
Music: Michael Kamen
Production design: Carol Spier
Cast: Christopher Walken (*Johnny Smith*), Brooke Adams (*Sarah Bracknell*), Martin Sheen (*Greg Stillson*), Sean Sullivan (*Herb Smith*), Jackie Burroughs (*Vera Smith*), Herbert Lom (*Dr Sam Weizak*), Tom Skerritt (*Bannerman*), Anthony Zerbe (*Roger Stuart*), Nicholas Campbell (*Frank Dodd*), Peter Dvorsky (*Dardis*) and others
100 mins, 35mm

1985
Cronenberg made a cameo appearance in John Landis's *Into the Night*.

1986

The Fly
Brilliant young scientist Seth Brundle meets science journalist Veronica at a convention. Unwisely, he takes her to his laboratory to demonstrate teleportation: the successful disintegration and reintegration of inanimate matter through space. Veronica is eager to write a story about this astounding breakthrough, but Brundle convinces her to keep his secret until he can perfect the teleportation of living matter. A romance develops, but Stathis Borans – Veronica's jealous ex-lover and editor of *Particle* magazine – begins to interfere. Through his relationship with Veronica, Brundle begins to understand 'the flesh', and teaches this to his computer, which finally teleports a living baboon successfully. However, one night, Brundle – misunderstanding Veronica's relationship with Borans – teleports himself and an unseen housefly. They are genetically spliced, and Brundle, initially super-strong and healthy, begins to mutate into something grotesque. Veronica, pregnant with his baby, is kidnapped from an abortion clinic by Brundlefly, who plans to fuse them both together to help make himself more human. Veronica is saved by Borans but Brundlefly is accidentally fused with a telepod. The resulting monster silently pleads for release. Sobbing, Veronica shoots it.

Production company: Brooksfilms
Producer: Stuart Cornfeld
Director: David Cronenberg
Screenplay: Charles Edward Pogue, David Cronenberg, from a story by George Langelaan
Cinematography (colour): Mark Irwin
Sound: Bryan Day
Editor: Ronald Sanders
Music: Howard Shore
Production design: Carol Spier
The Fly created and designed by Chris Walas Inc.
Cast: Jeff Goldblum (*Seth Brundle*), Geena Davis (*Veronica Quaife*), John Getz (*Stathis Borans*), Joy Boushel (*Tawny*), Les Carlson (*Dr Cheevers*), George Chuvalo (*Marky*), Michael Copeman (*second man in bar*), David Cronenberg (*gynaecologist*), Carol Lazare (*nurse*), Shawn Hewitt (*clerk*) and others
92 mins, 35mm

1987

Faith Healer
(Episode 12 of the TV series 'Friday the 13th')
Bogus healer Stewart Fishoff finds an old glove in an alley. He discovers that it holds the miraculous power to absorb afflictions and transfer them to others. However, unless the glove quickly touches another person, the absorbed ailment is turned back on the wearer. Fisher achieves dizzying heights of fame, enabling the crippled to walk, the blind to see and the deaf to hear while secretly causing the deaths of innocent people. Catching his TV show, Jack Marshak recognizes the glove as an item from the antique store, and the true nature of Fishoff's miracles. Marshak enlists the help of a friend, Jerry Scott, a man famous for exposing frauds. Unbeknownst to Marshak, however, Scott's interest in the glove is personal. Suffering from a terminal illness, Scott needs the glove to cure himself . . . even at the expense of his old friend's life.

Production company: Paramount Television Inc.
Executive producer: Frank Mancuso, Jr.
Producer: Iain Paterson
Director: David Cronenberg
Teleplay: Christine Cornish
Cast: Christopher Wiggins (*Jack Marshak*), Miguel Fernandez (*Stewart Fishoff*), Robert Silverman (*Jerry Scott*), John D. LeMay (*Ryan*), Robey (*Micki Foster*) and others.
26 mins, colour

1988

Dead Ringers
In Toronto, Elliot and Beverly Mantle are famous. Not only are they identical twins, but they run a successful gynaecology clinic. They live together and share everything: glory, emotions, experiences and women. Visiting actress Claire Niveau attends the clinic, unable to bear children. The twins discover that she is a rare trifurcate, possessing three entrances to her womb. After Elliot sleeps with her and passes her on to his 'baby' brother, Beverly begins to fall in love with Claire. On discovering that she has been sleeping with two men, Claire is disgusted, leaving Beverly distraught and Elliot unmoved. Beverly's love for Claire begins to come between the brothers. Haunted by fears of separation, he begins – like Claire – to take more and more 'prescribed' drugs. As Elliot continues to climb the career ladder and Claire leaves for another film assignment, Beverly descends into a pill-popping melancholia and madness. The brothers are finally suspended from practice because of Beverly's attempted operation on a woman with instruments he has had made for operating on 'mutant women' – custom-built by sculptor Wolleck. As Beverly's mind goes, so does Elliot's. In an apartment they try to 'separate' with the help of self-surgery: Beverly cuts Elliot open. The next day, they are both on the floor dead.

Production company: Mantle Clinic II Ltd, in association with Morgan Creek Productions Inc. With the participation of Telefilm Canada.
Executive producers: Carol Baum, Sylvio Tabet
Producers: David Cronenberg, Marc Boyman
Director: David Cronenberg

Screenplay: David Cronenberg, Norman Snider, based on the book *Twins* by Bari Wood and Jack Geasland
Cinematography (colour): Peter Suschitzky
Sound: Bryan Day
Editor: Ronald Sanders
Music: Howard Shore
Production design: Carol Spier
Cast: Jeremy Irons (*Elliot and Beverly Mantle*), Geneviève Bujold (*Claire Niveau*), Heidi von Palleske (*Cary*), Barbara Gordon (*Danuta*), Shirley Douglas (*Laura*), Stephen Lack (*Anders Wolleck*), Nick Nichols (*Leo*), Lynn Cormack (*Arlene*), Damir Andrei (*Birchall*), Miriam Newhouse (*Mrs Bookman*), and others.
115 mins, 35mm

1989

During this year, Cronenberg starred in Clive Barker's film *Nightbreed*, and completed the first draft of *Naked Lunch*. His only directing was for the following commercials:

Hydro

Client: Ontario Hydro
Product: Energy conservation
Agency: Burghardt Wolowich Crunkhorn
Production company: The Partners' Film Company Ltd
Format: 4×30-second commercials
Titles: Hot Showers, Laundry, Cleaners, Timers

1990

During the time it took to finance and prepare *Naked Lunch*, Cronenberg continued to direct commercials, as well as returning to television drama. He directed two episodes of the Canadian Broadcasting Corporation's series *Scales of Justice:* 60-minute docu-dramas which re-enact actual criminal cases that have been through the Canadian courts.

Caramilk

Client: William Neilson Ltd
Product: Cadbury Caramilk
Agency: Scali McCabe, Sloves (Canada) Ltd
Production company: The Partners' Film Company Ltd
Format: 2×30-second commercials
Titles: Bistro, Surveillance

Cronenberg was one of a number of 'name' directors invited by Nike to create their own commercial to launch a new shoe.

Nike

Client: Nike International
Product: Nike Air 180
Agency: Wieden and Kennedy
Production company: The Partners' Film Company Ltd
Format: 1×15-second/4×30-second commercial
Title: Transformation

Regina Versus Horvath

British Columbia, the 1970s. When the bludgeoned body of Mrs Horvath is found in her Vancouver home, her seventeen-year-old son John becomes a suspect. There is little evidence against him, but in a lengthy, uncannily skilful and meticulously recorded interrogation, Vancouver super-cop Larry Proke gets young Horvath to confess to matricide. The problem is that Proke's interrogation is skilled enough to amount to hypnosis. If it is, can the confession still be voluntary and admissible?

Production company: Canadian Broadcasting Corporation in association with Scales of Justice Enterprises Inc.
Executive in charge of production: Carol Reynolds
Producer: George Jonas
Director: David Cronenberg
Screenplay: Michael Tait, George Jonas
Photography (colour): Rodney Charters
Sound: Bryan Day
Supervising editor: Ronald Sanders
Music: Howard Shore
Production design: Carol Spier
Cast: Justin Louis (*John Horvath*), Les Carlson (*Larry Proke*), Len Doncheff (*John Molnar*), Kurt Reis (*Mr Justice Gould*), Michael Caruana (*Mr R. D. Schantz, Crown*), David Gardner (*Mr D. G. G. Milne, Defence*), James Edmond (*Dr Gordon Stephenson, psychiatrist*), Frank Perry (*Dr Coady, Coroner*) and others.
48 mins, Betacam

Regina Versus Logan

Ontario, 1980. A group of black teenagers try to rob a Mac's milk store in Toronto. During the attempt, part-time cashier Barbara Turnbull is shot and rendered quadraplegic. A court case from the victim's point of view, which highlighted aspects of the Toronto Caribbean black community.

Production company: Canadian Broadcasting Corporation in association with Scales of Justice Enterprises Inc.
Executive in charge of production: Carol Reynolds
Producer: George Jonas
Director: David Cronenberg
Screenplay: Gabriel Emmanuel, George Jonas
Photography (colour): Rodney Charters
Sound: Bryan Day
Supervising editor: Ronald Sanders
Music: Howard Shore
Production design: Carol Spier
Cast: Barbara Turnbull (*as herself*), Richard Yearwood (*Cliff*), Desmond Campbell (*Hugh*), Mark Ferguson (*Warren*) and others
44 mins, Betacam

70 David Cronenberg in Clive Barker's *Nightbreed*.

1991

Naked Lunch

1953. New York. Former junkie Bill Lee is an exterminator. His wife Joan, like the insects, has become hooked on the bug poison. Taken in by two narcotics agents, Bill is confronted by a giant beetle which claims to be his controller for a bizarre spy operation. Joan's addiction has become serious. The sinister Dr Benway prescribes a stronger narcotic cure, made from Brazilian centipedes. After shooting his wife by accident, Bill goes on the run. In a series of encounters, each more hallucinatory than the last, he meets a mugwump, a powerful and sexually sinister alien from Interzone. Lee becomes an operative for his typewriter, which has by now transformed into a giant beetle. Writing dubious reports on his insect typewriter in Interzone, Bill becomes involved with Joan and Tom Frost, decadent American writers with a dark secret. He loses all sense of time, space and himself; moreover, he's running out of junk. He is, in fact, writing what will become one of the most influential novels of the century, a series of 'reports' eventually to be called *Naked Lunch*.

Production company: Recorded Picture Company, with the participation of Telefilm Canada and the Ontario Film Development Corporation.
Producer: Jeremy Thomas
Co-producer: Gabriella Martinelli
Director: David Cronenberg
Screenplay: David Cronenberg, based on the novel *The Naked Lunch* by William S. Burroughs
Cinematography (colour): Peter Suschitzky
Sound: Bryan Day
Editor: Ronald Sanders
Music: Howard Shore
Production design: Carol Spier
Creatures created and designed by Chris Walas Inc.
Special-effects supervisor: Jim Isaac
Cast: Peter Weller (*Bill Lee*), Judy Davis (*Joan Lee, Joan Frost*), Roy Scheider (*Dr Benway*), Ian Holm (*Tom Frost*), Julian Sands (*Yves Cloquet*), Michael Zelniker (*Martin*), Nicholas Campbell (*Hank*), Monique Mercure (*Fadela*), Joseph Scorsiani (*Kiki*) and others.
115 mins, 35mm

After *Naked Lunch*, Cronenberg's continuity man Dug Rotstein enlisted the director to play himself in an episode of the Canadian comedy series *Maniac Mansion*, which followed the trials and tribulations of the Addison family who, in attempting to harness the energy of a meteorite which has crashed into their swimming pool, have undergone the odd mutation (e.g. Harry has turned into a fly). In the episode 'Idella's Breakdown' – directed by Rotstein – Cronenberg is worried about directing a non-horror movie and seeks psychiatric help. Idella Addison goes to the same psychiatrist – unable to deal with being married to a fly. Cronenberg later meets Harry the fly – a fan of the director's movie and even keener on *Fly II*. Cronenberg points out that he didn't direct that one.

1992

In March, Cronenberg starred in the Canadian short *Blue*, written and directed by Don McKellar. Made at the Canadian Film Centre, Cronenberg plays carpet king Tom Cramer, a man obsessed with porno magazines and prone to masturbating in his office, while his faithful secretary pines for his attention and love. The film opened in Toronto supporting the British documentary *Damned in the USA* and was described as 'a shorter version of *sex, lies and videotape*, minus the yuppied angst'.

1992/93

M. Butterfly

1964. René Gallimard, an accountant for the French Embassy in Beijing, falls under the spell of beautiful Chinese diva Song Liling. Initially reticent, the shy Song ultimately reciprocates his passion, though never completely disrobes before René. Excited even more by this, René begins to transform from the meek accountant to a man of confidence. Encouraged in his affair with Song by his own embassy, who believe they will gain important insights into the Chinese, René is promoted to Vice Counsel. However, Song is a spy for the Chinese Ministry, eliciting information from René about American troop movements in Vietnam. Song suddenly leaves Beijing, apparently pregnant with their child. By her return, the Cultural Revolution is already underway. René sees his son briefly before Song is sent to a re-education camp. A victim of Song's misinformation, René is sent to '68 Paris, demoted to government courier. Years later, Song reappears. To protect their son back in China, René agrees to give her access to diplomatic pouches. Arrested for espionage, René is finally forced to face the fact that Song is a man. Song is extradited to China and René is imprisoned in France, where he puts on his own version of Madame Butterfly, slitting his throat before his fellow inmates.

Production company: Geffen Pictures in association with M. Butterfly Productions Inc.
Executive producers: David H. Hwang & Philip Sandhaus
Producer: Gabriella Martinelli
Director: David Cronenberg
Screenplay: David H. Hwang, based upon his play
Cinematography (colour): Peter Suschitzky
Sound: Bryan Day
Editor: Ronald Sanders
Music: Howard Shore
Production design: Carol Spier
Cast: Jeremy Irons (*René Gallimard*), John Lone (*Song Liling*), Barbara Sukowa (*Jeanne Gallimard*), Ian Richardson (*Toulon*), Annabel Leventon (*Frau Bauden*) and others.
102 mins, 35mm

1996

Crash

James Ballard and his wife, Catherine, are locked into a practice of compulsive sex with strangers. They compare notes, seeking any physical experience that makes sense in a bleak, passionless world of multi-lane freeways. Ballard becomes involved with Helen Remington after he accidently ploughs into her car, killing her husband. Their mutual crash-victim status brings them together, ultimately delivering them into the sump-oiled world of the pathological Vaughan – a renegade scientist and leader of a strange subterranean group who spend their time looking at videos of simulated car accidents, fucking in cars or attending Vaughan's own 'illegal' performances, such as his restaging of James Dean's

'Death by Porsche'. Ballard, Catherine and Helen Remington are all drawn into Vaughan's crazed orbit, and his dream of a new conceptualized relationship of flesh and metal: man and machine. When Vaughan is killed in a motorway car crash, Ballard takes his place and the cycle continues. The film ends with Ballard caressing Catherine after he has forced her car off the motorway.

Production company: Alliance Communications Corporation
Executive producers: Robert Lantos and Jeremy Thomas
Co-executive producers: Andras Hamori and Chris Auty
Co-producers: Stephane Reichel and Marilyn Stonehouse
Director: David Cronenberg
Screenplay: David Cronenberg, based on the novel by J. G. Ballard
Cinematography: Peter Suschitzky
Editor: Ronald Sanders
Music: Howard Shore
Production designer: Carol Spier
Costume designer: Denise Cronenberg
Casting: Deidre Bowen
Cast: James Spader (*James Ballard*), Holly Hunter (*Helen Remington*), Elias Koteas (*Vaughan*), Deborah Unger (*Catherine Ballard*), Rosanna Arquette (*Gabrielle*), Peter Mac-Neil (*Colin Seagrave*) and others.

Bibliography

Andrew, Geoff, *The Film Handbook*, Longmans, London (1989)

Drew, Wayne (ed.), *David Cronenberg: Dossier 21*, British Film Institute, London (1984)

Handling, Piers (ed.), *The Shape of Rage*, Academy of Canadian Cinema, General Publishing Company, Canada (1983)

McCarty, John, *Splatter Movies*, FantaCo Enterprises Inc., Albany, NY (1981)

Merck, Mandy (ed.), 'Body Horror', *Screen*, Vol. 27, No. 1, January/February 1986.

Newman, Kim, *Nightmare Movies*, Bloomsbury, London (1988)

Wood, Robin and Lipp, Richard (ed.), *The American Nightmare*, Festival of Festivals, Toronto (1979)

Selected Interviews/Articles

Ayscough, Susan, 'Sex . . . Porn . . . Censorship . . . Art . . . Politics . . . and Other Terms: Interview with David Cronenberg', *Cinema Canada*, December 1983, pp. 15–18

Beker, Marilyn, 'David Cronenberg', *Expression*, March/April 1989, pp. 148–56

Billson, Anne, 'Cronenberg on Cronenberg: A Career in Stereo', *Monthly Film Bulletin*, 56/660, January 1989, pp. 3–6

Chesley, Stephen, 'It'll Bug You' [on *Shivers*], *Cinema Canada*, No. 22, October 1975, pp. 22–25

Chute, David, 'He Came from Within', *Film Comment*, Vol. 16, No. 2, March/April 1980, pp. 42

Creed, Barbara, 'Phallic Panic: Male Hysteria and *Dead Ringers*', *Screen*, Vol. 31, No. 2, Summer 1990, pp. 125–46

Delaney, Marshall, 'You Should Know How Bad This Film Is. After All, You Paid for It' [on *Shivers*], *Saturday Night*, September 1975, pp. 83–5

Garsault, Alain, 'Scanners', *Positif*, No. 242, May 1981, pp. 78–9

Harkness, John, 'David Cronenberg: Brilliantly Bizarre', *Cinema Canada*, No. 72, March 1981, pp. 8–17

Hofsess, John, 'Fear and Loathing to Order' [on *Rabid*], *The Canadian*, 26 February 1977, pp. 14–17

Jaehne, Karen, 'Double Trouble' [on *Dead Ringers*], *Film Comment*, Vol. 24, No. 5, September/October 1988, pp. 20–7

Jones, M. J., 'Cronenberg on Wheels: *Fast Companies* (2)', *Cinema Canada*, No. 49–50, September/October 1978, pp. 17–19

Link, André, 'Delaney's Dreary Denigration' [on *Shivers*], *Cinema Canada*, No. 22, October 1975, p. 24

Loorson, Charles, 'No Guts, No Glory', *Première*, October 1988, pp. 58–62

Lucas, Tim, 'The Dead Zone', *Cinéfantastique*, Vol. 14, No. 2, December/January 1983–4, pp. 24–31, 60–1

Lucas, Tim, 'Videodrome', *Cinéfantastique*, Vol. 14, No. 2, December/January 1983–4, pp. 32–49

Lucas, Tim, 'The Fly Papers', *Cinefex*, No. 28, November 1986, pp. 4–29

Rickey, Carrie, 'Make Mine Cronenberg', *Village Voice*, 1 February 1983, pp. 62–5

Rolfe, Lee, 'David Cronenberg on *Rabid*', *Cinéfantastique*, Vol. 6, No. 3, 1977, p. 26

Sammon, Paul M., 'David Cronenberg', *Cinéfantastique*, Vol. 10, No. 4, spring 1981, pp. 21–34

Schupp, Patrick, 'Les monstres de l'été' [on *The Brood*], *Sequences*, No. 98, October 1979, pp. 27–32

Shay, Don, 'Double Vision' [on *Dead Ringers*], *Cinefex*, No. 36, November 1988, pp. 32–49

Snider, Norman, 'Just Two Innocent Canadian Boys in Wicked Hollywood', *Saturday Night*, July 1974, pp. 17–22

Stanbrook, Alan, 'Cronenberg's Creative Cancers', *Sight and Sound*, Vol. 58, No. 1, Winter 1989–90, pp. 54–6

A Note on the Editor

Chris Rodley is an independent producer, director and writer. Since 1983, he has made a number of documentary films for British television concerned with cinema, including: *Out of the Blue and into the Black* (about the late-1960s American independent company BBS); *Long Live the New Flesh* (on the work of David Cronenberg); *Motion and Emotion: The Films of Wim Wenders*; *Pictures of Europe* (on the future of European cinema in the 1990s) and *Naked Making Lunch* (about the production of the film *Naked Lunch*). He continues to work on documentary and feature-film projects.

Index